A CROSS-CULTURAL REDEFINITION OF RATIONAL EMOTIVE AND COGNITIVE BEHAVIOR THERAPY

This unique volume integrates history, mythology/folklore, and theory and research to bridge the gap between Western and Middle Eastern approaches to and understanding of psychotherapy, particularly cognitive behavior therapy (CBT) and rational emotive behavior therapy (REBT).

Part I lays the foundation with an overview of the theoretical essentials of REBT and CBT in the West, the goals and assumptions of REBT and CBT in the Middle East, and what Middle Eastern clients understand about cognitive distortions, irrational beliefs, and emotions. In Part II, chapters delve more deeply into how psychology is placed in the context of Middle Eastern folklore. The author provides a summary of the history of psychology in the Middle East; an analysis of the relevance of Sufism to self-acceptance, acceptance of others, and life acceptance; and an evaluation of the use of metaphor in psychotherapy from the Middle Eastern perspective. Finally, the author provides case studies that show how these concepts are applied in practice.

This text is ideal reading for researchers and clinicians who study Middle Eastern psychology and who work with Middle Eastern clients, as well as for Middle Eastern psychologists and clients.

Murat Kaan Artiran, Ph.D., is a psychotherapist, clinical psychologist, director of the Albert Ellis Institute Affiliated Training Center in Turkey, and a certified CBT and REBT supervisor. He has translated three books on clinical psychology, REBT, and emotional regulation and has published six peer-reviewed articles on REBT and CBT and self-determination theory.

A CROSS-CULTURAL REDEFINITION OF RATIONAL EMOTIVE AND COGNITIVE BEHAVIOR THERAPY

From the West to the Middle East

Murat Kaan Artiran, Ph.D.

Routledge
Taylor & Francis Group

NEW YORK AND LONDON

First published 2020
by Routledge
52 Vanderbilt Avenue, New York, NY 10017

and by Routledge
2 Park Square, Milton Park, Abingdon, Oxon, OX14 4RN

Routledge is an imprint of the Taylor & Francis Group, an informa business

© 2020 Taylor & Francis

Library of Congress Cataloging-in-Publication Data
A catalog record for this book has been requested

ISBN: 978-0-367-22792-0 (hbk)
ISBN: 978-0-367-22793-7 (pbk)
ISBN: 978-0-429-27687-3 (ebk)

Typeset in Bembo
by Apex CoVantage, LLC

Visit the eResources website: www.routledge.com/9780367227937

CONTENTS

FOREWORD

We live in an increasingly diverse society that necessitates cultural sensitivity in the field of psychotherapy. As Dr. Murat K. Artiran so aptly stated in the first chapter of this book: A client is like a hero in a novel, with a unique, personal history. This unique history must inform therapy in order to assure a better therapeutic outcome. Therefore, the sensitive psychologist must consider not only the theoretical approach that guides the therapy but also the cultural context.

A Cross-Cultural Redefinition of Rational Emotive and Cognitive Behavioral Therapy: From the West to the Middle East is a welcome addition to the RE & CBT literature. While practitioners throughout the world employ this theory with clients from diverse cultures, there is a still a real need for information about specific cultural adaptations. Dr. Artiran's book focuses specifically on the applications of RE & CBT from the perspective and expectations of Middle Eastern clients. He makes the point that it can be difficult to adapt a foreign theory to a different culture and stresses the importance of careful consideration of cultural as well as subcultural differences before initiating any therapeutic approach.

While many practitioners acknowledge the importance of conceptualizing client problems based on theory as well as cultural realities, this is different than knowing how to do it. In this book, Dr. Artiran does an excellent job of pointing out the differences between a Western perspective and a Middle Eastern perspective where the society is more collectivist and people do not readily seek counseling from a professional. In fact, mental health is a misunderstood concept and treatment is considered a taboo, although that appears to be changing with younger generations. He discusses how various concepts such as the *self* are perceived differently based on cultural values, history, and social rules. He highlights the Middle Easterners' interpretation of cognitive distortions and other aspects of RE & CBT theory, helping readers understand the cultural backdrop that must inform practice.

While this book does a thorough job of presenting the way clients from Middle Eastern cultures experience the world, it goes a step beyond this and describes specific factors that should be useful to practitioners who are working with clients from this cultural perspective. For example, he discusses the use of metaphors, idioms, proverbs, and folk sayings that will make counseling much more relevant for these clients. He outlines the structure of a session with culturally sensitive adaptations, which should be extremely beneficial in working with clients from Middle Eastern cultures. Throughout the book there are numerous helpful examples that should help professionals with an individualistic, Western perspective develop a more culturally refined framework when applying RE & CBT with Middle Eastern clients.

It is my pleasure to write this foreword for a book that so thoroughly translates theory to practice within the cultural framework of the Middle East.

Ann Vernon, Ph.D.

ACKNOWLEDGEMENTS

Thanks (Teşekkür)

SWT. I would like to express my thanks to my family—especially my wife Aynur, my daughter Dora Defne, my mother Feriha, my sister Suna, and my brother Mehmet; they motivated me.

Additionally, I would like to thank my supervisors Professor Raymond DiGiuseppe, Professor Windy Dryden, John Viterito, Dr. F. Michler Bishop, Dr. Kristene A. Doyle, Dr. Michael Hickey, and others who taught me RE & CBT. I wish to thank Ann Vernon, John Viterito, and Dr. F. Michler Bishop for valuable feedbacks.

Many thanks should be extended to my clients and assistants who supported me at the Affiliated Center of the Albert Ellis Institute in Turkey. I also thank Steve Leyland, not only as an English language editor but also as a friend, coach, and frequent inspiration. He coaxed and guided me in all sections of the book.

ABOUT THE AUTHOR

Dr. Murat Kaan Artiran was born in Istanbul in 1975. After moving to the US in 2001, he studied psychology at Eastern Kentucky University. After graduating in general psychology in the Master of Arts Program in USA, he completed his doctoral program in clinical psychology. He became a supervisor of Rational Emotive & Cognitive Behavior Therapy following training in psychotherapy at the Albert Ellis Institute in New York. After returning to Turkey in 2013, he opened a private practice and is the director of the Affiliated Center of the Albert Ellis Institute. He generally works with children, adolescents, and young adults, providing supervision to clinical psychology students, teaching RE & CBT techniques at both his center and various universities in Istanbul.

PREFACE

Rational emotive and cognitive behavior therapy helped me in my own time of psychological distress, and in my personal development. However, after living and working in the US for 11 years, and then again in Turkey, when applying and using the theories for myself, my students, and my clients, due to cultural differences, semantic barriers, and different expectations from a therapeutic treatment, I observed some misunderstandings and missing points.

After attending great training sessions with professors and practitioners and having performed therapy with many Western (American, English, Australian, Russian, Spanish, Greek) and Middle Eastern (Turkish, Iraqi, Iranian, Syrian, Azerbaijani, and Lebanese) clients, and after working for the Albert Ellis Institute and lecturing at Turkish universities, participating in psychotherapy international congresses around the world, following a lot of brainstorming and discussions with Steve, and my colleagues from the West and Middle East, I identified a gap in the psychotherapy field for a book like this.

Before starting to write, I didn't know that with the combination of all my experiences it would take such a long time. My days and my nights, together with language editor/redactor Steve, have been filled with the book. If I had known that it would be so difficult to write such a book beforehand, I am not sure I would have wanted to start it, to be honest. However, later I understood that it has been worth it. When the finishing line got closer our enthusiasm increased. The book acquired a shape and started to make sense.

During the writing process, some days I was not sure if I was regurgitating what I already knew, whether I was aiming at a religious text, a scientific one, a book of theory, or even a book about history, semantics, and linguistics, or even geography and sociology. It was necessary to draw on a huge variety of texts, in books from personal collections, from libraries, online libraries, and, of course, scientific journals, and also texts and reportages published on the Internet and our own observations of different cultures. Physically it has been an exhausting and time-consuming journey, and I would like to thank my supporters for their sincere good wishes. It has been impossible for me to take a break for 12 months—and there was a long period of gestation before we started work on the book. Sometimes it is necessary to take a break and walk away, to get some respite, as a kind of word blindness sets in. The Middle East itself is a mosaic, and we drew on sources *far and wide*, from all over the world. The book is about cross-cultural psychotherapy, with an attempt to demystify some parts of Eastern thought and approaches to psychology, and to blend it with modern techniques of Western psychology. The purpose of the book is set out very clearly, and I hope you will enjoy learning something new and interesting, as well as updating what you already know, and—most particularly, Middle Easterners—will discover a way to understanding the mind in a deeper way, with opportunities for knowledge to be put into practical use. This is no mean feat, as readers are doubtless aware. A cross-cultural redefinition of RE & CBT from the West to the Middle East was hard; however, I have enjoyed it immensely. I hope you will too. *M.K.A.*

INTRODUCTION

Many schools of therapy and psychotherapy have been introduced by Western culture to the world and offer a plethora of basic, similar methodologies. Others offer specific, relatable hypotheses and particular, precise methods. The good news is that all are useful to a variety of differing cultures. In the wake of Western psychotherapies, if the cultural aspects are not ignored, we may obtain optimal benefits for non-Western cultures (e.g., Middle Eastern) in therapeutic treatments. Each psychotherapeutic approach has its own structure, hypotheses, and assumptions about human psychological well-being. Some of them are scientifically proven and applied all over the world, providing benefit to those in need. Although theoretical assumptions are applicable to clinical and nonclinical populations, each approach may not be culturally adaptable, nor is it necessarily capable of being adaptable to a different culture, due to its complex nature. In Western societies, diverse schools of psychotherapy have been condemned for their inability to welcome an ethnodiversity to their methodologies.[1]

Since psychotherapy sessions are individually beneficial, therapy necessarily has to be tailored to the needs of each client. Western philosophy and embedded cultural factors offer their own approach and perspectives to clients. Psychotherapists from non-Western cultures may have difficulty in applying such knowledge to sessions, without modifying applicable methodologies to their own culture. Language differences and cultural semantics are another huge obstacle in this process. Other aspects like life circumstances, socioeconomic levels, religions, race, family structure, educational systems, political dissimilarities, understanding of psychological illnesses, and attitudes towards an 'understanding' of psychotherapy vary from culture to culture and so, cultural pluralism needs to be addressed in a unique cultural formulation of a variety of therapeutic processes.[2] Therapists need to adjust their interventions using their own fundamental roots, in terms of academic theory, language, beliefs, and superstitions. The objective of this book is to convey an alternative point of view to rational emotive & cognitive behavior applications considered the 'norm,' when pertaining to Middle Eastern culture. Science is not only a body of established and unquestionable facts. It is also a method of asking questions that—at their best—move us closer to an understanding of what is really going on. Many up-to-date pieces of information have been included, and it is hoped that more research-based references will latch onto this modernity effectively.

Throughout the book, theoretical information is given as simply as possible. Applications that can be used by clients and therapists are presented in boxes. This book intends to show unique examples of cultural differences in psychotherapy. It is not only Middle Eastern people that are interested in cognitive behavior therapy (Chapters 2, 3, 4, and 5), a history of the psychology of the Middle East (Chapter 6), Sufism (Chapter 7), and metaphors (Chapter 8). It is hoped that the general public from all walks of life, all over the world, not least academics, practitioners, clients, and students, will gain something from this work. Successful psychology counselors are able to utilize and adjust their own psychotherapeutic models to give structure while intervening in a patient's personal issues, characteristic features, and culture/cultural expectations, identity, and adaptation skills. This book can be considered a *qualitative* approach to all the issues, and it is hoped to be used as guidance for

* clients and practitioners
* academics and researchers

The first four chapters of the book provide information about the central concepts of REBT and CBT. The fourth, fifth, and sixth chapters start to reveal cultural factors and differences. In the second part of the book, some cultural elements are provided that will help as a reference for clients, therapists, and academics in the application of REBT and CBT (Chapters 7, 8, 9, and 10).

This book is an attempt to bring a new look to the purpose of therapy for Middle Eastern people, with the aid of various Eastern sources, using RE & CBT interventions.

References

1. Tseng, W. S. (2001). *Handbook of Cultural Psychiatry*. San Diego: Academic Press.
2. American Psychiatric Association. (2012). *Diagnostic and Statistical Manual of Mental Disorders* (5th ed.). Arlington, USA: American Psychiatric Association.

PART I
Western Theory

1

WHAT IS THIS BOOK FOR?

There is a life-force within your soul, seek that life. There is a gem in the mountain of your body, seek that mine. O traveller, if you are in search of that, don't look outside, look inside yourself and seek that.

—Rumi

Trying to apply a Western-based psychotherapy model with an 'appropriate' and 'effective' method of psychology techniques is more difficult than merely reading about the rhetoric of theoretical information in books. It also requires the understanding of a professional as to the needs of his or her client and then empathizing with the client, planning treatment, and providing 'examples,' within a treatment plan.

Think, if you will, that a client is like a hero in a novel, with a unique, personal story. To achieve a better outcome in any treatment, it is necessary for a sensitive psychologist to understand the client's story well. Therefore, to assess the culture from which she springs become necessary. A practitioner needs to conceptualize a client's problems based on theoretical essentials as well as cultural facts. A culturally redefined theory helps us to figure out the cultural backdrop, in a scientific way. Psychotherapy is a reflection of the science of psychology in practice. It is a blend of 'science, art, literature, and life experience.' It is a tool that progresses in the light of scientific data. On the other hand, the results may depend on a discovery of the client's own story, using her own skill and life experience.

Therapist: What bothers you mostly?
Client: I question our existence, religion and life. Why do people have children? I worry when I think about what I really want to do with my life. I am sometimes depressed when thinking about whether I should

live in this country or move abroad. I want you to give me some ideas and suggestions about these questions. And there are uncertainties in my life. I am seeking answers . . . meanings . . .

If a client is originally from Iraq, Saudi Arabia, Egypt, the United States, the United Kingdom, Ireland, Australia, Germany, Italy, China, Thailand, Cuba, or Brazil, how can one type of therapy deal with such questions? Helping a client is not only about applying a single psychotherapy theory but also about unique cultural aspects, history, values, definitions, expectations, and social rules.

Famous psychologist Carl Rogers declared that *empathy* is the first and foremost issue in therapy.[1] If we do not touch on the culture, how can we apply 'empathy' in any therapy? Albert Ellis pointed out that the future of psychotherapy will be in the school system,[2] based on more 'teaching and learning' rather than classical 'talk therapy.' Careful consideration—of cultural and subcultural differences, in learning appropriation and behavior—needs to be made before applying any therapy.

East and West

'East–West' distinctions in the articles of scientific journals and magazines are frequently discussed. Cultural and subcultural differences in learning behavior fail to address the diversity of their learners.[3,4,5] It is argued that 'Eastern' culture and 'Western' culture are separate, or claimed that they are opposite, in terms of cultural structure. Is this true or not? We don't have an exact answer. Nevertheless, a theoretical approach, principally, cannot make such distinctions; a theory can only reveal its own rules and principles. Cultural differences, meanwhile, can be applied only by a therapist in practice.

Although science may be a universal concept, any theory needs to be provable and display a certain flexibility so that, at times, it is also culturally adaptable. Due to its nature this is truer for psychotherapy theories. In this book, a 'constructive' and 'processed-based' perspective is put forward, with a culturally redefined approach. In psychotherapeutic interventions a therapist has a responsibility to understand and communicate with clients by conceptualizing their problems, not only using theoretical points of view but also by considering certain cultural aspects. George Kelly's work[6] helped the birth of cognitive psychotherapists (e.g., REBT and CT). Kelly's use of constructs is what modern theorists explain as 'schemas.'[7] An individual's way of conceptualizing life, from her own particular constructs, must be appreciated. Hopefully, this book will lead to a continuation of this 'constructive' route, *culturally speaking.*

It is assumed that the theory of psychotherapy is applicable anywhere in the world. In order to utilize Western psychotherapy to empathize with Middle Eastern people, to reveal a different and more 'culturally compatible' mental health treatment approach, this book hopes to address some concerns of practitioners. In order to understand clients better, more than just an awareness of culturally embedded issues should be included in therapy sessions. However, as mentioned, when it comes to the psychological counseling process in general, the issue becomes more complicated than 'just applying the essentials of a psychotherapy theory.'

A Scientific 'Middle Eastern Mind'

The opinion that the 'rational' or 'scientific mind' originates in the West and that the world of the Middle East is light years away from having a scientific perspective is not correct. It is certainly not completely true, as history has shown. Harezmi in mathematics,[8] Al-Ghazali in philosophy,[9] Ibn-i-Sina (Avicenna) in medicine,[10] and Ibn Rushd (Averroes) in philosophy[11] all put forward rational and scientific theories, and they have been transferred to, and utilized by, *the West*. It is true, however, that Islamic countries have not followed their own theoreticians, nor have they embellished recent scientific knowledge (some caveats to this sentence are dealt with in later chapters). As a consequence, it is observed that rational and/or scientific knowledge is frequently exported from the West to the Middle East. The following chapters will discuss and provide some suggestions and examples about this topic.

Taboo

Generally speaking (there are exceptions) in the Middle Eastern population, psychological ill health is a taboo, or an unmentionable subject. When asked, many clients report that mental illness is not understood in their families/cultures at all and dismissed. They verbally or nonverbally link psychological problems to stigmas, such as being miserable, lazy, guilty, or crazy, and psychopathology is something which is forbidden. Additionally, according to some people, unfortunately, it is frequently seen that anyone who admits to seeing a mental health professional may be viewed as a lunatic, weak, shameful, unreliable, or/and fragile. Some Middle Easterners believe that mental illness may be seen as a lack of religious practice, or 'disbelief' in Islam.

In Middle Eastern countries many people still seek support from *hodjas* (Islamic teachers) for their mental health problems.[10] In larger Turkish cities this is less true, though the practice continues, and the rise in the amount of practicing psychologists is proof that Western ideas are desired. The efficacy of some of these counselling centers is discussed in later chapters.

Middle Eastern societies tend to be collectivist and patriarchal. Western psychotherapy may offer an individual an approach based on an individualistic society from which it is generated, but psychotherapy, and even cures, transferred from Western to other cultures may differ during that transmission.[12]

Cultural Sensitivity

Culture-sensitive approaches to psychotherapy would seem to be a necessity in our digitalized global world. For mental health professionals, it is very easy to copy-paste a theory to their own culture; however, it is very complicated to 'adapt' a foreign theory to a different culture and then adopt it, in situ, in practice. For instance, when we use the terms *self-actualization* (in humanistic psychotherapy) or *cognitive distortions* (in cognitive psychotherapy), some clients may understand these thoughts are related to 'anti-religious' or 'anti-traditional' ideas in the Middle East, and clients usually give curious looks at the therapist, as if their spiritual values are being attacked. A borderline personality disorder client reported that when she was doing her 'therapeutic' homework, her mind went off in a different direction, sometimes, to that which was focused on during a session, and she started to pray to God for a release from her problems. Practitioners feel under pressure to apply the concepts of RE & CBT when transferring the aforementioned conceptualizations to the client, and need well-explained, clearly defined statements, and a clearly defined approach. Another client asked whether religious beliefs are irrational. According to Taskin, Muslim people often seek a cure for their psychological problems through the power of prayer.[10] This may also be true for practicing Christians. It is desired that some of the chapters of this book (e.g., Chapter 7) will help many clients understand how we can use religious figures, such as Rumi (and Sufism), in psychotherapy, without direct use of religious concepts, in order to introduce scientific principles to bring about psychological well-being.

Another issue crops up with the 'self.' Many psychotherapies based on personality theories are interested in the conceptualization of the 'self.' The 'Self' has been taken as a social-cognitive framework and a constellation of cognitive schemas.[13] According to cross-cultural researchers, the self is culturally constructed.[14] For instance, Western societies create an individualistic model of personality theories.[15] Nevertheless, cross-cultural research points out that members of many collectivistic cultures (e.g., Turkey, Syria, Egypt, and Iraq) see a person as part of a social network, rather than as a unique individual.[16]

Hofstede's Theory

According to Hofstede's theory of cultural differences, people in collectivist societies tend to emphasize the obligations they have towards their in-group members, and are willing to sacrifice their individual needs and desires for the benefits of the group.[17] Hofstede developed a 100-item measurement and scale for people from different cultures.[18] Hofstede's work clearly shows that we cannot consider any theory without the cultural aspects. Aspects of cultural differences may vary in many fields of psychology too.

This book focuses on psychotherapy and the psychological counseling side of the cultural differences that are frequently encountered outside the West, and suggests some applications and interventions. The weight of the cultural dimensions of learned values, beliefs, and attitudes that shape cognitions, perceptions, emotions, and behavior cannot be stressed enough. To sum up, this book is for clients, practitioners, and academics who wonder what happens when Western psychotherapy is 'transplanted' or redefined to work in the (Middle) East and how to apply it in an appropriate way.

What Is in This Book?

Throughout the book readers will find:

- The essentials of rational emotive & cognitive behavior therapy
- Qualitative discussions about an 'Eastern' and 'Western' understanding of RE & CBT theory (cognitions, emotions, and behaviors)
- An introduction to cultural aspects of therapy
- An attempt at new, Middle Eastern-based 'goals' of treatment
- Some information about the history of Middle Eastern psychology
- Culturally redefined example sessions, protocols, and interventions
- Some materials for activities and homework

Conclusion

The practice of psychotherapy and psychiatric treatments has historically been provided by Western clinicians. Most of them are trained to address mental health problems and their hidden components directly. The question arises as to whether such an approach is completely true. Cultural competence is the capability to engage in performance, or produce conditions, so as to maximize the best possible progress of the client.[19] In order that Middle Easterners can become less fearful of Western methods, psychotherapists who have a culturally redefined framework and outlook will help academics, clinicians, practitioners, and students to gain a greater understanding of the work involved. It is a truism to say that psychological treatment is too frequently misunderstood in the Middle East and often muddled with medical treatment, which is dealt with in later chapters in more detail. It is good news that some of the young generation do not hesitate to talk about depression or anxiety and psychosomatic symptoms with their friends and relatives. Psychology and mental illness are becoming better understood and less taboo for some Middle Eastern people, though a distinction between rural and urban people must be made, even if they have relations who live elsewhere.

For psychologists (practitioners, academics, and students) trying to understand clients from the point of view of their own cultural identity, it is sincerely hoped that this book will aid the development of cross-cultural psychology and psychotherapy in the world. It is also hoped that it will be enjoyed and used as a reference, not only by Middle Eastern clients and practitioners but also for all those who seek respite and clarity in changing times all around us.

References

1. Rogers, C. R. (1959). *Client-Centered Therapy: Its Current Practice, Implications, and Theory*. Boston: Houghton Mifflin.
2. Epstein, R. (2001). The Prince of Reason. Retrieved from: https://www.psychologytoday.com/us/articles/200101/the-prince-reason
3. Mushtaha, A., & De Troyer, O. (2007). Cross-cultural understanding of content and interface in the context of E-learning systems. In N. Aykin (Eds.), *Usability and Internationalization: HCI and Culture, UI-HCII 2007: Lecture Notes in Computer Science* (Vol. 4559). Berlin and Heidelberg: Springer.
4. Fletcher, R. (2006). The impact of culture on web site content, design, and structure: An international and a multicultural perspective. *Journal of Communication Management, 10*(3), 259–273. https://doi.org/10.1108/13632540610681158
5. Hughes, H., & Bruce, C. (2006). Cultural diversity and educational inclusivity: International students' use of online information. *International Journal of Learning, 12*(9), 33–40.
6. Kelly, G. A. (1955). *The Psychology of Personal Constructs, Vol. 1: A Theory of Personality, Vol. 2: Clinical Diagnosis and Psychotherapy*. New York: Norton. (2. printing 1991. London: Routledge).
7. Leahy, R. L. (1996). *Cognitive Therapy: Basic Principles and Applications*. Bergen County, NJ: Northvale.
8. Capak, İ. (2010). Harizmi'nin Mefatihu'l-Ulumunda Mantik. *İslami İlimler Dergisi 5*(2), Güz, 47–58.
9. Griffel, F. (2016). *The Stanford Encyclopedia of Philosophy* (Winter 2016 ed.) (E. N. Zalta, Ed.). Retrieved from https://plato.stanford.edu/archives/win2016/entries/al-ghazali/
10. Reisman, D. C., & Al-Rahim, A. H. (Eds.). (2003). *Before and after Avicenna*. Proceeding of the First Conference of the Avicenna Study Group. Printed in Netherlands, Danvers, MA.
11. Tbakhi, A., & Amr, S. S. (2008). Ibn Rushd (Averroës): Prince of science. *Annals of Saudi Medicine, 28*(2), 145–147.
12. Taskin, E. O. (2007). *Stigma: Ruhsal hastaliklara yonelik tutumlar ve damgalama* [*Stigma: Attitudes of Mental Diseases and Stigmatization*]. Izmir: Meta Basim Matbaacilik.
13. Raney, S., & Çınarbaş, D. C. (2005). Counseling in developing countries: Turkey and India as examples. *Journal of Mental Health Counseling, 27*(2), 14.
14. Segal, Z. V. (1988). Review Appraisal of the self-schema construct in cognitive models of depression. *Psychology Bulletin, 103*(2), 147–62.9–160.
15. Lam, A. G., & Zane, N. W. S. (2004). Ethnic differences in coping with interpersonal stressors. *Journal of Cross-Cultural Psychology, 35*(Suppl 4), 446–459.
16. Markus, H. R., & Kitayama, S. (1991). Culture and the self: Implications for cognitions, emotion, and motivation. *Psychology Review, 98*, 224–253. http://dx.doi.org/10.1037/0033-295X.98.2.224
17. Neftçi, N. B., & Barnow, S. (2016). One size does not fit all in psychotherapy: Understanding depression among patients of Turkish origin in Europe. *Noro Psikiyatr Araştırmaları, 53*(1), 72–79.

18. Hofstede, G., Hofstede, G. J., & Minkov, M. (2010). *Cultures and Organizations: Software of the Mind.* New York, NY: McGraw Hill.

19. Whaley, A. L., & Davis, K. E. (2007). Cultural competence and evidence-based practice in mental health services: A complementary perspective. *American Psychologist, 62*(6), 563–574. doi:10.1037/0003-066X.62.6.563

2

THE ESSENTIALS OF RE & CBT

Rational beliefs bring us closer to getting good results in the real world.

—*Dr. Albert Ellis*

In this chapter some of what rational emotive behavior therapy (REBT) and cognitive behavior therapy (CBT) involves, together with information about some key people in its formation, is mentioned. The purpose of this chapter is to introduce readers to some aspects of RE & CBT, to prepare them for the rest of the book. It is intended only to give an overview of the mainstream cognitive behavioral therapies, which take many forms. There are obviously additional sources to learn more about RE & CBT therapy. Other cognitive behavioral therapies (e.g., mindfulness-based therapies, acceptance and commitment therapy, dialectic behavior therapy) are omitted. However, in Chapters 4 and 7, readers will find traces of 'third-wave' cognitive therapies (e.g., mindfulness-based therapies). REBT theory relies on both structuralist (certain schemas of the mind) and functionalistic approaches (processes of the mind) to cognition.[1] Recently in REBT literature, the four irrational beliefs have been called *cognitive processes* rather than the *structure* of the mind. In the past, the term 'cognitive process' was not used much and Ellis and other CBT therapists used the terms of many dysfunctional thoughts and beliefs as schema. Cognitive processes describe a number of tasks the brain does continuously. Seeing thoughts as an ongoing activity has some advantages in therapeutic interventions and gives motivation to clients. For instance, instead of saying to a client she has some deeply ingrained thoughts, a therapist could say that psychological well-being depends on the choice of our thoughts. Therefore, in this way, the client will be able to actively 'watch' and 'choose' her own thoughts, rather than fighting with them and trying to fix them. It is imperative to continue the dedication to maintaining healthy thought processes.

Cognitive behavioral therapy emerged as a combination of behavioral and cognitive theories.[2] CBT is a form of psychotherapy that focuses on the role of cognition in the expression of emotions and behaviors.[3] The first version of CBT was established by clinical psychologist Dr. Albert Ellis in 1955 and was called rational psychotherapy. REBT, which was formulated by Ellis, to be used in clinical settings, is greatly respected among cognitive behavioral therapies. Rational psychotherapy was named rational emotive behavioral therapy after 1992.[4,5] REBT was the first approach of the cognitive behavioral therapies. In the first CBT approach, Ellis employed a number of philosophical sources for his theory. He introduced the idea to the psychotherapeutic community that our thoughts and beliefs determine our emotions and behavior. This was a revolutionary movement in psychology because Sigmund Freud and his followers' approach to human beings was that they are psychologically sick in the first place and are then fixed by psychoanalysis, rather than believing that a human is born to be well, autonomous, competent, skillful, and functional. The Freudian approach dominated all areas of psychotherapy and psychiatry for many years till the late 1970s. The Freudian approach involved discovering the causes of psychological sickness during childhood. This is unlike the REBT and CBT approaches, which believe that psychological disorders are mainly related to our thinking and behaviors, and also to the human potential to solve psychological problems.

Stoicism

From a philosophical point of view, there are views similar to cognitive understanding found in the teachings of the Stoic school in ancient Greek philosophy. Stoic philosophy points out that the happiness of the individual depends on understanding what he can and cannot control. According to Epictetus, when individuals accept that there are situations, experiences, and events that they can and cannot control in life, and when they are able to distinguish between these two facts, they reach happiness and inner peace. Life continues to operate according to principles within itself, while the happiness of people is possible by understanding and complying with this process. Socrates also stated that 'True wisdom comes to us when we realize how little we understand about life, ourselves, and the world around us.'[6] Similarly, Italian philosopher Gianni Vattimo wrote, 'There are no facts, only interpretations.'[7]

REBT and CBT developed rapidly after the 1980s. The theory, enriched by many theoreticians and clinicians, has spread to many psychopathology treatment interventions, especially for mood disorders, personality disorders, and schizophrenia. As a result of the integration of behavioral and cognitive approaches in the 1980s, the CBT movement emerged, and this has been one of the most successful examples in the field of psychotherapy. CB therapies are evidence-based therapies and they are open to being tested and investigated. Although many models emerged after Ellis and Beck, the approaches they developed (REBT and CBT) are the most common and the most widely used.[8]

Challenging Harmful Thoughts

In the face of stressful events, our interpretations and evaluations determine how we respond to them emotionally and/or behaviorally, so that behavioral and emotional changes are cognitively mediated. That is to say, our thoughts determine our emotions and our behavior. Our emotional and/or behavioral responses can be healthy and helpful or unhealthy and unhelpful, sometimes called functional or dysfunctional. Rational and functional thoughts lead to psychological well-being in clients. Cognitive behavior therapy is a type of psychotherapy that believes in challenging and changing 'harmful' and dysfunctional thoughts. The theory suggests that cognitive, emotional, and behavioral components play a key role in pathological disorders.[9,10] It uses a variety of methods to treat pathological disorders within the model of event, belief, and emotional/behavioral result, which is defined as the ABC model.[9,10]

The ABC Model

Cognitive behavioral therapies define the framework of psychotherapy treatment in the context of the ABC model set forth by Dr. Albert Ellis. The ABC model means (A) the event, (B) the thoughts or beliefs about the event, and (C) the results (feelings and behavior).[10] RE & CBT therapists use the ABC model in therapy. In CBT, therapists assume that between A and C we have B. B can be defined as explicit or implicit information processing or cognitive schemas that affect our thinking and beliefs about a life event, ourselves, and other people. Events and situations do not cause anxiety and depression.[11] However, what people believe about them is that, if they are irrational, they will reveal anxiety and depression.

This is true for REBT and CBT. In the ABC model, B is the most important part for the model because the main assumption of all CBT theories focuses on changing dysfunctional cognitive structures to obtain healthy emotions and behavior (the C part of the ABC model). For example, a car accident (A) can be seen as a catastrophic event for one person, while for another it can be evaluated as a 'lucky' moment because it wasn't fatal (B). The former may feel scared and may be traumatized, while the other may feel happy or just 'sad' (C). The RE & CBT therapist tries to help the client by dealing with various cognitive factors (B) to evaluate the situation in a way that is logical, functionalistic, realistic, semantic, metaphoric, rational, and pragmatic. These methods are called disputation techniques (see Chapter 3).

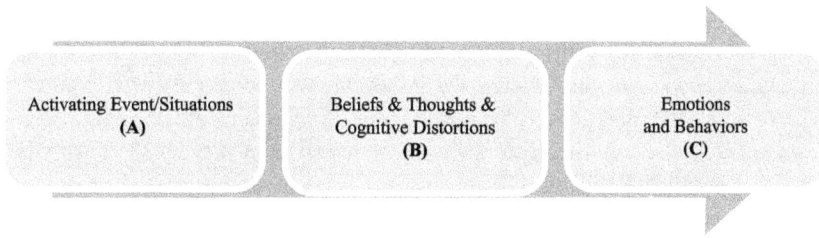

| Activating Event/Situations (A) | Beliefs & Thoughts & Cognitive Distortions (B) | Emotions and Behaviors (C) |

FIGURE 2.1 The ABC model: beliefs and thoughts are a mediator between A and C.

General Semantics

Ellis was also influenced by the general semantics theory of language. The main assumption of this assumes that we consciously make things abstract, which may be considered 'advanced thinking.' Therefore, our thinking, reasoning, and meaning we give to the world, our 'self,' and others depend on how we use language. In a RE & CBT therapy session, the therapist always watches the client's language and use of words when expressing his or her problems. By expanding our vocabulary and modifying our behavior, scientifically and mathematically, we develop clearer thinking about ourselves and improve our understanding of ourselves and others—and our relationships in the world we live in. Language evolves with structural flaws, in that the language we use does not completely reflect the world we experience 'out there,' not only in terms of semantics but also in terms of a world view, which involves different written and spoken languages.[12] In subsequent chapters we will develop this idea further, not only because of the vocabulary that we use in everyday life—in terms of grammar and syntax—but also because of how language is used differently from culture to culture, nation to nation.

Semantics in Different Cultures

Clinicians must be very careful when applying any type of therapy in dealing with clients who come from a different origin than their own—no easy task! The gap between thoughts and verbal expression makes a difference during treatment. If a bridge is not achieved, therapy remains on a level of just an 'educational activity,' without a therapeutic purpose. However, if a therapist catches on to a person's linguistic style, gauged not only socioeconomically but also by ascertaining which region he or she comes from, then the therapist can try to understand if there is a closer nexus to understanding how and why the person came to the point of needing to see a therapist in the first place. Most CBT therapists get stuck at this point, and unsuccessful CBT treatment fails at the level of 'semantic difference' between client and therapist. How can the average person relate to ideas of semantics when he or she is beset with everyday problems? How can you change the Asian/Muslim/Middle Eastern mind-set when nature, nurture, geography, government policies, and other outside forces (e.g., economic) do so much to make things harder than they are? Is this mind-set change, which REBT, CBT, and so forth hope to enable, a kind of restructuring of dysfunctional thought schemas? These questions will be discussed and answered throughout the book.

REBT

REBT shows us that cognitive processes are irrational and rational beliefs, but categorizes them into two different concepts.[13] Rational beliefs in REBT are thought to be healthy and beneficial, but irrational beliefs are seen as the main cause of psychological disturbances. The irrational beliefs that determine feelings and behaviors have been extensively studied. It is found that irrational beliefs lead to feelings such as anxiety, hostility, and guilt. According to much research[5,10,11] irrational beliefs can be linked to failure in dealing with problems in life, and operate as an obstacle to happiness.

Irrational Beliefs (IrBels)

Rational means not irrational, *irrational* means not rational, and *arational* means not rational *AND* not irrational. Arational is something that has no relation to reason (e.g., things related to instinct or intuition and, in general, that exist in nature—like stars, rocks, and trees). Or 'love.' Love is neither rational nor irrational. CBT does not mention arational in the ABC model. The ABC model describes REBT's view of psychopathology and human psychology and is used in the practice of psychotherapeutic treatment processes. Belief in the model assumes a decisive role.[9,15] In the ABC model beliefs (B) may be rational or irrational. If irrational, they are unhealthy, nonfunctional, incompatible, nonlogical, and/or non-overlapping.[16] If rational, then beliefs are healthy, functional, harmonious, logical, and/or coincide with reality[14] for therapeutic models and not personality types.

In REBT terminology, there are four core IrBels: irrational demandingness, catastrophizing/awfulizing, frustration intolerance (or low tolerance beliefs), and depreciation beliefs (sometimes called downing; see Chapter 3 for details). IrBels are considered to be extreme, rigid, and illogical. In contrast, there are four rational beliefs (RaBels): nondemanding preferences, anti-catastrophizing/anti-awfulizing, rational frustration tolerance (or high tolerance), and unconditional acceptance beliefs (of self, others, and life). Rational beliefs are considered to be non-extreme, flexible, and logical. IrBels have been shown to be related to various psychological

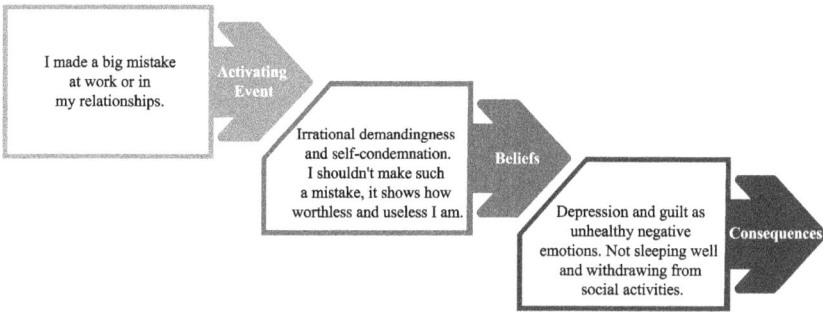

FIGURE 2.2 Example of an ABC model.

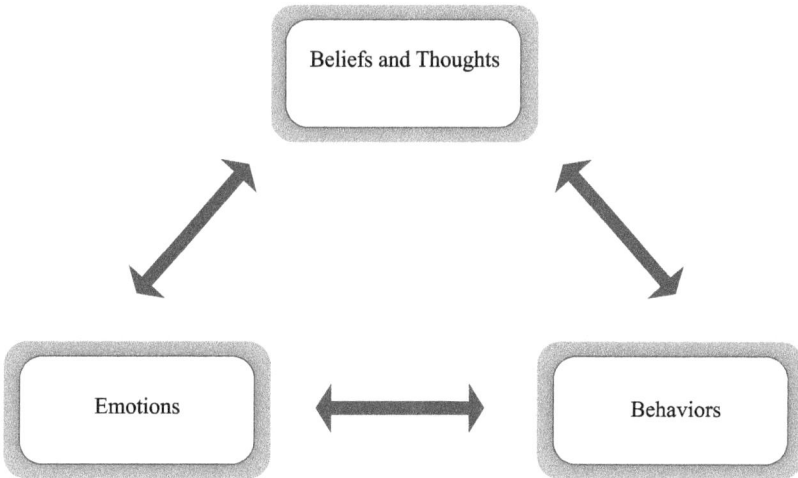

FIGURE 2.3 Beliefs, emotions, and behaviors affect each other.

disorders[17] and psychological distress.[18] IrBels are considered to be a barrier to good mental health or psychological well-being.

Psychological unhealthiness is essentially an illogical and unrealistic evaluation of events and situations by which, during the evaluation process, the client regularly distorts reality in a self-defeating way. Thus, it is the client's belief that causes emotional pain and countless, difficult behavioral patterns. RaBels in REBT are viewed as healthy and beneficial to people in the long run. IrBels can be associated with failure in dealing with the problems faced in life and function as an obstacle to happiness. In REBT, the therapist plays an active and directional role, enabling the client to replace IrBels with RaBels, and as a guide to avoiding emotional difficulties.

Positive Versus Rational Thinking

The importance of a change in clients' thinking, due to REBT interventions, is exemplified in the studies of positive effect. The study by Pressman and Cohen that found that positive effect was directly related to better health, higher recovery rates, and more favorable self-evaluations of health, in healthy and mildly psychologically ill individuals, is a seminal work.[19] The findings suggest that REBT contributes to a more positive outlook and may be very beneficial to a person's health on many levels. The same study found that a positive effect had a negative influence on health outcomes for terminally ill individuals and institutionalized older adults, suggesting, once again, that the emphasis on rational thinking, which REBT provides, is indeed beneficial. The researchers suggest that the negative effect of positive thinking is most likely as a result of the irrational beliefs that they are less affected by ill health than others, leading them to take less care of themselves. It is easy to see how thinking more realistically and rationally can have a great positive effect on an individual's health, rather than simply 'positive' thinking. The goals of the therapy are discussed in Chapter 4.

Elements of cognitive structures are known differently in REBT and in CBT; while REBT takes IrBels as the most important part of the 'B,' CBT assumes that 'automatic' thoughts and core beliefs are the most crucial. Their function is similar: helping the clients to reach healthy thinking, which is discussed, in detail, in Chapter 3. However, a therapist is trained in both theories and uses these concepts interchangeably in interventions. Therapists trained as a REBT or CBT practitioner may utilize different approaches in dealing with dysfunctional, unhealthy cognitions. Most of the time, whatever the different approaches are, the goal is essentially the same: to change someone's thoughts and beliefs, by regulating his or her emotions, so he or she will live a healthier and happier life. REBT and CBT is applied on the client to achieve a more philosophical outlook on life, where he or she stops thinking in absolute terms, and allows reality to take place, without having a strong adverse reaction to it.[20]

REBT and CBT training seminars and studies are carried out at the Albert Ellis Institute (AEI) and affiliated centers of the AEI, but cognitive behavioral therapy training sessions and studies are carried out at the Beck Institute in various countries around the world. There are also various associations around the world interested in CBT and REBT, such as the Association for Behavioral and Cognitive Therapies and the International Association for Cognitive Psychotherapy, the European Association for Behavioral and Cognitive Therapies, and also the Irish Association of Behavioral and Cognitive Psychotherapy, the Italian Association for Behavioral and Cognitive Therapy, the Association of Rational Positive Psychology—Turkey, and the British Association for Behavioral and Cognitive Psychotherapy. There are many scientific journals in which research on both types of therapy is found (e.g., *The Journal of Rational-Emotive &*

Cognitive-Behavior Therapy, *Cognitive Therapy and Research*, and *Behavioral and Cognitive Psychotherapy*—Cambridge University Press).

A note to clients: Psychological problems are not necessarily treated using medicine and psychotherapy. It is true that most people get over their problems trying many things, but REBT and CBT offer exemplary, evidence-based advice. If you step into a RE & CBT therapist's office you will receive structured guidance to help you solve your main problems in a clear and simple way. Have you ever heard anyone say, 'I went to the psychologist and she told me that. . .' or, 'I am not feeling good, I think I am depressed, I need some pills to feel better . . .'? Why not take a close look at what kinds of treatments are available for psychological problems? Many problems are never treated using medicine. They can be dealt with in a social setting with friends and close ones, or with books you buy.

Contributors to REBT & CBT

Besides Ellis and Beck, many others have contributed to cognitive behavioral approaches. The aim of the following information is to provide a limited history about cognitive behavior therapies and some of the people (directly or indirectly) who led to its foundation. This book does not intend to review REB and CB therapies so not all contributors are added to this section.

Wilhelm Wundt and John B. Watson

Wilhelm Wundt was born in Mannheim, Germany. He was the founder of psychology as a formal and academic science and established the first psychology laboratory, prepared the first psychology journal, and brought experimental psychology to the world of science as a science. Wundt's interests included: sensation and perception, attention, emotion, reaction, and association. He was interested in cognitive psychology, which is a subdiscipline of psychology that contends that an understanding of internal states is essential to an understanding of behavior. Furthermore, these episodes are physically embodied. In humans and other organisms, these mechanisms in the 'mind' are embodied in the brain and nervous system. Wundt studied anatomy, physiology, medicine, and chemistry but realized that he would prefer to work on physiology. After some time with well-known physiologist Johannes Muller, in Berlin, Wundt returned to Heidelberg to complete his doctorate in 1855, where he worked as an associate professor until 1864. The practice of introducing new students bored him, but, in 1864, he became an adjunct professor and remained in Heidelberg until 1874. While in Heidelberg, the idea of psychology as an independent and experimental science had begun to wane, but in Wundt's mind his first thoughts about psychology as a new science were revealed in his book *Contributions to the Theory of Sensory Perception: On the Methods in Psychology*. In his book, Wundt described his original experiments at home and included his views on the methods of this new psychology. It discussed several problems that attracted the attention of experimental psychologists for many years. The word 'behavior' in cognitive behavior therapy owes its existence to Wundt's work. He especially influenced the founder of Behaviorism, John B. Watson. Although Wundt, who was the father of experimental psychology, and interested in exploring human conscious experience, Watson used experimental psychology to explore, record and measure human behavior.

According to Watson, psychology only becomes scientific if it focuses on the tangible aspects of human behavior rather than cognition. Albert Ellis and Aaron Beck gathered together these ideas into one work: CBT.

Albert Bandura

Social learning theory, which emphasizes that learning is not only behavioral but also a cognitive process, in a social context, created significant awareness by emphasizing the effectiveness of cognitive processes in human behavior. One of the precursors to the improvement of CBT was the emergence of Bandura's social learning theory, and it played an important role in the emergence of cognitive understanding.[21] Dissimilar to the psychodynamic or behavioral views of psychological disturbance, according to Bandura, people interact consciously and actively within their environment.

Arnold Lazarus

Multimodal therapy (MMT), which is a systematic and comprehensive psychotherapeutic approach, was created and developed by Dr. Arnold Lazarus, a clinical psychologist. MMT gives almost equal weight to all modalities, whereas, especially for Ellis and Beck, cognitions are a priority. Lazarus was very influential in the development of CBT. He was awarded the Albert Ellis Humanitarian Award for his contribution to CBT in 2013. For the first time, Lazarus introduced scientific literature about 'behavioral therapy' to show that behavioral interventions are the basis for clinical practice.[22] Later, Lazarus broadened the therapeutic spectrum of therapy[23] because of the high incidence of reoccurrence in the follow-up studies of those who applied only behavioral methods. He preferred to tackle his studies in a multifaceted way, in order to be able to provide clearer answers to the questions 'for what problem, under what conditions, who and what best provides treatment?,' and he was methodical in both the application and measurement of therapy. Although the measurement in MMT is 'multi,' the treatment is actually more 'unimodal' or 'bimodal.' Lazarus is seen as the predecessor of those who established behavioral therapies, but a wide range of strategies is applied in MMT. Multimodal theory is interchangeable with behavioral therapy, rational-emotional-behavioral therapy, and other cognitive therapies.

Donald Meichenbaum

Dr. Donald Meichenbaum followed the Gestalt, psychoanalytic, and semantic practice techniques prescribed by the American Psychological Association (APA) congress in 1963. His contribution to the cognitive learning theory began with his doctoral dissertation. He was interested in the role of 'self-directing' in areas of human behavior, such as skill acquisition and problem-solving. Meichenbaum was interested in teaching internal speech that provided personal control over external verbal behavior.[24,25] According to Meichenbaum, the instructions that people give themselves reveal the desired behavioral changes by providing a passage through inharmonious and nonfunctional disturbing thoughts to a harmonious and healthy mind. The aim is to provide skills to cope with stressful situations, to develop personal control strategies, and to provide 'learned skills' resources that can be replaced by 'learned reactions,' which will become a natural part of one's character. This includes RE & CBT methods, such as didactic training, Socratic discussion, cognitive restructuring, problem-solving, relaxation training, behavioral and imagery rehearsal, personal monitoring, personal training, personal reinforcement, and efforts to change the environment.

Karl R. Popper

Karl R. Popper was a philosopher, not a psychologist, and his ideas have influenced many CBT contributors. His understanding of a variety of philosophical sources was influenced by destructive ideas, such as totalitarianism and fascism, which were prevalent during his lifetime. He shaped and improved his own philosophy in the light of such political activity. Criticism, which is not necessarily a negative thing, is a part of Popper's philosophical attitude. He adopted criticism as a criterion of rationality. Popper suggested that without criticizing theories, there is no possible room for improvement in science. Many world leaders have been influenced by his discoveries. Ellis was very impressed with the idea of 'the principle of falsifiability' as the basis of Popper's theory of science. Dr. Ellis continuously improved, corrected, and modified his own theory. According to Popper, theories can never be experimentally verified because of the invalidity of the induction principle, but this could be wrong. It is therefore necessary for a theory to be scientific to be able to be mistaken. Popper was interested in Albert Einstein's theory of relativity, Karl Marx's understanding of history, Sigmund Freud's theory of psychoanalysis, and Alfred Adler's individual psychology theories. He criticized Freud's approach for not being scientific because Freud presented his theory as if it could not be falsified. According to Popper, psychoanalysis is not a scientific approach to the study of the mind. Popper noted that the theories of Marx, Freud, and Adler did not specify under which conditions their clients would refrain from repeating the same behavior, and that they would continue to maintain old thought patterns. Despite a possible recognition that things were not going correctly, clients and therapists simply imagined a change may occur by osmosis. As a result of this, Popper divided theories into 'scientific' and 'unscientific.' It is easy to find experimental support under certain conditions, whatever a theory may be, and it is easy to find empirical support of any given theory; however, it is essential to determine under what conditions the theory is wrong.

> Tbox: Karl R. Popper wrote, 'Good theory is a theory that can be falsified, refuted—depending on time.' This also applies to psychotherapeutic theories. It is important that any techniques used are in accordance with scientific knowledge, and have been scientifically proven.

Albert Ellis

Dr. Albert Ellis is known as the grandfather of cognitive behavior therapies. He originally trained in psychoanalysis and initially carried out therapy processes in line with this school. For 15 years he continued to work within this theoretical framework. He then began to see clients in his New York office after years of psychoanalysis training. Over time, he realized that clients did not change much, although they had a very good insight into psychoanalytic therapy. After seeing the inadequacies of Freudian theory, and even, in some cases, the harmful aspects of it, he began new investigations. He documented, collated, archived, and established what he discovered as scientific knowledge and put forward an effective evidence-based psychotherapy approach. He concluded that the cognitive functions of individuals were not taken into consideration in the psychoanalytic process. Individuals are conditioned during their childhood years so that in their later lives they feel and behave in a way appropriate to these conditions. During the therapy process, the individual is expected to get rid of the effects of these conditions and to see that the fears she experiences are not suitable for the situation. Ellis supported his ideas with philosophical information and turned it into scientific knowledge by putting forward an effective evidence-based psychotherapy approach. Some important elements of CBT were spawned from his ideas, such as demandingness, irrational beliefs, unconditional self-acceptance, frustration intolerance, awfulizing, downing, two categories of emotions (healthy and unhealthy negative emotions), and the techniques of rational imagery, the ABCDEF model, and rehearsal of RaBels. It is noteworthy that Ellis's proposal of the benefits of unconditional acceptance and frustration tolerance especially, in psychological health, is closely related to Middle Eastern culture, as well as third-wave cognitive therapies.

Aaron Beck

Immediately after Ellis, Aaron Beck, a psychiatrist and cognitive behavioral therapist, made a great contribution to cognitive therapy (CT). He created a treatment protocol for depression. Later it became a cognitive therapy to treat many disorders. According to him, clients with depression can be defined thus:

there are certain cognitive contents that cause them to look badly on their current lives and the future. In this respect, the aim of therapy is to define and change cognitive distortions, prejudices, and the client's specific schemas and thinking. CT became CBT and included behavioral techniques in its treatment protocols. According to Beck and Padesky, the fundamental difference between REBT and CBT is that REBT is philosophically based psychotherapy, while CBT is empirically based psychotherapy.[26] Instead of confronting clients with their irrational beliefs and thoughts, as in REBT, Beck's approach looked to join with a client in a course of collaborative discovery, tempting her to be involved, as a scientific observer of her own experience, as the psychotherapist guided her towards an alternative outlook through Socratic dialogue.[27]

Cognitive Therapy

Clients are taught to see and respond more rationally to negative automatic thoughts by labeling a variety of cognitive distortions, and subsequently engaging in cognitive reformation with the therapist and in journaling activities.[27] According to Beck's cognitive theory, there is an interaction between how the individual perceives himself/herself, his/her environment, the future, and how he/she feels/behaves.

Cbox: If one or more of these thoughts bother you and disturbs your functionality, please see a mental health worker.

In Figure 2.4, there are three examples of our dysfunctional thought processes according to CBT.

About self—'nobody likes me.'
About the world—'the world is a bad place.'
About the future—'I will always be bad.'

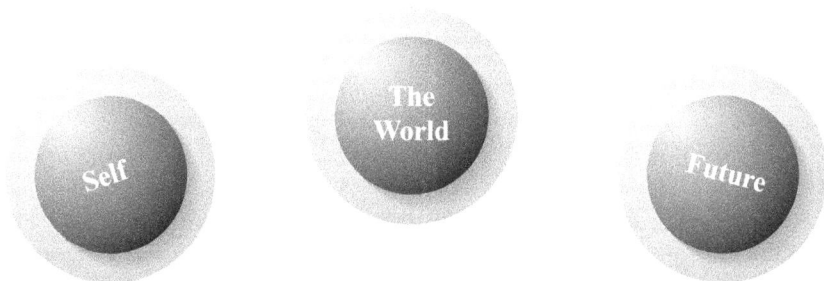

FIGURE 2.4 Beck's model assumes that there are three3 types of automatic thoughts.

CBT proposes three components for dysfunctional thoughts. They are that individuals, who are in psychological distress, may have dysfunctional thoughts about themselves, life, and the future. For instance, if one has dysfunctional thoughts about the future one may have hopeless feelings about the future and may therefore be in depression. That is to say, the emotional response of the individual depends on the way she perceives, recognizes, and interprets events.[28] Individuals constantly evaluate the meaning of events in their environment and their cognitive processes are often accompanied by emotional reactions. Cognitive processes that disrupt this adaptation can trigger emotional and physiological responses.[29] Cognitive behavioral theorists assume that cognitive elements that cause problem behaviors contribute to mental disorders and to their maintenance. Cognitive behavioral therapy is thought to prevent the recurrence of problems after therapy[30] by determining and analyzing emotions, thoughts, and behaviors that cause problems in the individual's life.

Cognitive theory examines cognition under two main headings of schemas and automatic thought, which is one of the variables examined in research. Cognitive theory is the interpretation of what influences human emotions and the physiological and behavioral responses associated with it.[29] Cognitive theory examines three main themes: cognition, automatic thought, and schemas. Schemas are identified as intermediate and core beliefs. It is thought that it would be useful to examine schemas, intermediate beliefs, fundamental beliefs, and irrational beliefs, in addition to automatic beliefs, in order to better understand cognition and to make it easier to distinguish automatic beliefs in others. According to Beck, automatic thinking is, in fact, the repetition of a sentence, automatically and subconsciously, that people say to themselves repetitively under certain situations.[31] It generally tends to be negative, carrying with it the attitudes, prejudices, and other 'voices' of parents, peers, and family from an early age. Psychological problems arise when people consistently have negative thoughts. The situation itself does not directly determine how they feel or what they do; how they perceive the situation determines what their emotional response will be. Insisting on repeating negative mantras cannot change anything. The ability to explore and express how individuals feel and behave emotionally, how they interpret a situation, and how they think about it is the way to a greater understanding of how to act and react.

Contemporary Practitioners and Academics

Nowadays, there are many psychologists who actively conduct studies, give seminars, and write books about CBT, such as Windy Dryden, James McMahon, Arthur Freeman, Stefan G. Hofmann, and Raymond A. DiGiuseppe. The latter is one of the authors of the book *A Practitioner's Guide to Rational Emotive Therapy and a Primer on Rational Emotive Behavioral Therapy.* He established a firm conceptualization of REBT based on rational and irrational beliefs. He works on the development of the theory, practice, and support of empirical research of rational emotive behavior therapy and cognitive behavior therapies. He developed a measurement (Attitude and Beliefs Scale—II) (ABS-II) based on Ellis's concept of irrational and rational beliefs and their relationship to other cognitive behavior constructs. Prof. DiGiuseppe was elected president of the Association for Behavioral and Cognitive Therapies (ABCT), which is the most influential organization for cognitive behavior therapies. Contemporary practitioners and scientists still contribute to CBT development. Some of the past presidents of the ABCT were famous psychologists, such as Joseph Wolpe, Alan E. Kazdin, David H. Barlow, Arthur Freeman, Steven C. Heyes, Steven D. Hollon, Artura M. Nezu, Marsha M. Linehan, Robert L. Leahy, Debra A. Hope, Stefan G. Hofmann, and Jonathan Abramowitz. They have all been influential in the world of REBT and CBT studies and their development.

Since there are more people who live in the East, and Africa, than in the West, and even more who seek mental health professionals' advice, it is a strange dichotomy that there is *no one* from the East in this list. Why are Middle Eastern practitioners not mentioned? For sure, they have no theories, but their experience must be invaluable. What theories do Eastern psychotherapists suggest? Iranian Nossrat Peseschkian, who is known as a German scientist, created positive psychotherapy. However, for instance, when you watch YouTube to hear his views they are all in German—there is nothing in English. Tayyab Rashid helped to create another type of positive psychotherapy, but he is known as a Canadian therapist, not Middle Eastern.

Conclusion

The important thing about RE & CBT is to regulate feelings through cognition. We must recognize and practice the effort of directly editing our emotions and behavior. Analyzing our thoughts and examining our core beliefs, as well as our irrational beliefs, may provide us with an enduring method of dealing with stressful events. With a more complete understanding of the essentials of REBT it will be easier for Middle Eastern clients, especially, to tackle some of the practical suggestions in the second part of this book and be able to relate it to some of the deeper concerns of an approach to REBT using alternative cultural resources, such as Sufism. With this in mind, the next chapter sets out the goals of rational emotive & cognitive behavioral therapy.

References

1. Ruggiero, G. M., Spada, M. M., Caselli, G., & Sassaroli, S. (2018). A historical and theoretical review of cognitive behavioral therapies: From structural self-knowledge to functional processes. *Journal of Rational-Emotive & Cognitive-Behavior Therapy*, 1–26.
2. Courtney, L. B., Connor, M. P., & Settipani, C. A. (2011). History of cognitive-behavioral therapy (CBT) in youth. *Child and Adolescent Psychiatric Clinics of North America, 20*, 179–189.

3. Turner, R., & Swearer, S. M. (2010). Cognitive Behavioral Therapy (CBT). In *Encyclopedia of Cross-Cultural School Psychology* (pp. 226–229). Boston, MA: Springer.

4. Ellis, A. (1994). *Reason and Emotion in Psychotherapy* (Re. ed.). Secaucus, NJ: Birch Lane.

5. Collard, J., & O'Kelly, M. (2011). Rational emotive behaviour therapy: A positive perspective. *Journal of Rational-Emotive & Cognitive-Behavior Therapy, 29*(4), 248–256.

6. Campbell, P. (2016). *The Story of Civilization: VOLUME I – The Ancient World*. Charlotte, NC: TAN Books.

7. Gianni Vattimo (1936–). (n.d.). Retrieved from: https://www.iep.utm.edu/vattimo/

8. Kaymakcan, R., & Şirin, T. (2013). Bilişsel-Davranışçı Psikoterapi Yaklaşımı ile Bütünleştirilmiş Dini Danışmanlık Modeli'nin Din Eğitimi Alan Erkek Üniversite Öğrencilerinin Durumluk ve Sürekli Kaygı Düzeylerine Etkisi. *Değerler Eğitimi Dergisi, 11*(26), 111–148.

9. Ellis, A. (1962). *Reason and Emotion in Psychotherapy*. Secaucus, NJ: Lyle Stuart.

10. DiGiuseppe, R. A., Doyle, K. A., Dryden, W., & Backx, W. (2014). *A Practitioner's Guide to Rational Emotive Behavior Therapy* (3rd ed.). New York: Oxford University Press.

11. Ellis, A., & Dryden, W. (1997). *The Practice of Rational: Emotive Therapy* (2nd ed.). New York: Springer.

12. Verbal Awareness. (n.d.). Retrieved from www.generalsemantics.org/the-general-semantics-learning-center/overview-of-general-semantics/basic-understandings/

13. Ellis, A. (1997). Albert Ellis on rational emotive behavior therapy. Interview by Lata K. McGinn. *American Journal of Psychotherapies, 51*(3), 309–316.

14. Bernard, M. E. (2010). *Rationality and the Pursuit of Happiness: The Legacy of Albert Ellis*. West Sussex, UK: Wiley Blackwell.

15. Ellis, A. (2003). The relationship of Rational Emotive Behavior Therapy (REBT) to social psychology. *Journal of Rational-Emotive & Cognitive-Behavior Therapy, 21*(1).

16. Dryden, W. (2009). *Understanding Emotional Problems, the REBT Perspective*. New York, NY: Taylor & Francis Group.

17. DiGiuseppe, R., Leaf, R., Gorman, B., & Robin, M. W. (2018). The development of a measure of irrational/rational beliefs. *Journal of Rational-Emotive & Cognitive-Behaviour Therapy, 36*(1), 47–79.

18. Vîslǎ, A., Flückiger, C., Grosse Holtforth, M., & David, D. (2016). Irrational beliefs and psychological distress: A meta-analysis. *Psychotherapy and Psychosomatics, 85*(1), 8–15.

19. Pressman, S. D., & Cohen, S. (2005). Does positive affect influence health? *Psychological Bulletin, 131*(6), 925.

20. Engels, G. I., Garnefski, N., & Diekstra, R. F. (1993). Efficacy of rational-emotive therapy: A quantitative analysis. *Journal of Consulting and Clinical Psychology, 61*(6), 1083.

21. Turner, R., & Swearer, S. M. (2010). Cognitive Behavioral Therapy (CBT). In *Encyclopedia of Cross-Cultural School Psychology* (pp. 226–229). Boston, MA: Springer.

22. Lazarus, A. A. (1958). New methods in psychotherapy: A case study. *South African Medical Journal, 32*(6).

23. Lazarus, A. A. (1971). Where do behavior therapists take their troubles? *Psychological Reports, 28*(2), 349–350.

24. Meichenbaum, D. H., & Goodman, J. (1971). Training impulsive children to talk to themselves: A means of developing self-control. *Journal of Abnormal Psychology, 77*(2), 115.

25. Meichenbaum, D. (1977). Cognitive behaviour modification. *Cognitive Behaviour Therapy, 6*(4), 185–192.

26. Padesky, C. A., & Beck, A. T. (2003). Science and philosophy: Comparison of cognitive therapy and rational emotive behavior therapy. *Journal of Cognitive Psychotherapy*, *17*(3), 211.
27. Thoma, N., Pilecki, B., & McKay, D. (2015). Contemporary cognitive behavior therapy: A review of theory, history, and evidence. *Psychodynamic Psychiatry*, *43*(3), 423–461.
28. Beck, A. T. (1967). *Depression: Clinical, Experimental, and Theoretical Aspects*. Philadelphia: University of Pennsylvania Press.
29. Jesse, H. W., Basco, M. R., & Thase, M. E. (2006). *Learning Cognitive-Behavior Therapy: An Illustrated Guide*. Arlington, VA: American Psychiatric Association Publishing.
30. Gladding, S. T. (2015). *Family Therapy: History, Theory, and Practice*. Essex: Pearson Education Limited.
31. Beck, C. T. (2001). Predictors of postpartum depression: An update. *Nursing Research*, *50*(5), 275–285.

3

THE B OF THE ABC MODEL

The knowledge of anything, since all things have causes, is not acquired or complete, unless it is known by its causes.

—*Avicenna*

In the following pages the main features of cognitive behavior therapy are introduced. How do our thought processes work? What are the components of our cognitive schemas? Why do we feel how we feel? In Chapter 2, the ABC model was briefly mentioned, but in this chapter, beliefs and thought processes, known as B, will be scrutinized.

In the face of any stressful event our emotions are activated by our thoughts and beliefs. According to the ABC model, the most important aspect of human psychology is not the *A*s (activating events) but the *B*s. With some knowledge of the ABC model, cultural differences can be evaluated when, during therapy, it is applied to Middle Eastern people. REBT and CBT share common ground about *B*s, though some small differences exist. The following chapter (Chapter 4) will focus on the '**Cs**' (emotions) of the model.

In CBT, the effect of an event on a person is measured by her thoughts. In other words, we live according to what we think of the events. The reason why unhealthy emotions and unhealthy behavior are experienced, such as anger, anxiety, and depression, is not the events but our thoughts concerning these events. Therefore, one of the most important points in psychological well-being is to analyze unhelpful, unreasonable, unrealistic, dysfunctional cognitive schemas and replace them with alternatives (e.g., functional thoughts, rational beliefs). In order to change our dysfunctional cognitive schemas, applications/interventions need to be made with therapeutically and scientifically proven evidence-based

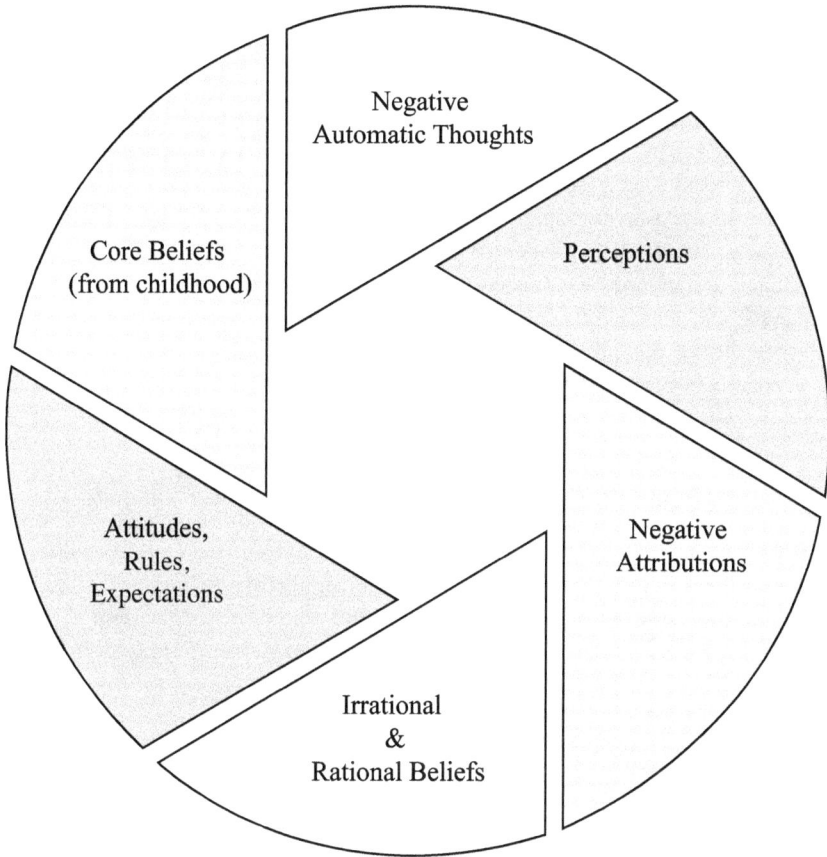

FIGURE 3.1 Bs of the ABC model: an integrated model for Ellis's and Beck's approaches.

techniques. Interventions are divided into three categories in CBT: cognitive, behavioral, and emotional. This book focuses mainly on cognitive and emotional interventions alone.

Here, to gain a more advanced knowledge about what CBT does in the Bs, a look at the most recent features of REBT (known as the Ellis approach) and CT (known as the Beck approach) is put forward.

Distinct Features of REBT

REBT is one of several psychotherapeutic approaches that can be differentiated from other types of cognitive behavior therapies. CBT therapists often apply REBT components in their therapies (and their books) but they call their approach CBT. Also, some REBT therapists use the Beck approaches (e.g., automatic thoughts) in their therapy. Empirical research in REBT practice has frequently been evaluated under the name of CBT. These studies show REBT is an effective therapy. A meta-analysis of psychotherapy outcome studies indicates that REBT has the second highest effectiveness and usefulness in terms of effect size after systematic desensitization and before behavioral modification, Adlerian therapy, client-centered, psychodynamic, transactional analysis, and eclectic therapies.[1]

REBT focuses on irrational and rational beliefs and not on automatic thoughts and core beliefs as in the Beck approach. It also tries to qualitatively change emotions, as opposed to the Beck approach, which tries to reduce the intensity of dysfunctional emotions (e.g., anxiety, guilt) quantitatively. Thus, in REBT, for example, sadness is exchanged with depression, concern with anxiety, and regret with guilt, in order make the process from unhealthy/dysfunctional emotions to healthy/ functional emotions. REBT uses the Socratic questioning and didactic method to dispute (restructure) irrational beliefs and rehearse rational beliefs in session.[2]

Irrational Beliefs (IrBels)

Irrational beliefs are related to various psychological disorders[3] and psychological distress.[4] That is to say, IrBels are considered a hindrance to mental health and psychological well-being. According to REBT there are some dysfunctional cognitive processes, called irrational beliefs, which cause psychological ill-being. They are known as:[5]

1. irrational excessive demandingness
2. awfulizing (unrealistic negative evaluation)
3. frustration intolerance (low tolerance)
4. global condemnation of human worth (also called self, other, and life downing or depreciation beliefs)

IrBels are considered to be extreme, rigid, unrealistic, and illogical (see some examples in Figure 3.2 and at the end of the chapter). They cause certain unhealthy negative emotions. For a lengthier discussion about emotions please see Chapters 4 and 5. Starting with Chapter 4 of this book, readers will discover rational beliefs interventions using Middle Eastern sources.

For more about irrational and rational beliefs, readers are encouraged to read the book *Rational and Irrational Beliefs: Research, Theory and Clinical Practice* (Oxford University Press).

Rational Beliefs (RaBels)

A therapist and client try to replace irrational beliefs with rational alternatives during therapy together. RaBels are not 'positive' or 'optimistic' but rather realistic, logical, pragmatic, and flexible cognitive processes. There are four rational beliefs:[2]

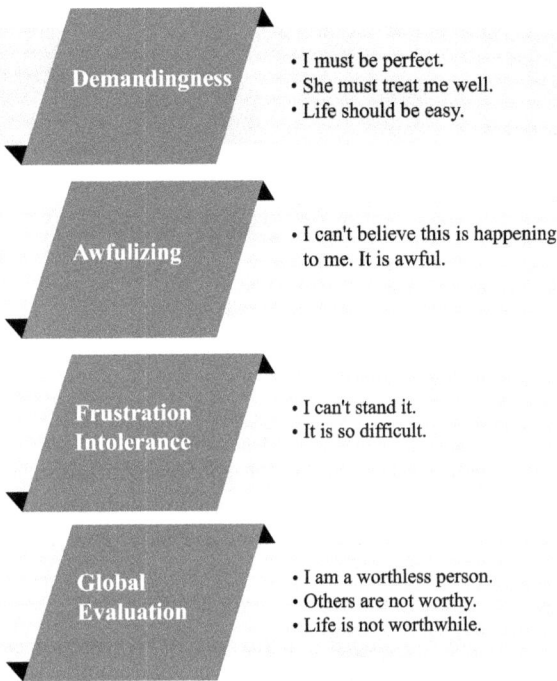

FIGURE 3.2 Demandingness is the primary irrational belief and others are evaluative irrational beliefs.

1. Preferences (nondemanding wants and wishes)

    'I prefer people to treat me well, but nowhere is it written that they must.'

2. Anti-awfulizing (realistic negative evaluations)

    'It is a bad thing; however, it is not awful.'

3. Frustration tolerance (high-tolerance beliefs)

    'It is a bit of a pain but I can still stand it.'

4. Acceptance beliefs (of self, others, and life) (or, as proposed in this book, 'love of self, love of others, and love of life' beliefs).

    'Regardless of what my failures are, I am still a worthwhile person.'

Note: A list of irrational and rational beliefs can be found at the end of this chapter.

More on REBT

Dr. Ellis focused mainly on irrational beliefs and psychological *ill-being* relationships and, for a long time, rational beliefs remained behind the scenes. In recent years, Albert Ellis Institute faculties have tended to investigate and apply rational beliefs

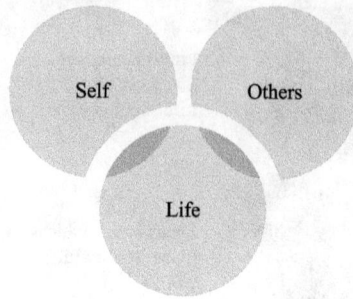

FIGURE 3.3 Our irrational beliefs have three dimensions.

more than irrational beliefs in practice. Ellis's students want to know about the effectiveness of rational beliefs on psychological *well-being*. An investigation of the effect of rational beliefs on psychological conditions may help us to see some of the factors that make clients live satisfactory lives and have positive feelings.

T and C box: Readers are encouraged to obtain more information about these issues from other REBT and CBT books—for example, A Practitioner's Guide to Rational Emotive Behavior Therapy (Third Edition).

REBT claims that demandingness and self-depreciation (global evaluation) irrational beliefs have three dimensions: self, others, and life. For instance, a person may believe that others must respect them (demand from others), or, she must be perfect at all tasks (demands of herself), or a student may believe that an exam should be easy (demands of life). Global evaluation irrational beliefs express themselves in a similar way: a suicidal person may believe that life is not worth living, a person who has narcissistic tendencies believes that others are worthless, or a person who gets fired from her job believes that she is worthless.

Context-Specific Irrational Beliefs

Recent development in REBT and CBT theories points out another approach to irrational beliefs that is called *context-based* IrBels. This area of REBT and CBT is very interesting and ripe for research. The context-based approach focuses on irrational beliefs about specific life issues or motivational aspects of human behavior. Some investigations have focused on the irrational beliefs of three basic psychological needs.[6]

For instance, irrational beliefs in the context of basic psychological needs (autonomy, competence, relatedness) are very new concepts that help the client to recognize and overcome her irrational beliefs to satisfy those psychological needs.[3,7] The idea behind context-specific irrational beliefs is that the therapist is not only dealing with activating events (e.g., asking the client, 'What is a recent example of your stress?') but also dealing with clients' psychological needs. The therapist identifies the problems with a client's autonomy, competence, and relatedness needs and then relates them to irrational beliefs.[8] In this way, clients try to dispute and eliminate (and replace with rational beliefs) any irrational beliefs that prevent her reaching basic psychological needs. Such intervention can also be used in dealing with automatic thoughts and cognitive distortions.

Similar *context-based* irrational beliefs made by others include: (1) DiGiuseppe's[8] IrBels and RaBels on three content areas of achievement, affiliation, and comfort and (2) Lindner et al.'s[9] demand for fairness, need for achievement, and need for approval.

Emotional Disturbance

As mentioned previously, REBT views emotions qualitatively rather than quantitatively, as in CBT. There is a difference between the unitary (Beck's approach) and the binary (Ellis's approach) of emotions and the implications for theory and practice of therapeutic approaches. Different perspectives on the unitary and binary model of emotions are considered the fundamental difference between cognitive therapy and rational emotive behavior therapy.[2,10]

Not everyone knows emotions are semantically different from each other. Can you recall what 'depressed' or 'angry' feels like? It is not about the degree (intensity) of your feeling, such as feeling bad, or feeling 'so so,' or even feeling great. It is about categorizing your emotions qualitatively, not quantitatively. Wouldn't it be amazing to be able to choose what emotions you want to feel? This is so casual . . . scientists do not think like this—it is a completely different style. Not only Ellis but also famous psychologist Alfred Adler suggested a binary model of emotions. While a unitary model suggests that human behavior disturbances can be explained only in intensity of emotions,[2,11] a binary model suggests that functional and dysfunctional emotions are qualitatively different, based on rational or irrational beliefs.[2] Anxiety as an emotion is *qualitatively* different to concern, and likewise, depression versus sadness, anger versus annoyance, guilt versus regret, and shame versus disappointment. 'These emotions rest in two different emotional continua.'[12] This approach provides clients with a tool for understanding and changing emotions. It may be very important to take either one of two perspectives for therapists, because the emotional goal of the therapy will be changed accordingly. Both therapist and client together will aim to reduce the intensity of dysfunctional emotions, or they will aim to qualitatively differentiate alternative emotions to replace negative unhealthy emotions. This distinction affects how to apply cognitive disputation techniques. REBT works on irrational beliefs, to replace them with rational beliefs, in order to take the client from unhealthy negative emotions to healthy negative emotions. In quite the opposite way, Beck's (CBT) work is placed on reducing the number of, and intensity of, negative automatic thoughts, to reduce the level of dysfunctional emotions (e.g., from 1 to 10 anxiety level). According to research outcomes both approaches work!

Elegant Solution

In REBT, the term 'elegant solution,' in therapeutic intervention, refers to disputing irrational demandingness and evaluating irrational beliefs (e.g., catastrophizing/awfulizing), in order to create and maintain philosophic change. Philosophic change is defined as: changing IrBels to RaBels permanently—in a timeless, placeless, and causeless manner, rather than changing inferences and automatic thoughts in the face of stressful events.

Asking for evidence regarding a client's 'catastrophe' is an inelegant intervention—for instance, asking, 'Do you have evidence that everyone in the classroom thought you were a terrible teacher?' Rather, asking a client, 'What is the worst thing that could happen if we assume you are bad teacher?' will lead her to find an elegant solution. A solution to this could be that she believes in the possibility of choosing to accept herself, independent of her teaching ability.

To sum up, REBT focuses on disputing irrational beliefs that a client holds in everyday life, while CBT focuses on dealing with cognitive distortions and other components of cognition, such as automatic thoughts and core beliefs in specific incidents. Elegant solutions are claimed to be beneficial for long-term philosophical change and they are considered superior to disputing cold cognitions for some therapists. However, research suggests that any kind of harmful and dysfunctional beliefs and thoughts are worthy of disputation in order to become psychologically well.

Disputation

We rarely fight, but sometimes we do. Fighting with our thoughts happens too! However, imagine that you do not know how to fight! RE & CBT teach you to deal with your own unhealthy, dysfunctional, repetitive, stubborn, and useless thoughts without fighting and wallowing! You can use RE & CBT disputation techniques to your advantage. They are the centered assignments in CB therapies. Disputation is restructuring the cognitive schemas to gain a better life and self-acceptance, take emotional responsibility, increase tolerance of uncertainty and discomfort, improve skills in flexible thinking, obtain the ability of self-direction, end utopic thoughts, pursue realistic thinking, and achieve and maintain behaviorally functional living (e.g., practicing a sport, socializing, and enjoying life in general).

Disputation is a method of changing irrational beliefs and negative automatic thoughts to a healthy, rational, and useful type of thinking. A therapist can use various kinds of disputation styles to help a client get rid of dysfunctional thoughts.[13]

There are four major styles in disputation:[2]

1. The Socratic style
2. The didactic style
3. The humorous style
4. The metaphoric style

Using any one of these styles, there are many types of disputation: semantic, logical, functional, and evidence-based. Teaching or, rather, giving cold hard facts about which thoughts or beliefs can be beneficial to clients is also considered to be disputation (didactic disputation). For instance, giving a client homework, and asking her to repeat rational beliefs to herself, may help her to change her irrational beliefs to rational ones. The Socratic style includes asking critical questions to a client to 'force' her to discover her irrational thoughts and challenge her illogical, unrealistic, and harmful points of view. In Part II of this book, based on didactic, humorous, and metaphoric styles, it will be observed how Eastern sources can be used in disputations. Sufic instruction, 'wise old sayings,' and session protocols have been carefully structured to support clients in a rational and positive way. Chapters 5, 7, 8, 9, and 10 are all about disputation. However, as mentioned, this book tends to focus on RaBels, rather than irrational ones, and provides examples from the Middle East to be used in a variety of ways, including didactic, humorous, and metaphoric styles. This type of disputation is briefly explained ahead, using the Socratic and didactic styles.

> **Semantic disputation** is generally applied by drawing attention to the 'meaning' of words in the client's beliefs or thoughts. Thus, a therapist may ask a client, 'What do you mean by saying, "I can't stand it"? Could you explain to me what "can't stand" means? When you "can't stand it," what do you do? I acknowledge that we cannot stand being hungry, thirsty, or sleepless. How about in your situation? Do you really mean "can't stand it" or in some way and at some point, you have a hard time dealing with it?'
>
> **Functional disputation** directly focuses on the functionality of beliefs or thoughts themselves: From a pragmatic perspective, asking a client how the beliefs they hold serve their goals. A therapist may ask the client, 'How can having all kinds of destructive, noisy, helpless, awful thoughts lead you to what you want to reach (i.e., psychological well-being, passing the exam, or having a peaceful life)?'
>
> **Evidence-based disputation** is making a client collect evidence against dysfunctional thoughts, such as the thought 'No one loves me' can be disputed by collecting evidence on any given day. By giving homework, a client can try to find out if 'no one loves me' is 'not true.' A brief note: this

kind of work can be done only if a therapist is sure that the client really has some people around her who potentially love or like her. Another point in evidence-based disputation is that clients need to collect data against the irrational beliefs of dysfunctional thoughts, not the opposite.

Logical disputation is a good one but a harsh one! The client is asked whether there is a rule or law about her demands. For instance, the therapist asks the client, 'You keep saying the person must love you. If he doesn't like you, moreover we assume that he will never like you; then could you tell me where it is written that 'he must like you'?! The purpose of a therapist asking such a question is that it shows the client that 'must' is a problematic word in the belief. Ellis suggested that rational beliefs like 'I prefer (or wish) him to like me' is a logical thought; however, 'I must be liked by other people' is not a logical belief because 'must' is an absolute term and when you say 'must' then it *must* be so 100% of the time. In real life, however, things do not occur like that, so it is not logical!

Philosophic disputation is used when a therapist is faced with a client who displays a tendency to awfulize things or self/life downing. With this technique, the therapist reminds her that, indeed bad things happen, but her life is not only filled with negativity, and subsequently asks whether she can still try to find a bit of happiness, peace, or meaning in her life. RE & CBT therapists usually use stoic-epicurean philosophy when they use this type of disputation. However, in this book, Sufism and Middle Eastern 'wise old sayings' are suggested when using such philosophic disputation, as culturally defining.

Some More Examples

The following dialogues are taken from actual sessions with Turkish clients in Istanbul.

Example 1: Semantic Disputation

Notes: A 19-year-old client was rejected by a girl whom he liked. The essential components of REBT were introduced to the client during the first and second sessions. Disputations took place concerning the belief of catastrophizing/awfulizing. In order to reach an elegant solution, the therapist accepted the 'badness' of the situation without judging. The therapist wanted to lead the client to the rational belief: 'Being rejected is unfortunate but it is simply bad. It is not awful or terrible.' The client was then asked if being rejected was the worst thing in the world.

T: Is being rejected the worst thing in the world?
C: For me, yes, it's the worst thing in the world.

T: I understand you. Let's suppose that's true. I also understand that you never want to experience such heartache but to re-evaluate the situation, I am asking you what you mean by the 'worst thing in the world'?

C: I mean it is kind of the worst, at least, at the moment, I feel this way.

T: I hear you. I just wanted to point out that you gave a meaning to being rejected as the worst thing in the world. If you would, could you give any other definition to it? Maybe a helpful one, or a functional one.

C: I feel kind of upset. I cannot generate any other meaning. However, I get your point, I guess. Calling it the worst thing in the world is kind of exaggerating.

T: When we think about your situation, could we say that it is not the worst thing in life, but it is very bad in your life?

C: Yes, I can say that there have been other experiences my life when I felt really bad.

Example 2: Logical Disputation

A 45-year-old woman wants to play in a drama. She goes to the audition; however, she was not chosen for the play.

C: Can you explain why something is found funny? I mean, I may find something—that is to say, I have appraised it as funny. But someone else may not find it amusing. Is this an irrational belief?

Note: At this point, if you discuss with the client whether her joke is funny, or why the listener found the joke funny or not, it will lead you in the wrong direction—which would be an inelegant solution. For an elegant solution this could be used:

T: Do you mean they must find your joke funny?

C: I wanted them to laugh at my joke.

T: Yes, but did they have to? I mean, which one is it better to believe: 'they have to laugh at my joke' or 'I prefer, or, I wish them to find my joke funny'?

C: I guess I believe I must make them laugh. I keep asking myself why they don't laugh when I do something I think is funny, but they do laugh at other points, when I see no reason for it. Should I be pleased with this surprise?

T: Where is written that you must make them laugh?

C: I must because I need the role in that play.

T: It is true that, in order to get chosen, you'd better make them laugh. If it is a comedy. However, is there any rule or law saying they must laugh or that you must make them laugh?

C: No, there is no law or rule. It's just that I really badly wanted to be in that play.

T: Yes, you really wanted it, but there is no place that says you must make them laugh, nor that you will get the job, even if you do.

Basics of CT

Aaron T. Beck introduced the essentials of cognitive therapy with his first book, *Depression: Clinical, Experimental and Theoretical Aspects*, in 1967. He was influenced by Albert Ellis's works and also by George Kelly, and further developed his ideas. Beck was the second scientist in history after Piaget to mention cognitive schemas whereby our thought processes screen, decode, and evaluate the stimuli around us.[14]

Unrealistic cognitive evaluations of certain life events affect our emotions and behaviors negatively. The CT (or CBT) approach emphasizes that systematic errors in thinking, and cognitive distortions of events, may lead to negative emotions and incongruent behavior.[14] Cognitive distortions are slightly different to Ellis's proposals about irrational beliefs. They are not as deep as IrBels are; they are mostly on the surface. Cognitive theory explains the cognitive structure of an individual and exploits two basic concepts. These concepts are automatic thoughts and schemas. Schemas can be divided into two groups: intermediate (attitudes or rules) beliefs and basic (core) beliefs. These three groups of cognition (core beliefs, intermediate beliefs, and automatic thoughts) are thought to be intertwined rings, with automatic thinking in the surface ring, intermediate beliefs in the middle ring, and core beliefs in the innermost ring.

Cognitive Schema

As an information processing theory, CT is interested in cognitive structures. When we say cognitive schemas, we are actually talking about core beliefs.[14] According to Beck, a cognitive structure is used for screening and evaluating the activating (stressful) event.[15] Schemas starting in childhood and developing into adult life, with constant and permanent characteristics, are constantly supported by cognitive distortions. According to Beck, because cognitive schemas are acquired very early, individuals have not yet reached the capacity to question them correctly and effectively.[15]

Cognitive schemata are mental activity patterns that are determined by the past experiences and learning of the person, shaping the situations that are encountered by the individual in sorting, distinguishing, and coding.[16] The schema concept has been determined as the end result of the previous experience and past learning of the person. The stimuli encountered by the person are defined as the pattern of mental activities that form their cognition in shaping them through discrimination, sorting, and coding.[16,15]

Core Beliefs

Core beliefs are methods of thinking and conditional beliefs are underlying assumptions.[14,16] Individuals develop ideas about themselves, others, and the world from their childhood, and they accept these ideas as absolute truth.

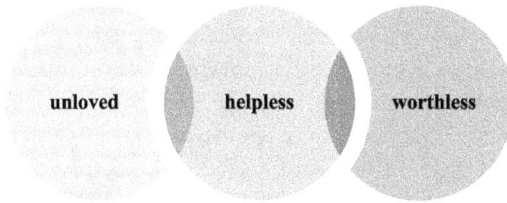

FIGURE 3.4 Three common core beliefs.

These fundamental beliefs are deeply rooted because individuals do not often express (verbalize) themselves to others.[15] Core beliefs are usually extreme generalizations.[17,15] They are defined as generalized, absolute, fundamental, and inflexible beliefs that people have about themselves, others, the world, or the future.[18,17] These beliefs are the most well-established beliefs and constantly affect our lives. Generally, well-established core beliefs allow individuals to interpret, evaluate, and respond to life events in a realistic and adaptable way. However, when core beliefs are wrong, useless, or judgmental, the individual's self-concept has a profound impact on self-efficacy and vulnerability to emotional disturbances.[14,18] Core beliefs are gathered into three groups: unloved, helpless, and worthless.

For instance, a basic formulation may be helplessness consists of a lack of success, power, performance, ineffectiveness, loss, incompetence, obsession, disability and frailty; these elements come from negative core beliefs, such as being unloved, helpless, or worthless.[16] So, a person may think she/he is in danger or she/he does not deserve to live a good life.

Maladaptive Automatic Thoughts

Beck's cognitive model suggests the existence of some cognitive appraisals on the surface level: automatic thoughts.[19] Positive or negative automatic thinking is found in all people and influences behavior. What affects individuals' emotions and behavior is not an event and/or a condition but an automatic reflection of that event and/or situation. Automatic thoughts are thoughts which are verbal or image-like and can emerge from the mind—rapidly, automatically, and involuntarily. Automatic thoughts are related to content and meaning in the mind. They may cause internal dialogues about the world, the self, and the future. According to CBT, emotions are not internal dialogue but thoughts are. CBT investigates an individual's private interpretation of events and tries to discover what kinds of dysfunctional emotions and behaviors she has. These are some examples of clients' negative automatic thoughts: 'I'm stupid,' 'I can't make it,' and 'Life is difficult.' When a situation or event is encountered, it appears spontaneously without conscious effort. Automatic thoughts are defined as thoughts or images that occupy the vast majority of the mind in moments of emotional distress.[20] Beck states that negative thoughts appear very quickly and automatically.[17]

Cognitive therapists focus on the client's cognitive distortions and negative automatic thoughts. For example, negative automatic thoughts and negative viewpoints of oneself increase anxiety and depression.[21] At the same time, negative automatic thinking can lead to distress, such as despair.[20]

Note: A list of automatic thoughts can be found at the end of this chapter.

Intermediate Beliefs

Intermediate beliefs are often described as assumptions, biases, attitudes, rules, expectations, or conditional expressions. They lie between automatic thoughts and core beliefs in our cognition. Intermediate beliefs are expectations and assumptions about ourselves and connections and circumstances around us. They are rules and guidelines that we keep in our mind. Priorities and predispositions that we hold in the face of stressful life events impact the way we think and shape our reactions.

Some examples of intermediate beliefs are: 'If I ignore my weight I will be disliked by other people,' 'People don't care about each other because they are selfish,' and 'No one wants to hear my problems.' 'I must always be successful in my work,' 'I should not ask for help from others while working,' and 'I must be perfect in my job to avoid being a weak person' are absolute thoughts in cognitive distortions. Intermediate beliefs are found in individuals, with or without psychological distress, as are negative automatic thoughts. However, intermediate beliefs may be more negative and violent than automatic thoughts.[22,23] These beliefs are seen as important rules and assumptions that often apply to an individual's everyday life.[17,18]

For example, a person with a core belief in 'helplessness' lives with the rule: 'I need to take all school classes,' and may continue with a negative intermediate belief, such as 'It is a failure if my overall grade is less than 100 points from all my lessons.' Examples of irrational beliefs are 'It would be terrible to get something less than 100,' or, as an example of how the world works, 'Successful people should take lessons from their failures.' The problem with these intermediate rules and hypotheses is that they may be rigid and inflexible. Core and intermediate beliefs can lead to negative automatic thoughts and cause the client to feel dysfunctional emotions and behave maladaptively, and thus encounter psychological troubles.

Cognitive Distortions

In Beck's model, cognitive distortions are at the center of CBT. Dysfunctional (negative) automatic thoughts fall into categories of '*cognitive distortions*,' otherwise known as *thinking errors*.[16] In many cases, it is difficult to separate cognitive distortions (as in CBT) from irrational beliefs (as in REBT). It is not the aim of this book to distinguish or discuss the terminology of both therapies. Readers can assume that one can use these terminologies interchangeably many times, in different cases. Some examples of cognitive distortions are *all-or-nothing think-ing*, where things are perceived on the cusp of good-bad. For example, a person who fails at a project at work might think, 'I am not successful in my job, so I am a failure.'[14,15]

Tbox: A client may ask: 'The information you gave me about how our cognition is structured is good but shouldn't you provide solutions here?' The answer could be this: CBT does not only show you what the problems are but also tells you the solutions. Yes, solutions come from many techniques and that is what CBT is for. However, there are no quick answers for any problems. Certainly, we need to do our homework first, and then activities, together, to 'attack' these 'bad' thoughts and beliefs.

Types of Cognitive Distortion

The main task for a cognitive therapist is to find out the distortions associated with a client's thinking process and dysfunctional automatic thoughts.[24] Readers may find, at first, some cognitive distortions seem similar to each other (e.g., all-or-nothing thinking and excessive generalization) or that they are used inter-changeably without certain classification. It is difficult to think of cognitive distortions as independent from each other, and the definition of a given cogni-tive distortion may be valid for other distortions.[15,18] Here is a list, and some examples, of common cognitive distortions:

All-or-nothing thinking is a distorted thought process that has no 'middle.' There are only two categories in which a person perceives the world: good or bad, black and white, all or nothing, love or hate. Example: 'I have suc-ceeded at nothing in this life.'

Negative catch-up is where an event or situation is assessed only negatively. It is a kind of all-or-nothing thinking without the 'all' side. Negative expectations lead the behavior without evaluating all the results. Example: 'I see that her decision made everything difficult so I'd better seek some other companies to continue this project.'

Modals of obligation are where an individual has a clear set of rules in the face of events or situations and does not change them. This cognitive distortion is the same as the irrational beliefs of demandingness in Ellis's model of CBT—for example, 'I should never make mistakes in my work' or 'I must be competent in my all tasks.'

In **emotional inference**, a person believes results only when she feels it in the moment, without evidence, or even when there is evidence to the contrary. For example, she thinks that she will experience an event parallel to the emotional state of the person.[23] 'I feel kind of bad, today. I know something terrible will happen to my relationship with my partner.'

Personalization is related to perceptions. For instance, a client thinks that bad things happen to her as if they were planned: 'My boss is acting this way on purpose; he doesn't want me here.' **Blaming** is another distortion, similar to personalization; however, this time the person shifts it to others. 'They didn't give us the project but it's my colleagues' fault.'

A person may attempt **mind reading** with no real evidence when others are responding negatively to her. For instance, she may say or think automatically, 'I know they are thinking badly about me.'

> *Tbox: A client may have all-or-nothing thinking, blaming, and labeling cognitive distortions when in depression.*

The cognitive distortion of **excessive generalization** is the equivalent of catastrophizing/awfulizing in REBT—for example, 'If I cannot decide what I want to do, it is terrible!' or 'It is awful if I lose my position in my job.'

Labeling can happen to self, others, life, or things in life. Someone with labeling distortion tends to negatively label almost everything: 'I am a boring person,' 'They are stupid,' or 'I knew that he is incompetent.'

The distortion of **selective abstraction** is where an event or circumstance, without evidence or contrary evidence, ignores other important features, by highlighting a detail that the person chooses, instead of evaluating the whole picture. Another kind of thinking error is **extreme enlargement and reduction**, where an enlargement of adverse events and a reduction of positive events are seen. When an individual evaluates herself, a situation, or someone else, she tends to enlarge negative points, unreasonably, and downsize positive events.[17,18]

Conclusion

Considerable detail and care have been used to explain the importance and complexity of REBT and CBT, but it must be appreciated that there is a huge body of work in existence that can also be sourced. It must also be noted that the Bs of the ABC model can always be used interchangeably. Another way of saying this is that certain therapists label cognitions 'negative automatic thoughts' or 'cognitive distortion,' yet others call them 'irrational beliefs.' In essence, there is a case of basically harmful, dysfunctional, and irrational thoughts and beliefs at work. For instance, when a therapist worked with a 6-year-old client, she summarized them into two words: 'Bad thoughts'!

In Part II of this book, an attempt is made to provide some solutions to these thoughts and beliefs, using diverse cultural sources (e.g., Sufism), on the proviso that the aim is not to divide REBT and CBT into two different approaches.

A List of Irrational Beliefs

1. If people who are important to me do not like me, it is because they are worthless.
2. People who think that I do poorly on an important task are of no value.
3. If people I value do not like me, I accept that they are good people, even if they dislike me.
4. It is disappointing to be disliked by people who are important to me, but it is only disappointing and not awful.
5. I can't stand a lack of consideration from other people, and I can't bear the possibility of their unfairness.
6. It's awful to be disliked by people who are important to me.
7. It is a catastrophe if they don't like me.

Note: Taken from Attitude and Beliefs Scale—II (DiGiuseppe, Robin, Leaf & Gorman, 1988, DiGiuseppe, Leaf, Exner, & Robin, 1989) and Shortened General Attitudes and Beliefs Scale (Lindner, Kirkby, Wertheim, & Birch, 1999).

A List of Rational Beliefs

1. It is unfortunate when I am frustrated by hassles in my life, but I realize it is only disappointing and not awful.
2. I do not like to feel uncomfortable, tense, or nervous, but I can tolerate the feelings.
3. I do not want to fail at important tasks but I realize that I do not have to perform well, just because I want to do well.
4. When I feel uncomfortable, I realize it is not awful to feel this way but only unfortunate.
5. If I am rejected by someone I like, I can accept myself and still recognize my worth as a human being.
6. It is important that people treat me fairly most of the time; however, I realize I do not have to be treated fairly just because I want to be.

Note: Taken from Attitude and Beliefs Scale—II (DiGiuseppe, Robin, Leaf, & Gorman, 1988, DiGiuseppe, Leaf, Exner, & Robin, 1989).

A List of Negative Automatic Thoughts

1. Most people are against me.
2. I am an idiot.
3. How stupid they are!
4. Poor me!
5. Life sucks!
6. Things will get worse!
7. So much!
8. My pain means my illness is getting worse.
9. My appearance is a problem.
10. Oh, no. Not again!
11. Enough is enough!

References

1. Smith, M. L., & Glass, G. V. (1977). Meta-analysis of psychotherapy outcome studies. *American Psychologist, 32*(9), 752.
2. DiGiuseppe, R. A., Doyle, K. A., Dryden, W., & Backx, W. (2014). *A Practitioner's Guide to Rational Emotive Behavior Therapy* (3rd ed.). New York: Oxford University Press.
3. Artiran, M. (2015). *Title: A New Scale Based on Rational Emotive Behavior Therapy and Self-Determination Theory: The Development of a Rational Emotive Self Determination Scale (RESD).* This study was presented at ICCP 2017, the 9th International Congress of Cognitive Psychotherapy. 29th of June–1st of July 2017. Cluj-Napoca, Transylvania, Romania.
4. DiGiuseppe, M. (2014). Representing nature of science in a science textbook: Exploring author-editor-publisher interactions. *International Journal of Science Education, 36*(7), 1061–1082.
5. Vîslă, A., Flückiger, C., Grosse Holtforth, M., & David, D. (2016). Irrational beliefs and psychological distress: A meta-analysis. *Psychotherapy and Psychosomatics, 85*(1), 8–15.
6. Dryden, W. (2009). *Understanding Emotional Problems, the REBT Perspective.* New York, NY: Taylor & Francis Group.
7. Artiran, M. (2018). *Development and Validation of a Scale for Measuring Work Related Irrational Beliefs of Basic Psychological Needs in the Health and Behavioral Sciences.* Master's thesis in Clinical Psychology. Istanbul, Turkey: Arel University. Study presented at 48th Annual Congress of European Association for Behavioural and Cognitive Therapies in Sofia, September 5–8, 2018.
8. Artiran, M. (2015). Title: A New Scale Based on Rational Emotive Behavior Therapy and Self-Determination Theory: The Development of a Rational Emotive Self Determination Scale (RESD) Doctoral thesis. Istanbul, Turkey: Istanbul Arel University
9. DiGiuseppe, R., Leaf, R., Gorman, B., & Robin, M. W. (2018). The development of a measure of irrational/rational beliefs. *Journal of Rational-Emotive & Cognitive-Behaviour Therapy, 36*(1), 47–79.
10. Lindner, H., Kirkby, R., Wertheim, E., & Birch, P. (1999). A brief assessment of irrational thinking: The shortened general attitude and belief scale. *Cognitive Therapy and Research, 23*(6), 651–663.

11. Hyland, P., Shevlin, M., Adamson, G., & Boduszek, D. (2014). The organization of irrational beliefs in posttraumatic stress symptomology: Testing the predictions of REBT theory using structural equation modelling. *Journal of Clinical Psychology, 70*(1), 48–59.

12. Russell, J. A., & Carroll, J. M. (1999). On the bipolarity of positive and negative affect. *Psychological Bulletin, 125*(1), 3.

13. Ellis, A., & DiGiuseppe, R. (1993). Are inappropriate or dysfunctional feelings in rational-emotive therapy qualitative or quantitative? *Cognitive Therapy and Research, 17*(5), 471–477.

14. Beal, D., Kopec, A. M., & DiGuiseppe, R. (1996). Disputing clients' irrational beliefs. *Journal of Rational-Emotive and Cognitive-Behavior Therapy, 14*(4), 215–229.

15. Padesky, C. A. (1994). Schema change processes in cognitive therapy. *Clinical Psychology & Psychotherapy, 1*(5), 267–278.

16. Beck, J. S. (2011). *Cognitive Behavior Therapy: Basics and Beyond.* New York: Guilford Press.

17. Cully, J. A., & Teten, A. L. (2008). *A Therapist's Guide to Brief Cognitive Behavioral Therapy.* Houston: Department of Veterans Affairs South Central MIRECC.

18. Beck, A. T. (1967). *Depression: Clinical, Experimental, and Theoretical Aspects.* New York: Harper & Row.

19. Beck, J. S. (2001). *Bilişsel terapi: Temel ilkeler ve ötesi.* Ankara: Türk Psikologlar Derneği.

20. Gilbert, P., & Leahy, R. L. (Eds.). (2007). *The Therapeutic Relationship in the Cognitive Behavioral Psychotherapies.* Abingdon, UK: Routledge.

21. Schniering, C. A., & Rapee, R. M. (2004). The relationship between automatic thoughts and negative emotions in children and adolescents: A test of the cognitive content-specificity hypothesis. *Journal of Abnormal Psychology, 113*(3), 464.

22. Tümkaya, S., Hamarta, E., Deniz, M. E., Çelik, M., & Aybek, B. (2008). Duygusal zeka mizah tarzı ve yaşam doyumu: Üniversite öğretim elemanları üzerine bir araştırma. *Türk Psikolojik Danışma ve Rehberlik Dergisi, 3*(30), 1–18.

23. Karahan, T. F., Sardoğan, M. E., Şar, A. H., Ersanlı, E., Kaya, S. N., & Kumcağız, H. (2004). Üniversite öğrencilerinin yalnızlık düzeyleri ile benlik saygısı düzeyleri arasındaki ilişkiler. *Ondokuz Mayıs Üniversitesi Eğitim Fakültesi Dergisi, 18*(2004), 27–39.

24. Freeman, A., Simon, K. M., Beutler, L. E., & Arkowitz, H. (Eds.). (1989). *Comprehensive Handbook of Cognitive Therapy.* New York: Plenum Press

4
THE GOALS OF THERAPY

Yesterday I was clever, so I wanted to change the world. Today I am wise, so I am changing myself.

—Rumi

What action do clients want to take, or what are their goals, when they come to therapy? What are the primary and secondary goals of therapy? How about cultural differences? Can a different culture be a determinant for the goals of therapy? Is the main (or final) goal of therapy feeling positive emotions, finding the ultimate meaning in life, solving relationship problems, being functional, gaining motivation, becoming happy, or none of them? It all depends on clients' attitudes, beliefs, genes, a therapist's approach, the nature of the case, and the society and the culture client lives in. Also, many Western psychotherapy theories answer these questions from different perspectives. When it comes to a cross-cultural consideration of psychotherapeutic interventions the answers may become more complicated.

REBT and CBT use a multi-model approach to analyze, define, explain, and offer formulizations to deal with emotional disturbances. How should we redefine the term 'emotional disturbances' for a Middle Eastern understanding? What about psychological well-being or happiness? Is the meaning of happiness in the West the same as in the East? When considering the concepts of self-actualization, or unconditional self-acceptance, considerable obstacles appear. What do they mean to a Middle Easterner? Undoubtedly, appropriate, understandable, and clear redefinitions are needed. There is a famous vox pop on YouTube. It took place in Turkey in 2018 (youtube.com/watch?v=bs49T83C6F8). A 55-year-old man was asked by a reporter, '*What is the secret formula to being happy?*' He became angry and told the reporter, '*Hey! That's none of your business. It is between my wife and I. What kind of a question is that!' (He understood that the question was about sex, and sex is not easily spoken about openly in the Middle East.)* Different cultural and educational backgrounds cause different outcomes. Some types of goals/ expectations for cultural consideration in any therapy can be listed thus:

1. Clients' expectations from therapy (e.g., to get over depression).
2. Clients' desire to solve real-life problems (e.g., finding a partner and getting involved in a romantic relationship).
3. Theoretical goals (e.g., expecting a client to learn and apply RE & CBT and the ABC model).
4. Therapists' expectations from clients, such as gaining insight, learning from mistakes, increasing frustration tolerance, or reducing the number of negative automatic thoughts.
5. General therapeutic goals (e.g., gaining a new perspective towards life, others, or self; being functional, living rationally, self-actualization, and so on).

A Case Example

This is a typical example of working at cross purposes, where the opportunities for misunderstanding are rife. The therapist's goal was to work with a 32-year-old female Middle Eastern client towards an awareness and understanding of the deep underlying dynamics of her psychology. The therapist tried to search for unhealthy cognitive distortions and dispute them. However, this was not the purpose of the client, when she asked for an appointment. The therapist asked many questions about the client's emotions, followed by her thoughts, perceptions, and evaluations of her own stressful circumstances. The client tried to answer all of the questions but she was uncomfortable in the session. She also felt pressured to answer the therapist's questions, even though the questions were warm and sincere. She, on the other hand, merely wanted to solve some relationship issues and was under the impression that therapists understand their clients and can relate, appropriately, to their problems. She wanted to be directed more, with an active approach from the therapist. She sought for advice, saying, 'I need to know what the right behavior is.' This is just one example and cannot be generalized for all clients or all cases. However, it is obvious that the nature and direction of therapy for Middle Easterners need to be 'redefined.'

The goal of REBT and CBT is to remove or regulate dysfunctional emotions. CBT claims that, if a client has negative thoughts about themselves, life, others, or the future, then that client has dysfunctional/unhealthy negative emotions. Consequently, if the client has unhealthy negative emotions, she will have dysfunctional behaviors that will certainly affect her happiness and satisfaction in life. *Some* of the major *goals of any therapy* are to ensure the happiness and life satisfaction of a person by regulating or overcoming her emotional disturbances. Emotional disturbance means 'the dysfunctional emotions' that people are disturbed by. Since the actual goal of therapy is to maintain happiness and increase life satisfaction, then when your emotions are disturbed, you will have disturbed behavior, which causes a dysfunctional, noncreative, unproductive, problematic, and stressful life.

Positive Goals

Case formulations and conceptualizations of RE & CBT need to aim not only to transform dysfunctionality into functionality but also to target positive components (e.g., enjoyment, enthusiasm, love, meaning in life, long-term pleasure, being autonomous, being competent, and motivation) in treatment. This is especially true for Middle Easterners, who sometimes, impatiently, have difficulty in seeing what the purpose of the disputation of cognitive distortions and irrational beliefs is, and how therapy will help them, pragmatically, with real-life problems (e.g., relationship problems). It is imperative that this is made clear to them. Most Middle Eastern clients are not interested in *self-actualization* or *functionality in life.* Some of them want to learn the 'secret' of their own (or their children's) personality, or try to gain 'wisdom,' in general, in solving their own life problems, and can't wait to see what the therapist will tell them to deal with their issues.

Classic REBT and CBT conceptualizations do not include strengths, talents, happiness, life satisfaction, and subjective well-being components in a treatment plan. However, as CBT proposes, it cannot be claimed that functional behaviors and emotions alone will lead to a happy life. The structure and style of CBT are very effective in helping clients quickly because its 'symptoms-based interventions' are well developed.

On the other hand, the REBT approach is based more in taking clients towards a hedonic and eudemonic happiness rather than just reducing symptoms.[1] Since REBT aims to philosophically change a person's life, a client will have the opportunity to reach a positive psychological competence for herself. It is not possible, however, to be happy all the time in our lives.

In REBT, while dysfunctional thoughts and IrBels are linked with dysfunctional negative feelings, rational beliefs are associated with functional negative feelings.[1] Dysfunctional negative feelings in REBT are, in no particular order, as follows: hatred & anger, fear & panic & anxiety, depression, jealousy, envy, guilt, trauma & hurt, and shame. However, research is still needed to investigate whether functional thoughts and rational beliefs are 'strongly' related to happiness. To accommodate this, in REBT, emotions are divided into two main categories: healthy negative emotions (e.g., annoyance, concern, sadness) and unhealthy negative emotions (e.g., anger, anxiety, depression). Healthy emotions are not necessarily positive, but they are 'unharmful or nondestructive' emotions. According to Dr. Albert Ellis, we do not need 'to have positive feelings' *to feel better* in our life; 'having healthy but still negative emotions' is, however, realistic to *'get better'*! However, in the last ten years, recent research about positive psychological aspects of human emotions, cognitions, and behaviors have been investigated and researchers found some valuable information to pay more attention to more positivity in psychology.

Positive Sides of Psychology

In RE & CBT we do not fully know yet with how much therapy the goal of achieving a state of happiness for the client can be reached. It could be said that RE & CBT have not dealt much with positive constructions in this respect. Thankfully, the flexible and expandable nature of all cognitive behavior therapies will allow a positive psychology to integrate the RE & CBT approach.

Using a positive psychology approach, many 'life coaches,' or 'mentors,' offer very attractive systems of advice to people. One of them is Tony Robbins; he is a very talented and successful person at 'inspiring people.' There are also many so-called mentors who encourage people to find motivation in life. Some inspiration programs are cash cows and some are seen as 'fake' or a scam, much like a one-armed bandit, but their books and programs help a number of people. Positive psychology is not only about 'self-help' books or 'happiness' camps!

Many famous academics have recently been interested in developing CBT-coaching approaches. The idea of functioning as a clinician and how a border is to be drawn between clinical work and the life-coaching business is not clear. The concept that clinicians are creating programs on 'how to be happy' is a new trend. Some think that the idea of turning clinicians into life coaches is not ethical, nor is it a clinician's business. Some practitioners and academics say certain positive psychology and motivational aspects should be included in treatment. However, without trying to become a life coach, since the coaching process addresses specific personal projects, mental health professionals need to have something to offer clients to achieve happiness and life satisfaction.

Since the beginning of time people have looked for pleasure and happiness. Numerous views have been suggested with respect to what happiness is, and how individuals can be happy, and whether continuous, unchanging happiness can be achieved. According to Eckhart Tolle, if you live for 'I' (self), suffering will follow you everywhere. He suggests that living in the present moment is the solution, and much deeper than any concept of happiness.[2] Many researchers have shown progress in this regard. For instance, Veenhoven suggests[3,4] subjective well-being (SWB) is the level of quality of one's being, while, Vaillant[5] indicates that SWB represents the positive side of psychology. There are advantages if positive aspects of psychology are incorporated in CBT case formulations. Concepts that are close to happiness, such as excitement, enthusiasm, energy, and motivation, can be added to RE & CBT case formulations in order to improve the strengths and subjective well-being of the clients.

Adding the *Gp* to the ABC Model

The classic REBT model offers the ABCDEF model in therapy: (A) Activating event, (B) Beliefs, (C) Consequences, (D) Disputation, (E) Effective beliefs, and (F) Functionality. The model needs to be improved in order for it to be culturally attractive to Middle Eastern clients. The model can be extended by adding (Gp) Goals: *positive needs, traits, and states* to the model. Gp contains positive psychology aspects like strengths,[6] a search for meaning, peace, 'love' (as one of the two basic capabilities 'to love' and 'to know'[7]), and three basic psychological needs (autonomy, competence, and relatedness)—which come from the basis of self-determination theory.

The concept of life goals was primarily mooted in the 1970s as a dimension of motivation hypotheses.[8] When individuals described their ideas about living with pleasure and the meaning of life, they usually discussed their desires for the future.[9] A definition of 'life goals' is a desired state that people seek to get, continue or avoid, by means of cognitive and behavioral strategies.[10] According to Schmuck and Sheldon[11] life goals are the exact motivational objectives by which a person directs his life over time,' whereas Lock and Latham[12] have defined life goals as the special desires of individuals that they are aware of. For most people the word 'goal' carries exclusive meanings and ought to be measured in a different way to daily goals. In other words, life goals are individual and subjective and span a lifetime.[13]

This kind of model may appear to be a very attractive direction for Middle Eastern clients. In psychotherapy, Middle Easterners may expect to not only to solve their problems or get better but also feel a need to gain enthusiasm, energy, motivation, and, ultimately, peace and love in their lives. When disputation on irrational beliefs is carried out, this may be linked to positive aspects of human psychology in treatment. Part II of this book provides some oriental suggestions on this issue. The model ahead (Figure 4.1) represents many aspects of the psychological ill-being process concerned with social factors from the perspective of a Middle Easterner.

'Collectively' Subjective Well-Being

Positive psychology is interested in eudaimonia and hedonism. Psychology literature shows that studies have focused more on psychopathology, which represents the negative aspects of mental health.[3] There are rare studies of different cultures that handle the subjective well-being of humans in conjunction with their life goals and strategies to encourage subjective well-being. The methods of people to spread their personal well-being are known as subjective well-being increasing strategies.[14] Tkach and Lyubomirsky[15] determined that various devices are effective in increasing subjective well-being. These strategies are: having community relations, taking part in activities vigorously, defining and reaching goals, displaying behaviors linked to SWB, taking part in spiritual activities, and having psychological control.

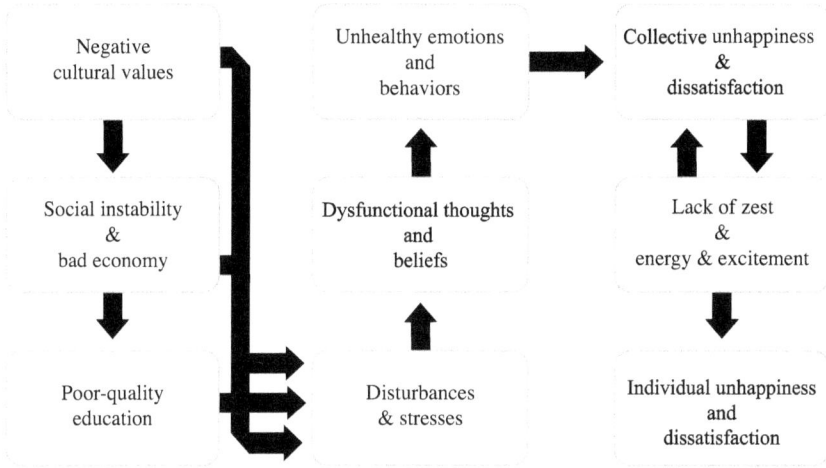

FIGURE 4.1 Ill-being processes with social factors in the Middle East.

People in the Middle East are from a collectivist society so that subjective well-being strongly depends on social well-being. With the world in a state of flux, and because the Middle East takes so much of the brunt of world's problems, everyone wants to know what is going on and how they will be affected. For instance, most Middle Easterners, unlike US citizens, watch news items containing political and social life every day (locally and internationally), and many watch them all day long. The majority of Middle Easterners use all types of social media too. People want to know what the President said, which soccer club hired what players, who formed a protest, what they protested about, and how many people were involved, what happened to the people in Syria, and what current exchange rates are or will be, as well as wanting to learn what the most recent economic news is, and so on. They are more concerned about the future than Western people because they do not have a guarantee of a relatively stable life, arguably as a result of economics.

Goals

Determining goals in therapy and 'life in general' is important for Middle Eastern people. Goals demonstrate a person's future orientation and knowing what those goals are will help her understand her present and future behavior better.[16] Kasser and Ryan divided life goals into two categories—intrinsic and extrinsic.[17] Intrinsic goals contain meaningful relations, community contributions and individual development. Extrinsic goals include money-related success, social gratitude, and physical attractiveness. The subjective well-being of individuals with intrinsic life goals is higher than those with extrinsic life goals and their sadness and anxiety levels are lower.[18,19] When people settle on their life goals, and strive to reach them, their subjective well-being levels increase.[20,21,22] This is a desired approach for Middle Eastern clients, due to their need to have a rationale for a goal, however much it may not be reached, and they realize it is not a target easily attainable in working life.

Related studies have analyzed the relationship between life goals and subjective well-being. For example, in the intercultural studies that Oishi and Diener[23] carried out, they concluded that determining a goal positively influences the subjective well-being of individuals. Similarly, Sheldon et al.[19] proposed that determining goals has positive effects on the subjective well-being of individuals. It has been determined that individuals with high levels of subjective well-being are creative and that they are better at coping with stress, they have better physical health, and they are better at interpersonal relationships.[24,25,26]

Motivation

It can be assumed that motivation can be linked with having inspiring thoughts, willingness, and clear goals, and developing personal skills and cognitive and emotional stability. The definition of motivation in the West has been established quite clearly, but it is based on an individual's perspective. In quite the opposite way, in the Middle East, motivation is initially perceived from a collectivist point of view, and is the norm. For instance, as far as motivation in classroom settings is concerned, Arab students are less threatened than US students when uncertain situations in classroom activities arise, because they like an unstructured way of learning.[27] They like to communicate with their teachers about nonacademic problems, and they tend to build a personal relationship with their teachers. They want to receive individual feedback.[28] They may want to talk about their culture and they love to share cultural exchanges and information. It can be concluded that motivation differs from culture to culture.

According to Bartol and Martin,[29] in order to reach a goal, motivation plays a role in forcing certain behavior that stimulates and leads direction. Kreitner and Kinicki[30] indicate that motivation is associated with a goal, and it is a behavior that produces emotional arousal, direction, and stamina. Pointing out the importance of learning procedures, such as arranging, monitoring, paying attention, and association skills, Turner[31] perceives motivation to be cognitive processes rather than behavioral. This makes sense, from a cross-cultural point of view, because people of different origins have different motivations.

Theories about motivation are categorized into three main groups: content, process, and consolidation theories. Motivation theories (e.g., goal-setting theory, motivation and equity theory, Alderfer's ERG theory) have been formed and developed in the West, and there are no well-developed theories by or specifically for Middle Easterners.

> *Tbox: When choosing the goal of the therapy, clients' cultural backgrounds need to be included in the formula.*

REBT, CBT, and SDT

REBT, CBT, and SDT (self-determination theory) can be integrated to extend the goals of therapy.[32] SDT is interested in the intrinsic motivations of human behavior. Middle Eastern clients will be helped considerably by a study of intrinsic motivation in the therapeutic process. There are numerous studies on how cognitive processes cause emotional disturbances that interrupt happiness and motivation. For instance, RE & CBT can increase an athlete's self-determined motivation by helping her to reduce her dysfunctional cognitions.[33] Research suggests that one of the reasons that REBT is effective in promoting self-determined motivation is because the disputing of irrational beliefs and promotion of rational beliefs enhances an athlete's basic psychological needs satisfaction.[33]

Previously, content-based irrational and rational beliefs, and Gp as a component of the ABCDEF model, were mentioned. When considering the Middle Eastern population, through combining REBT and SDT, it might be possible to aid the development of basic psychological needs through the disputation and promotion of rational beliefs (i.e., cognitive restructuring).[32] However, the application of both SDT and REBT, in the prevention of unhealthy emotions and behavior, suffers from a lack of a theoretical model.[33] An integrative approach can be used in the Middle East, and for this purpose the three basic psychological needs of SDT can be combined in an economic model, under the umbrella of autonomous irrational beliefs, competence irrational beliefs, and relatedness irrational beliefs. The reason for this is that many Middle Eastern people want to see content-based goals with tangible results, rather than what are perceived, by them, as vague goals, like self-actualization and eliminating dysfunctional behaviors and unhealthy negative emotions. Many of them seek attractive goals and ideas that take them further to results they want. Motivation analysis may be needed during treatment in order to support Middle Easterners. Bringing together both approaches (SDT and RE & CBT) is an important method of putting forward an economical prevention and intervention model because offering intrinsic motivation to Middle Eastern clients may boost the positive outcome of treatment.

Peace vs. Happiness

The pursuit of happiness and meaning is the major source of motivation in life as well as psychological well-being. Happiness and meaning are linked to each other. We become happy doing meaningful things in our life. We do not usually continue with something that has no meaning for us. Meaning may not bring peace all the time and happiness may not guarantee that we will have peace either. However, besides happiness and meaning, people also need peace in their lives. The people of the Middle East often seek to be peaceful rather than happy. Conversely, within the culture it may appear strange to look 'very happy.' When we think of Middle Eastern culture, being peaceful is more valuable than being happy. Happiness in Western culture is perceived as fun, pleasurable, and joyful, while in the Middle East those things can be seen as 'bad' or 'immoral': 'When your brother is not happy, you should be sad too!' Aiming at individual develop-ment or 'happiness' is not appropriate when the community is in depression and traumatized due to wars, terror, and social, economic, and political turbulence.

There is also a paradox in seeking happiness and seeking meaning in life. For instance, the 'parenthood paradox':[34] parents report that having a baby made them happy; however, at the same time, some research says parents with children usually score very low in measures of satisfaction from life and happiness. It can be concluded that raising children may reduce happiness but increase mean-ing in parents' life. It is important to seek other variables when investigating meaning and happiness. This claim is truer for Middle Eastern cultures because Middle Eastern people, unlike Westerners, suffer from a lack of quality educa-tion, which may be as a result of economic hardship or the continuation of tribe culture. For Middle Easterners peace and meaning are more important than happiness.

Suffering

In Islam, ultimate happiness comes from 'reaching' Allah, and, in order to do this, many difficult situations or conditions in life need to be experienced to learn 'the true path.' One way of doing this for Muslims is by practicing suffer-ing. In some cultures people have positive attitudes to being sad and being in suffering.[35] In the Quran, suffering is a part of enlightenment, though many Muslims might misunderstand this message. Even smiling or laughing aloud may be considered 'wrong' for some Muslims. When you are not smiling, or looking sad, it may be viewed that 'you are part of the community and you suffer with others and it is a good thing to show you are a true brother or sister.' Western culture sees suffering as a negative thing, and does not relate it to the concept of happiness.[36] In Islam, suffering is considered a divinely intended experience leading to personal growth.[35] In Islam, a spiritual form of happiness does not describe happiness based on positive feelings.[35] Rather, fulfillment of essential spiritual needs and growth of character strength are suggested, as well as virtue and moral values.[36] The Islamic conceptualization of happiness underlines virtue and positive functioning as the main requirement of being happy.[37] Islam is more tolerant of sadness and suffering than contemporary Western society.[36] The reason for this might be that emotional suffering may be conceived as qualifying for religious blessing, reward,[38] and patience. The contemporary Western understand-ing of happiness generally focuses on self-indulgent pleasures, positive states of mind, and high-arousal emotions.[35] The hedonic aspects of happiness are more strongly emphasized in literature.[36] Another significant thing about Western society is that Westerners dislike suffering and negativity. For instance, in Ameri-can society, being positive, optimistic, and happy is a social requirement, while negativity and melancholy are seen as an unhelpful attitude.[37] The conceptualiza-tion of happiness for Western people is less tolerant of sadness and pain than for Middle Eastern people.

A Proposal

Philosophical change and trying to understand dysfunctional symptoms in feelings and behaviors are complicated. The cross-cultural practices of RE & CBT may be restricted to their roots in individualistic psychotherapy when a society is collectivist. Cooperation and collaboration can and should be used by Middle Eastern people to achieve their own goals. In some cases, REBT and CBT may be inadequate to help Middle Eastern people because people are happy doing things that make sense. Intrinsic motivation is something that people in the Middle East can focus on, together with meaning in their lives, and a search for inner and outer peace. Suggested components of RE & CBT in the Middle East may include goals as represented ahead in Figure 4.2.

In this model, the goals of therapy are extended from functionality (reducing dysfunctional symptoms) and philosophical change, which are two of the main goals of REBT, to the meaning of life, love of self/others/life, finding 'true peace,' and intrinsic motivation. These concepts can be itemized thus:

1. Maintaining functionality is the primary goal of CBT. It aims to help clients to achieve functional emotions and functional behaviors, along with good physical and mental health.

   A therapeutic question: How do my irrational beliefs and cognitive distortions disturb my functionality?

2. Philosophical change is the core goal of REBT theory. Ellis stated that, with philosophical change, clients may experience not only short-term but also long-term benefits from the therapy.

   A therapeutic question: What are my irrational beliefs about my 'self,' others, life, things in life, and the future?

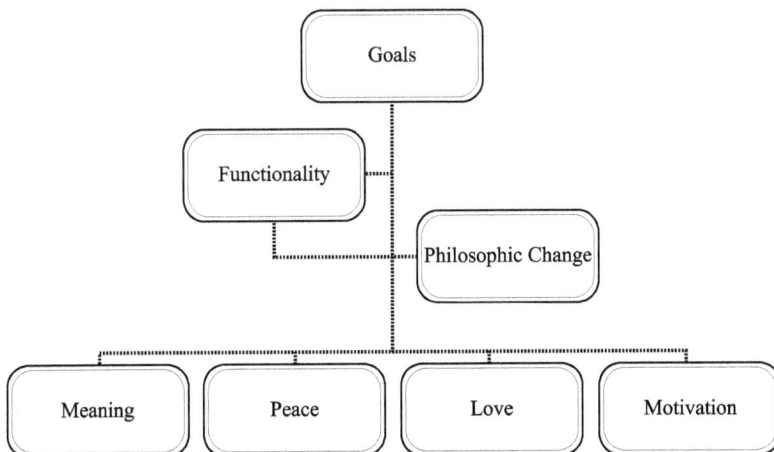

FIGURE 4.2 Proposed *culturally redefined* therapy goals.

3. Finding the meaning and purpose of life, as one of the main tenets for therapy, has been tested in the Middle East in the past. For instance, it is found that the meaning of life, in Turkey, significantly predicted the extent of subjective well-being.[38] Victor Frankl's work in a 'search for meaning' is famous. His logo therapy encourages spirituality and, according to him, spirituality makes it easier for people to find meaning.[39] Although this idea is parallel to Middle Eastern people's mind-set, it suggests that meaning should not be limited to spirituality (or cannot depend only on spirituality). There are many ways to live a fully meaningful life, such as bringing up a child, writing a book, traveling around the world, being a member of a music group, or working for charities.

   A therapeutic question: What kinds of irrational beliefs and cognitive distortions do I have that become blocks to finding meaning in my life?

4. Peace is one of the popular concepts in all religions, including Islam. Messages of peace are regularly given to Muslims and Middle Eastern people via verses of the Quran, anecdotes of the Prophet Mohammed's (S.A.V.) life (called hadiths), and other stories about the Caliphs. According to many Middle Eastern sources, one of the ultimate purposes of all creatures is to find peace. Chapter 7 contains Sufic teachings, integrated with unconditional acceptance, about this issue.

   A therapeutic question: What are the thoughts and beliefs I hold that create chaos in my life and that become a barrier to maintaining peace in my life?

5. Love is universal. Love has not received enough interest in psychological research, yet love is an important tenet of Sufism. Concepts of love of self, love of others, and love of life can extend the idea of Ellis's unconditional self/others/life acceptance theory to a further (or more emotional) point. Middle Eastern people like to talk about love more than talking about unconditional acceptance. With regard to love, the teachings of Sufism may be a good guide to clients.

   A therapeutic question: When considering my 'self,' others, and life, why is I 'love' important, and what are my irrational beliefs that hinder me from loving my 'self,' others, and life?

6. According to self-determination theory (SDT), intrinsic motivation comes from satisfying three psychological needs.[40] SDT is a well-proven theory and according to some research it is culturally adaptable.[41] SDT assumes that therapeutic change involves energizing and supporting inherent tendencies as patients take on the problems confronting them.[41] SDT, integrated with RE & CBT, gave some promising results and it is culturally beneficial in the Turkish population.[42]

   A therapeutic question: What are my irrational beliefs about being autonomous in my life and feeling competent and being related to others?

For those partaking in the courageous task of therapy, there are some prerequisites: on the therapist's side—a compassionate sensitivity of the highest degree and the capability to grasp, precisely, the anguish of the client. This must accompany consistency in the effort to be trustworthy and authentic and, lastly, the aptitude to exercise what one sees. A client, on the other hand, however uncomfortable the release of personal (mis)understandings, thoughts, deeds, and emotions may be, must be prepared to discuss problematic areas in a frank and honest manner. Dr. Carl Rogers's theory and the person-centered approach have been approved as effective as any other modern psychotherapy theory. It has become a litmus test and the core professional value of contemporary nurses, carers, and social and mental health workers.

Everybody has both gracious and imperfect attributes. This is where people have difficulty—not being able to concede they have defects, and, when they recognize their imperfections, many are unable to survive with these flaws. Further examination shows that high levels of self-acceptance can be improved by reducing the focus on unhelpful aspects of oneself, and increasing involvement in acts of self-*love*.

Growth requires that you understand your character and habits; inner *peace* comes when you stop comparing yourself and your achievements to others. Acknowledging your skills, or the lack of them, will bring happiness, or at least alleviate feelings of dissatisfaction, anger, resentment, or unhappiness. They are only the first step on the road to empowerment; they are not an excuse for staying as you are. To get the things you want, you need to learn to use affirmations effectively. There are hundreds of videos, books, and magazines about alternative lifestyles, though sadly lacking in Muslim countries, not least because of the price of paper! There is plenty of information on the Internet; many people seem to be looking for an answer to a lack of spiritual, physical, and moral enlightenment. Gone are the days of the hippy, unless you include the rainbow gatherings. Were those days real?! These are the days of the consumerist, ultracapitalist society, but not for all are there advantages, and certainly not for most, unless you look at all sides of the spectrum.

In subsequent chapters of the book a profile can be drawn that is appropriate to Middle Eastern culture. Of course, what is said here, as qualitative work, needs to be supported by quantitative research. Since RE & CBT are interested in clinical interventions and various mental disorders, their development, in the future, needs to aim to increase a positive route to mental health wellness. A scientific system, or structure, can be offered by clinical psychologists, in order not to allow the field to be overrun by life coaches or so-called mentors. Having made such a bold statement, Part II of this book is mostly concerned with rational beliefs and well-being, rather than irrational beliefs and ill-being.

References

1. DiGiuseppe, R. A., Doyle, K. A., Dryden, W., & Backx, W. (2014). *A Practitioner's Guide to Rational Emotive Behavior Therapy* (3rd ed.). New York: Oxford University Press.
2. Tolle, E. (2004). *The Power of Now: A Guide to Spiritual Enlightenment.* Novato, CA.
3. Hills, P., & Argyle, M. (2002). The Oxford Happiness Questionnaire: A compact scale for the measurement of psychological well-being. *Personality and Individual Differences, 33,* 1073–1082.
4. Veenhoven, R. (2008). Sociological theories of subjective well-being. *The Science of Subjective Well-Being, 9,* 44–61.
5. Myers, D. G., & Diener, E. (1995). Who is happy? *Psychological Science, 6*(1), 10–19.
6. Park, N., Peterson, C., & Seligman, M. E. (2004). Strengths of character and well-being. *Journal of Social and Clinical Psychology, 23*(5), 603–619.
7. Positive Psychotherapy: Peseschkian, since 1968. (n.d.). Retrieved from www.euro-psyche.org/contents/13148/positive-psychotherapy-peseschkian-since-1968
8. Stauner, N. (2013). *Personal Goal Attainment, Psychological Well-Being Change, and Meaning in Life* Doctoral Thesis). Social & Personality Psychology, Riverside, CA: Case Western Reserve University.
9. Brdar, I., Rijavec, M., & Miljković, D. (2009). Life goals and well-being: Are extrinsic aspirations always detrimental to well-being? *Psihologijske teme, 18*(2), 317–334.
10. Emmons, R. A., Colby, P. M., & Kaiser, H. A. (1998). *When Losses Lead to Gains: Personal Goals and the Recovery of Meaning.* Mahwah, NJ: Lawrence Erlbaum Associates Publishers.
11. Schmuck, P. E., & Sheldon, K. M. (2001). *Life Goals and Well-Being: Towards a Positive Psychology of Human Striving.* Seattle, WA: Hogrefe & Huber Publishers
12. Locke, E. A., & Latham, G. P. (1990). *A Theory of Goal Setting & Task Performance.* Englewood Cliffs, NJ: Prentice-Hall.
13. Austin, J. T., & Vancouver, J. B. (1996). Goal constructs in psychology: Structure, process, and content. *Psychological Bulletin, 120*(3), 338.
14. Eryilmaz, A., & Öğülmüş, S. (2010). Ergenlikte öznel iyi oluş ve beş faktörlü kişilik modeli. *Ahi Evran Üniversitesi Kırşehir Eğitim Fakültesi Dergisi, 11*(3).
15. Lyubomirsky, S., Tkach, C., & DiMatteo, M. R. (2006). What are the differences between happiness and self-esteem. *Social Indicators Research, 78*(3), 363–404.
16. Jungermann, H., Von Ulardt, I., & Hausmann, L. (1983). The role of the goal for generating actions. In P. C. Humphreys, O. Svenson, & A. Vari (Eds.), *Analysing and Aiding Decision Process* (pp. 223–236). Amsterdam: North Holland.
17. Kasser, T., & Ryan, R. M. (2001). Be careful what you wish for: Optimal functioning and the relative attainment of intrinsic and extrinsic goals. *Life Goals and Well-Being: Towards a Positive Psychology of Human Striving, 1,* 116–131.
18. Kasser, T., & Ryan, R. M. (1993). A dark side of the American dream: Correlates of financial success as a central life aspiration. *Journal of Personality and Social Psychology, 65*(2), 410.
19. Sheldon, K. M., & Kasser, T. (1995). Coherence and congruence: Two aspects of personality integration. *Journal of Personality and Social Psychology, 68*(3), 531.
20. Emmons, R. A. (1986). Personal strivings: An approach to personality and subjective well-being. *Journal of Personality and Social Psychology, 51*(5), 1058.
21. Omodei, M. M., & Wearing, A. J. (1990). Needs satisfaction and involvement in personal projects: Toward an integrative model of subjective well-being. *Journal of Personality and Social Psychology, 59*(4), 762.

22. Palys, T. S., & Little, B. R. (1983). Perceived life satisfaction and the organization of personal project systems. *Journal of Personality and Social Psychology, 44*(6), 1221.

23. Diener, E., Oishi, S., & Lucas, R. E. (2003). Personality, culture, and subjective well-being: Emotional and cognitive evaluations of life. *Annual Review of Psychology, 54*(1), 403–425.

24. Diener, E. (1984). Subjective well-being. *Psychological Bulletin, 95*(3), 542.

25. Diener, E., & Seligman, M. E. (2004). Beyond money: Toward an economy of well-being. *Psychological Science in the Public Interest, 5*(1), 1–31.

26. Lucas, R. E., Clark, A. E., Georgellis, Y., & Diener, E. (2004). Unemployment alters the set point for life satisfaction. *Psychological Science, 15*(1), 8–13.

27. Sumrain, I. A. (1987). *Academic Dishonesty: Comparing American and Foreign Students' Attitudes.* Thesis submitted to Oregon State University. Corvallis, Oregon.

28. Shafer, J., & Walker, A. (2012). *Beyond English III Saudi Arabian Students in U.S. Higher Education: A Case Study at the University of North Dakota.* TESOL Conference Presentation. Grand Forks, North Dakota.

29. Saleem, B. (2015). *The Impact of Motivation on Performance: Findings from Karachi Based Service Organizations.* Istanbul, Turkey. Istanbul Technical University. doi:10.13140/RG.2.1.2836.8488.

30. Kreitner, R., & Kinicki, A. (2008). *Organizational Behavior* (8th ed., International Student, Ed.). Boston, MA: McGraw Hill and Irwin.

31. Meyer, D. K., & Turner, J. C. (2002). Discovering emotion in classroom motivation research. *Educational Psychologist, 37*(2), 107–114.

32. Artiran, M. (2015). *Akılcı Duygucu Davranışçı Kuram Ve Öz-Belirlenim Kuramı Çerçevesinde Yeni Bir Ölçek: Akılcı-Duygucu Öz-Belirlenim (ADÖB) Ölçeği'nin Geliştirilmesi—Doktora Tezi.* Turkey: Istanbul Arel University. Istanbul, Türkey.

33. Pellegrino, A. B. W., Davis-Martin, R. E., Houle, T. T., Turner, D. P., & Smitherman, T. A. (2018). Perceived triggers of primary headache disorders: A meta-analysis. *Cephalalgia, 38*(6), 1188–1198.

34. Kaufman, J. C. (2016). *Creativity 101.* New York: Springer.

35. Joshanloo, M. (2015). Conceptions of happiness and identity integration in Iran: A situated perspective. *Middle East Journal of Positive Psychology, 1*(1), 24–35.

36. Singelis, T. M., Triandis, H. C., Bhawuk, D. P., & Gelfand, M. J. (1995). Horizontal and vertical dimensions of individualism and collectivism: A theoretical and measurement refinement. *Cross-Cultural Research, 29*(3), 240–275.

37. Joshanloo, M. (2014). Eastern conceptualizations of happiness: Fundamental differences with Western views. *Journal of Happiness Studies, 15.* doi:10.1007/s10902-013-9431-1

38. Joshanloo, M. (2013). A comparison of Western and Islamic conceptions of happiness. *Journal of Happiness Studies, 14*(6), 1857–1874.

39. Okan, N., & Ekşi, H. (2017). Logoterapi'de Maneviyat. *Spiritual Psychology and Counseling, 2*(2), 143–164.

40. Deci, E. L., & Ryan, R. M. (2008). Self-determination theory: A macro theory of human motivation, development, and health. *Canadian Psychology/Psychologie canadienne, 49*(3), 182.

41. Yu, S., Levesque, C. S., & Maeda, Y. (2018). General need for autonomy and subjective well-being: A Meta-analysis of studies in the US and East Asia. *Journal of Happiness Studies, 19*(6), 1863–1882. doi:10.1007/s10902-017-9898-2

42. Vlachopoulos, S. P., Asci, F. H., Cid, L., Ersoz, G., González-Cutre, D., Moreno-Murcia, J. A., & Moutão, J. (2013). Cross-cultural invariance of the basic psychological needs in exercise scale and needs satisfaction latent mean differences among Greek, Spanish, Portuguese and Turkish samples. *Psychology of Sport and Exercise, 14*(5), 622–631.

5

WHAT THE THEORY SAYS, WHAT THE CULTURE UNDERSTANDS

Maybe you are searching among the branches for what only appears in the roots.

—*Rumi*

In this section, RE & CBT theories are discussed qualitatively in the Middle Eastern population. Cultural differences affect how therapy is practiced in a session, and how Middle Eastern clients recognize, evaluate, and understand cognitive distortions, irrational beliefs, and emotions. In relation to this, a variety of socioeconomic factors, language differences, family dynamics, peer relationships, traditional and religious expectations, other relevant social values, and cultural factors are examined here in terms of psychotherapy in general and RE & CBT. In addition, a specific overview in understanding how the population may approach seeing a psychologist, and how this differs from seeing a psychiatrist, is included in this chapter. Cognitive and emotional differences in Middle Eastern cultures are not necessarily understood in the same way as in Western society. Many reasons can be cited for these differences. As a prelude, some issues in Middle Eastern culture, and the attitudes of its people, need to be mentioned.

First of all, the use of vocabulary in everyday speech, and meanings given by therapists and clients to thoughts, beliefs, and emotions, differs from culture to culture. Our experiences shape our language and our language shapes our experience. Benjamin Lee Whorf, a linguist, indicated that language shaped the way we perceive the world. The following pages provide some examples of how the meanings of emotions and thoughts differ in the Middle East to that of the West.

Secondly, when solving psychological problems, CBT therapists avoid building the A-C connection, or even solving it, because they believe that the root of the problem is in cognitions (Bs) (negative automatic thoughts and irrational beliefs)—as mentioned in Chapters 1, 2, and 3. Many Middle Eastern clients generally attend sessions with prejudices towards the ABC model (when it is first introduced by a therapist), and maintain a focus on link between A (activating event) and C (consequences). This is also true for clients in the West. Both sets of clients see that stressful life events and past experiences create psychological dysfunction and believe therapeutic treatment is only possible to solve stressful events and the past traumas. They ignore the power of thoughts to evaluate and overcome stressful life conditions.

Hofstede claimed that Middle Eastern people are collectivists rather than individualists.[1] Maybe, because they are the members of a collectivistic culture, Middle Eastern people are prone to want to appear 'good' in others' eyes, rather than taking part in individual development and individualistic worries. Most make the 'A-C' connection to express their problems and look for solutions in 'A.' This understanding affects the A-C connection because quite a number of clients think 'A' can be solved only if other people around them are being fixed, or vice versa—fixing themselves for others. In dealing with these types of problems, therapists face two problems with clients:

1. Overcoming the A-C connection and bringing the client to the B-C connection (our thoughts affect our behaviors, or emotions).
2. Explaining the 'C' when the primary goals of the therapy are emotional well-being, not finding practical solutions.

Third, in the Middle East, people may refrain from using psychological services for fear of stigmatization.[2,3] They may have extreme shame and anxiety, if they are called 'mentally ill' by others.[2,3] A mother may hesitate to tell a teacher her child goes to a psychologist. A bank worker who has company health insurance may refuse to report his visits to a psychologist, but instead pays the cost from his own pocket. Some, possibly, tell their relatives and close friends about what their psychological distress, concealing the truth from others.[3] Originating from a collectivistic culture, Middle Eastern people tend to keep their feelings and psychological disorders secret, or remain in denial. Many have closed families, where they do not talk about negative experiences with other people, and some of them prefer to use religious healers for psychological disorders. This in itself shows a different state of mind.

In conclusion, the fear of stigmatization interferes with many people receiving psychotherapy treatment. Luckily, some people are willing to get psychological support from a professional. The obstacle then faced, however, is that many of these same people know only about Freud, sketchily, who was an analyst and psychiatrist and not a psychotherapist. Additionally, there are some problematic perspective and 'rigid' thinking patterns concerning psychological treatments in the Middle East, which, in turn, affect an exact application of Western psychotherapy.

How Psychotherapy Is Viewed

This is a book written for academicians, psychotherapists and people who have met and interacted with therapists, in any capacity, and not a book about sociology. It is intended to help other types of guides, including university and school counselors. It is plain that deep research into this subject is surely the work of psychologists. However, there will of course be a need to enter social issues inevitably. Most Middle Easterners believe that past experiences cause their own set of psychological states. Perhaps this may be the reason why most clients think of Freud when they hear of psychological treatment. The bad news is that a large part of the population in the Middle East is ignorant, or has incorrect knowledge, and they are also badly educated about behavioral therapy and other psychotherapies in general. The good news is that many young people have become interested in receiving psychology training which contain cognitive and behavioral components in recent years. Turks have also, relatively recently, discovered cognitive behavioral therapy.

For the most part stargazing is still more popular (!) than therapy and, in the Middle East especially, coffee-cup fortune-telling is also popular with a considerable number of people. The popularity of the Freudian approach may also related to 'fortune-telling' for Middle Easterners. As the Freudian approach postulates, the hidden secrets of our childhood and how the unconscious mind processes 'who we are' may be understood as 'a scientific technique of fortune-telling.' Some Middle Eastern clients want to hear childhood 'secrets' about themselves, using psychoanalysis, but they miss the point that their problems are created by their thoughts and not their unconscious secrets. Psychoanalysts like such clients since psychoanalysis cannot be falsified (see Popper's falsification principle), anything that it, or psychodynamics, says is true for the therapist and the client during sessions. According to Popper, science contains the way of its own refutation and that the whole analysis might be erroneous. So, a quantity of superior ways to explore the world is to make clear how to perceive them if they might be wrong. No psychotherapy theory is 100 percent perfect, including all cognitive behavior therapies. Many Middle Eastern clients ignore Karl R. Popper's point of view because they do not usually follow contemporary issues about psychotherapy.

Psychoanalysis, however, is still popular in Turkey, Egypt, and Lebanon. For instance, in Lebanon, there are a couple of very active associations, such as the Lebanese Association for the Development of Psychoanalysis (ALDEP), which is affiliated to the International Psychoanalytical Association (IPA), and L'Association Libanaise Pour le Développement de la Psychoanalyse.

Tbox: Please investigate Karl R. Popper's falsification principle in other sources, carefully, to feed your practice with evidence-based therapeutic techniques.

A number of therapists who apply psychoanalysis, or similar approaches, in universities and private practices are influential in Turkey, Lebanon, and Syria. The acceptance, registration, and, particularly, the duration of the establishment, implementation, and subsequent maintenance of new approaches to psychotherapy take a long time because of the old approaches and methods that exist. Turkey is relatively more open to new psychotherapy approaches than other Middle Eastern countries. In this part of the world there are, however, other countries far behind Turkey. For example, cognitive behavioral therapy is not taught in the universities of Azerbaijan. Students claim that only a primitive version of psychoanalysis is taught in the capital city, Baku, and there is no proper training in cognitive behavioral therapy.

The Influence of Psychiatry

Another problematic issue for psychotherapy is the influence of psychiatrists in Turkey and the Middle East. Some psychiatrists are prejudiced about psycho-therapeutic treatment. A few of them even restrict their patients to receiving only medical treatment. Unfortunately, too many clients think that medication is the only way to heal, because of a psychiatrist's directives. On the other hand, there are no proper occupational laws (as of 2019) for psychologists, which decree that a graduate-level psychologist can perform psychotherapy. The laws in Turkey have been formed to protect psychiatrists in the use of psychotherapy. As a result of this, practicing therapy is difficult for clinical psychologists in the mental health field. Prejudicial thinking about clinical psychologists is mostly attributable to psychiatrists, in the Middle East at least. Psychiatrists are very influential in the mental health field, especially in the Health Ministries, and they govern who can, or who cannot, give treatment. Of course, the whole world knows that performing therapy as a clinical psychologist differs from that of a psychiatrist. The former receives a more humanistic education, relying more heavily on verbal communication and psychology, whereas the latter focuses on biology and the chemistry of the human body. These issues negatively affect psychotherapy development in the Middle East and will remain so, as long as the mental health field is dominated by psychiatry, despite the show of counsel-ing services that are available in Turkey.

A psychiatrist said, 'People frequently call me a psychologist. I'm a psychiatrist! After studying at the Faculty of Medicine (for six years), I received the title of medical doctor!' It appears that she feels she is superior to a psychologist because, in addition to four years of study as a medical doctor, she also studied adult psychiatry. The tone here, suggesting that being called a psychologist is somehow not worthy of respect, is impolite. Most well-trained clinical psychologists in Turkey have obtained a four-year bachelor's degree (in psychology). They then spend two years completing a graduate degree, and, subsequently, four more years of doctoral study, followed by a couple of years of psychotherapy training at various psychotherapy institutes. That makes a total of almost 12 years—and much of it in a foreign language. As someone who spends time considering human psychology and psychological disorders, as a clinical psychologist, it can be definitively stated that psychologists have more education, and experience, in psychology and psychological treatments (for all ages) than a psychiatrist. As a result of this work, an end to the *myth* that psychiatrists are superior to clinical psychologists in mental health is long overdue or, at the very least, a rethink might be in order.

Some psychiatrists do not accept that a clinical psychologist can treat a psychological disorder. One Iraqi client reported that there is no psychotherapy treatment available in the northern part of Iraq. If a patient needs to get psychological treatment then she has to go to a psychiatrist or a medical doctor to obtain medicine.

Discounting the affair with the West that the Arabs have, it must be borne in mind that for the Muslim world, Turkey is seen as a leader in the modern world, and to much of the Third World too. Turkey is a key player in bringing the modern world to Muslims and a bridge to a different world. Fortunately, in

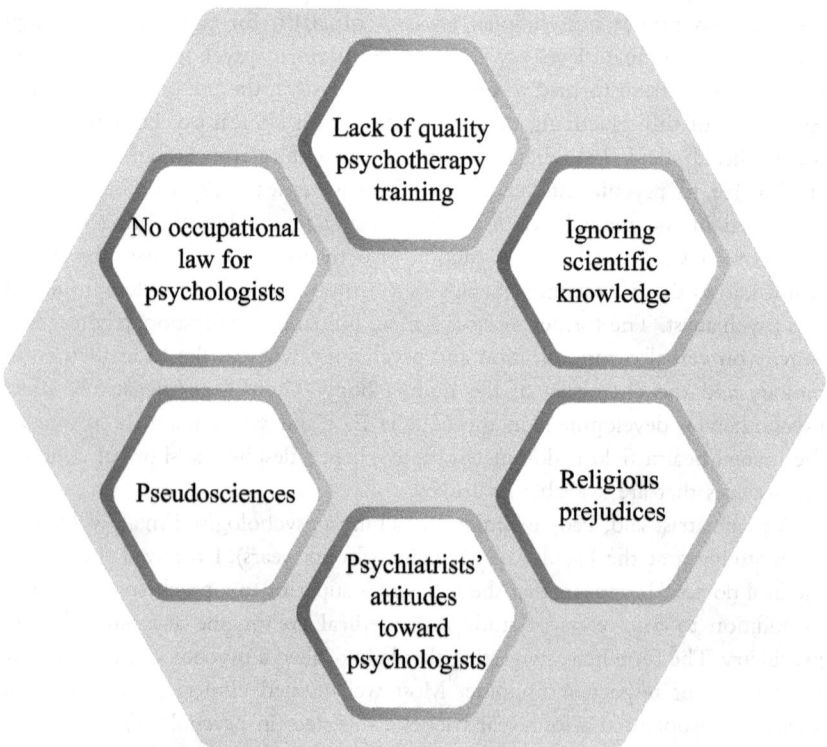

FIGURE 5.1 Problems faced in the field of psychology in the Middle East.

Turkey, the lack of availability of CBT training is changing rapidly in big cities, such as Istanbul and Ankara. Some Turkish clinical psychologists who have obtained degrees, diplomas, and licenses from the United Kingdom, Europe, and the United States have brought the knowledge they gained from their respective universities here. However, most psychology departments in graduate schools and CBT training programs in Turkey are provided by psychiatrists. Clinical psychologists or psychological counselors are viewed as 'assistants' to psychiatrists, and they do not feel they are given the scope to perform psychotherapy, and give training in psychotherapy, in an independent way.

Patriarchal Nature

It is important to mention the patriarchal nature of Middle Eastern society when making the distinction between psychotherapy and religiosity in the Middle East. Providing psycho-education about what therapy is and what therapy aims to achieve is necessary. For instance, many parents make life difficult for a therapist because many young clients (e.g., adolescents) seek autonomy and freedom from their families. Parents have a hard time in distinguishing between therapeutic goals, religious commands, and traditional rules. Therapy may support young Middle Eastern clients to achieve autonomy in their lives, but their family is afraid their child will get 'wrong' advice from a therapist. In a lot of cases, families want to stay in contact with the therapist during the therapeutic process. Some of them even want to be in the room during a session! Or after a session they want to know what has been talked about in the session! Such things can happen with not only adolescents but also even clients aged between 20 and 30.

An ingrained patriarchal nature also affects the relationship between younger therapists and older clients. Most Middle Eastern clients will not contemplate therapy with younger therapists and are unlikely to continue, if they begin. Younger therapists are also frequently not comfortable seeing older clients. In the Middle East 'experience in life' and 'being older' symbolize being 'wise.' Therefore it can be concluded that theory itself is not enough to be a practitioner.

Religious Clients

It has been suggested that REBT is an excellent option for deeply religious clients because the therapy is belief-based, and because most religions are in agreement with REBT's theoretical notions about irrational thinking.[4] The researchers report, however, that religious clients often become disturbed by their own faulty interpretations of religious texts, believing, for example, that they can never be good enough to please God, and this leads to emotional disturbances, depression and behavior problems, and so forth.[4]

REBT, in cases like these, can be applied by the therapist to demonstrate how a client's interpretation is at fault, and how a different, more rational way of thinking about a passage in the Bible or Quran, or any religious text, or a general religious belief, such as, 'God doesn't love me as much when I sin,'[4] can be applied.

Some researchers found that adopting a religiously accommodating approach to REBT resulted in significant reductions in depression, automatic thoughts, cognitive distortions, and general symptom distress, when clients were instructed to amass a body of faith-specific evidence from their religious texts to counter their irrational beliefs, and to use these daily in their thought processes.[4] In the Middle East, it is important for the client and the therapist to hold similar religious beliefs, or at least to allow, through rational thinking, for the possibility that someone else is entitled to hold beliefs that are somewhat different from her own.

Religious Sensitivity

Clients from an Islamic cultural background have a different perception of psychological disorders and treatment. Some of them do not appreciate modern therapeutic approaches. Rather they tend to find answers from their closest ones, friends, *abi*s and *abla*s (people who are older than them), preachers (imams), medical doctors, psychiatrists, and (finally!) psychologists and psychological counselors. Recently, Islamic psychological counseling has become popular in the Middle East.

For those who choose to visit a psychologist, taking a client's value system into consideration is important during sessions. Religious sensitivity has been demonstrated to be of great importance in therapy, as seen in studies. Shumway and Waldo examined whether there would be an interaction between participants' levels of religiosity and their anticipated working alliance with a counselor.[5] The participants were invited to sign a consent statement before a discussion of religious issues. The researchers' anticipation was that religious clients would show a higher anticipated working alliance in response to the invitation to address religious issues, and they did.

Therapeutic Relationship

In examining this interplay between religiosity and therapy, the researchers brought up the all-important issue of a working alliance between the client and the therapist. The working alliance consisted of three components: (1) agreement on in-counseling behavior and tasks; (2) mutually agreeing upon the outcome of therapy and goals; (3) the client/counselor trust, confidence, respect, and bond.[5] A working alliance presupposes that both parties must be allowed to contribute during therapy and therefore the client's perspective must be taken into serious consideration by the therapist. In fact, Flückiger et al. found that the introduction of a brief meta-communication intervention during therapy, or, in other words, valuing a clients' perspective, reinforced a client's alliance with his or her therapist over the course of therapy.[6] A brief meta-communication is not an option but a necessity for Middle Eastern clients. A study of different therapists produced different outcomes in clients, and showed that more effective therapists have higher expectations of positive therapy outcomes and a higher working alliance quality.[6]

For Western clients, a therapeutic relationship is shaped in a different way. Interestingly, Johnson, DiGiuseppe, and Ulven report that Dr. Albert Ellis was often described as cold, aloof, abrasive, and more interested in efficiency than in relationships.[7] Even more interestingly, however, is that Ellis was reported to have engaged in numerous mentoring relationships throughout his career, though he did not initiate most of them, and was said to have provided considerable support, acceptance, and encouragement to his protégés.[7] This suggests that though personality is important, in working relationships, as well as the working relationships between therapist and client, there are certain aspects of a therapist's personality that are more important than others. For example, a therapist who accepts a client unconditionally and allows her to express her ideas, before offering advice, might have a much better result with that client than a therapist who is quick to offer her corrections, based on the way she already thinks. Because of the close proximity in which a therapist and a client work on therapy issues, it is easy to see how a therapist's personality and level of belief in religiosity may be of great importance in therapy in the Middle East. Most Middle Eastern clients seek a psychologist who, at least, believes in God, but is not, maybe, too religious.

It is easy to imagine that opening up to a therapist may be extremely difficult for some clients. In fact, in a study of patients' disclosures to significant others, Khurgin-Bott and Farber found that not all therapy clients were comfortable disclosing information about their therapy to their confidants.[8] Conversely, we can infer that not all patients are comfortable disclosing certain information to their therapist, in which case, it is extremely important that the therapist acts in a way that ensures trust, especially when the therapy in question is REBT, where the client is expected to take direction from the therapist. Bearing these cultural factors in mind, RE & CBT may be a good choice for Middle Eastern clients when they are seeking psychological guidance.

Cognitions and Emotions: Examples From RE & CBT

Demandingness

If a therapist does not emphasize the words *should*, *have to*, and *must*, and subsequently does not also include an adverb, such as *definitely*, *absolutely*, or *always*, then Middle Eastern clients may misunderstand the irrational beliefs of demandingness. At any rate, in the Turkish language, reinforcement and emphasis must be done in this way. Therapists need to emphasize certain words to convey irrational beliefs to a client. There are many reasons for this, not only related to semantic differences. When discussing demandingness with only a single modal verb and not adding an adverb, to express the meaning strongly, a client may not understand that it is an irrational-harmful belief, so that he or she mistakenly understands that demandingness is a useful thought process, not a harmful one. Additionally, 'don't' and 'it is forbidden' are phrases endemic to Turkish culture and this sense of, and actual, prohibition needs to be overcome.

Example:

> Instead of a client saying to herself, 'I must finish my work on time,' the therapist needs to emphasize that 'I <u>definitely (or absolutely) have to</u> finish my work <u>exactly</u> on time!' is irrational.

Some interesting results were achieved from a study that was conducted with students in 2016.[8,9] When the participants answered the (Attitude and Beliefs Scales-II; ABS-II) questionnaire, they saw demandingness statements as normal and healthy ones. The outcome of the study showed correlations between demandingness and 'positive' feelings. This went against theoretical assumptions. This means that demandingness irrational beliefs are perceived as 'good' and 'healthy' thoughts. A number of phrases such as 'definitely must' and 'absolutely have to' were added to the items in the questionnaire; the results then changed dramatically and demandingness irrational beliefs were identified by the participants as negative and unhealthy beliefs. Therefore, in order to give the 'right' meaning to a demandingness irrational belief, the therapist may need to use adverbs. In this way it can be demonstrated, in order to convince clients that irrational beliefs are unhealthy cognitive structures, that certain words must be clearly defined. In fact, Albert Ellis often used the same strategy in his sessions.[10]

Middle Eastern examples:

1. Sentences such as 'I must do my job correctly' and 'I have to deal with the problems of my children' are invariably natural rhetoric for most people.

   A suggested usage is: 'I must **always** do my job correctly' or, 'I **always** have to deal—**I have no other choice**—with the problems of my children.'

2. In Western culture, when a person hears a sentence like 'You must do it,' then she usually questions the realistic reason behind the 'must.' On the other hand, in Turkey, 'You must do it' may not be perceived as a condition to be questioned. It is perceived as a responsibility, or a question of moral or community values.

Some differences between the two cultures can lead to change. For example, one of the socially accepted norms of Turkish people is that they may be extremely patient with extreme demands and subsequently endure suffering without complaint. However, independent, self-reliant, decision-making habits occur less frequently in Eastern culture compared to Western culture.

Some RE & CBT concepts differ culturally:

1. Demandingness irrational beliefs may appear normal because of cultural expectations.
2. Frustration intolerance irrational beliefs may be viewed as immoral, rather than abnormal, due to being seen as 'lazy,' or considered to be 'parasitic.'
3. Catastrophe/awfulizing irrational beliefs may activate feelings of embarrassment in a person, and even cause mockery in some cases. Panic disorder, for example, is likely to be seen as disgraceful.
4. Self-downing irrational beliefs may be situations viewed with sympathy in society, rather than as a psychological problem, due to collective depression.

One other possible reason is that there is a difference in cognitive distortion and irrational beliefs related to the family structure in Middle Eastern culture compared to Western culture. For instance, in Turkey, there are families who care for their children at home until a much greater age than in the West. Being dependent may mean the population possesses more 'frustration intolerance' beliefs. At what age parents cease supporting their children, to become autonomous, differs in both cultures. In Turkish families, becoming autonomous takes much longer than in Western families. When you reach 18 years of age, it is quite usual for many children to move away from their parents' home in Western culture. However, in Turkey, it is the norm that children live with their parents until the age of 25 or even 30! Someone married in their thirties may still ask their mother how to solve life's problems. This may occur because of financial or socioeconomic reasons. When compared to Western culture, in Turkey, children grow apart from their parents at a much later stage, and autonomy is rarely achieved. These circumstances also affect the way in which irrational beliefs are experienced as cognitive distortions. This trend is currently changing and, inevitably, this leads to more simple efforts to guide people in therapy.

Catastrophizing or Dramatization!

Being in a panic, or anxious, is seen as a weakness, especially for men, in the Middle East, and cannot be spoken about openly. Most clients use medicine to solve any problems, and not necessarily as a last resort. When a therapist conceptualizes a client's problem, she or he may use the word 'dramatization,' instead of catastrophizing or awfulizing. The irrational beliefs of catastrophizing and awfulizing need detailed explanation when dealing with anxious clients.

'Dramatizing' is a good word that remains in the minds of clients, especially those with depression. This is a relatively new phenomenon, especially with a burgeoning population, to which so many refugees are even now being added to, on a daily basis, but it previously existed because of laws that have been in favor of men—giving women an excuse to use emotional blackmail to dramatize their plight. Turkish teenagers love this concept, usually because they have watched their parents dealing with the latest calamitous state of affairs in Turkey, regarding everything from high drama in politics to the latest problem of dealing with life in an apartment—which is where most Turks now live. An alternative word for dramatizing is *exaggerating* (in Turkish: *abartmak!*), to describe awfulizing beliefs. The good news is that when using *exaggeration*, it contains a little bit of humor. There is even an idiom in the Turkish language that is often used in everyday conversations: 'making things bigger in your eyes.'

Frustration Intolerance

High tolerance and being patient are seen as virtuous, as a social value, in Turkey. There are many verses in the Quran about the benefits of being 'patient.' However, waiting for the doctor at the hospital, waiting in line at a grocery store, or sitting in the lecture room with a notebook and a (working!) pen is a problem for Middle Eastern people. Being polite and waiting in line may be considered a 'waste of time' for many. Examples of such social reality may challenge clients during treatment too. In therapy sessions many Middle Eastern clients want quick answers. In educating a client about frustration tolerance, it is better to be more direct and use the statement 'the benefits of being *patient.*' Unconditional life acceptance also works for clients with frustration intolerance. Social impatience may make a client think, 'Why should I be patient when nobody else is patient?' Actually, some Middle Eastern people already know the 'impatient' side of themselves. For instance, there is an *ekşi sözlük* (sour dictionary) that is a very widely used Internet forum. Many people read it and write on it. One of the discussions had the title 'Turks do not know how to get in line'!

At the 17th National Congress of Social Psychiatry, Prof. Dr. Şahin and his team presented some research outcomes. It was revealed that Turkish people were easily frustrated and fought each other, physically and verbally, sometimes resulting in harm to both doctors and even the structure of hospitals. The research also found that Turks acted selfishly in traffic and they also displayed a deep dislike of any form of criticism as well as having superstitious beliefs.[11]

Digesting is another idiom to be used when expressing low tolerance beliefs for clients in the Middle East. 'I can't digest . . . things in my life' can be used instead of 'I can't tolerate . . . things in my life.'

As a cognitive distortion Personalization is related to frustration intolerance especially in Middle Eastern social life. For instance, while driving, if you press the horn at the driver in front of you, he may get out his car and ask you, 'Do you know who I am?! How dare you sound your horn.' This kind of incident is likely to occur in many cities.

Acceptance or Love

Even though RE & CBT theory does not define acceptance as a condition of love for practical purposes, the term of unconditional acceptance is better redefined as *unconditional love of self/others and life* for Middle Easterners. Especially for Turks, semantically, acceptance does not carry any 'philosophical' or 'virtuous' meaning; rather it contains a more negative sense, possibly including a betrayal of not only ability but also self-worth. 'Acceptance' for them implies that they have 'lost the match' and that nothing will ever change, or that they will always be incompetent, which is black and white thinking wrapped up in 'it's my destiny' even after a hard struggle. If you use the word 'acceptance' with a client, when in session, he or she feels a disappointment, which is visibly recognizable physically in the slump of a body, and later it becomes very difficult to give psycho-education about what unconditional self-acceptance is. Instead, the word 'love' is a good replacement for 'acceptance' when introducing and discussing unconditional self-acceptance, because the word 'love' is not always used in the sense of romantic or sexual relationships. 'Love' represents acceptance in the Middle East, and clients do not become not defensive about the statement. In fact, just the opposite—they will respond positively to this word in sessions.

Here are two separate dialogues with students who were preparing for an important university entrance exam (similar to the SAT or GRE or A Levels) taken from a real session.

With client A.

Therapist:	Let's assume that you fail the exam and you will never be able to take it again. Will you still be able to accept yourself unconditionally?
Client A:	I've thought about that and tried it in my head, but I cannot accept myself unconditionally. It is true that people sometime fail, but it is really important for me, and I will be angry with myself. I cannot change these thoughts.

With client K.

Therapist:	Let's assume that you fail the exam and you will never be able to take it again. Will you lose your love of yourself?
C:	No, I will still love myself. However, I keep blaming myself too.
T:	You are saying that you still love yourself unconditionally. It doesn't depend on whether you fail the exam or not.

C: I will be angry with myself but, yes, I mean . . . I love myself, but it is not enough.

T: At least you still love yourself. (smiles)

C: Yes, that's true. (laughs)

T: How about acceptance . . . ? Will you be still able to accept yourself, unconditionally, even if you fail the exam?

C: No, I won't accept my self like that, I can do better, I need to work hard to improve.

Other Concerns

Here is a list of a cross-cultural redefinition of RE & CBT in the Middle East:

1. Men's anger problems, for which there are multiple causes, the same as women's, but in a different way, may not be seen as abnormal behavior. Since the majority of men regard their behavior as a right, in that they are the authority figure in society, many men refuse their partners the right to work. It is better to work on unconditional other acceptance with clients who have anger problems in session, rather than challenging frustration intolerance irrational beliefs.

2. Anger problems related to demandingness beliefs may become intense. When working with irrational demandingness, the concept of 'virtue' and 'forgiveness' may be necessary as a therapeutic goal. However, avoidance of logical disputation like 'Where is it written that people must respect you?' is suggested because most Middle Eastern clients would be irritated by such a question.

3. Over-generalization/catastrophe beliefs may be experienced because not attaining autonomy until one's thirties makes it difficult to build one's own decision-making skills. Therefore, homework on being autonomous in their life will help young Middle Eastern clients to overcome such irrational beliefs.

4. Terrorism and war have plagued the Middle East for many centuries, which is debilitating. Terrorism makes life feel worthless so that the value of human 'worth' is not similar to that of the West. Situations and events, with recurring regularity, make it difficult for a client and a therapist to talk about value systems, and even discussing having 'worth' or 'being worthy.' Instead of an individualistic way of looking at this, the problem of worthiness needs to be conceptualized in a collectivistic way for Middle Eastern clients. Refer to the information in Chapters 7, 8, and 9 (which contains Sufism teachings and wise old sayings) to deal with 'worthlessness,' rather than trying to point out the idea of 'we are worthy just because we are human beings.'

5. Some women are abused and beaten by their husbands/fathers/family members. As a result of this, it is difficult to apply any direction towards self-worth, or a humanistic philosophy approach, in therapy in the Middle East,

as opposed to in the West. Disputation on catastrophizing may be the best approach to work with clients who are abused, because they need to know they are not helpless.

6. Mind reading and fortune-telling are not always considered to be cognitive distortions; rather they are necessary for survival. A lack of admiration for science and poor scientific thinking skills support cognitive distortions. A therapist, too, may be material for mind reading! *'I guess my therapist thinks that my boyfriend doesn't love me!'* Some psycho-education about psychology science, before RE & CBT, would be great when working with such clients.

7. To convince clients that 'our thoughts determine our beliefs and emotions' is the most common obstacle in therapy in the Middle East. Emotional reasoning is also affected by nonscientific thinking. It may take a little bit more time for Middle Eastern clients to believe that their beliefs cause their problems compared to Westerners.

8. Some subcultures in the Middle East believe in *'namus.'* 'Namus' may be explained as a traditional rule that says no woman is allowed to have romantic (or sexual) relationships freely. For some, women are seen as the property of men. If *'namus'* is broken, then the woman and the man are executed. Therefore, many women feel guilty about their romantic relationships and it is difficult to discuss with the client concepts such as 'being autonomous' or 'freedom,' or some cognitive distortions, such as *all-or-nothing thinking and catastrophizing.* Being executed is a catastrophe! Isn't it? When disputing certain values in the Middle East, a practitioner needs to make sure as to what degree those values are important for a client, as well the suitability for her background and environment.

Emotions

> You are a lover of your own experience . . . not of me . . . you turn to me to feel your own emotion.
>
> —*Rumi*

Emotions are a universal construct. Where emotion comes from is not only explained in biological terms. In RE & CBT, the emotional regulation paradigm is a continuation of Richard Lazarus's appraisal theory. However, when defining emotions, many psychologists are interested in the environmental and relationship aspects. Additionally, when a foreign language is translated from one to another, perhaps one of the most challenging topics is emotions. As REBT and CBT try to impart or adapt functional feelings to clients, as therapeutic goals, RE & CBT researchers need to investigate what clients understand about emotions in qualitative studies because most of the time clients cannot differentiate between unhealthy negative (dysfunctional) and healthy negative (functional) emotions.

Markus and Kitayama introduced the term 'self-construal,' in order to define Western and Eastern cultures.[12] Independent self-construal is Western and inter-dependent, and self-construal is Eastern. People feel free to express their feelings in Western culture, while in Eastern culture[13] people pay greater attention to group values and harmony when expressing their feelings. Furthermore, in Turkey, an individual is seen as a selfish or self-centered if he or she 'expresses themselves,' and 'not expressing one's feelings' is 'respected' by society. In Western culture, high-arousal emotions, such as excitement, anger, alarm, fear, happiness, gladness, and joy,[14] are appreciated. They are valued and promoted more than low arousal emotions, such as calm, depressive, relaxed, gloomy, and satisfied.[15] In different cultures emotions may have different meanings. Separate words are used not only qualitatively but also quantitatively. There is very little quantitative or qualitative research about emotions in Turkey. Indeed, in the field of psychotherapy in general, research is very limited.

Emotions are spoken of sparingly in a Turkish family. It is not often that emotions are released, although there are strong emotional ties and closeness in Turkish families. However, 'ties' and 'closeness' are experienced differently to Westerners. For instance, Middle Eastern people usually pull a veil over or cover up/over what is done wrong or badly, and that is their understanding of how to deal with their emotions.

Families move with an instinct to survive. Instead of 'solving' problems, they are more interested in maintaining the ties of the family. Rather than looking to get help (from counselors) they hide the problem within the family. This is true for the physically, as well as the emotionally, disabled and may stem, in part, from religion and education—or the lack of it, or the quality of it, as well as, among other things, the geography and climate. A Turkish idiom expresses it appropriately: 'An arm is broken but the broken part remains within' *(Don't let it out of the room).*

Looking back on past generations and even to 20 or 30 years ago, fathers, especially, were distant and prescriptive to children and they managed them with fear and anger. In some families, fathers still try to direct the family by scaring or shouting at their children. It is also clear today that current generations of modern parents still have difficulty in talking of their feelings to a therapist. Fathers who do not speak loudly and who do not manage their children in anger or through fear may be tagged by society as passive or non-masculine men. Certainly, there are so-called metrosexual modern dads in Turkey, but they are relatively nonexistent as a result of the way society is made up.

Cbox: If you have difficulty talking about your emotions, then it is best to explain this to your psychotherapist. Psychologists cannot always predict that you are experiencing anxiety, nor when you want to talk about your emotions.

As a therapist, it is important to remember that a client may be encountering someone for the first time who genuinely listens to her or him and pays attention to her or his feelings, thoughts, and even words. If either sex, for whatever reason, is experiencing anger problems, they may have difficulty coming to therapy. Clients frequently find it very hard to talk about their feelings. It is best to treat them very sensitively, as they may need considerable help from the therapist to express their feelings. Perhaps the only place where they can talk about their feelings is in the psychotherapy session room. Unfortunately, on the other hand, many people do not come to psychotherapy at all, because they have difficulty in expressing their emotions and experience a kind of anxiety when they talk about their feelings. Speaking about and expressing feelings in Middle Eastern culture are frequently difficult, even fraught. Some clients see being emotional as a weakness. When clients have difficulty with their emotions, they hesitate to explain them. In order for them to open up about their feelings, if they experience cognitive distortions, irrational beliefs, or anxiety, it may be necessary to work on emotional issues first, on the anxiety of arousal. When this hurdle is overcome and clients feel 'safe,' hopefully they will start to talk about their feelings and subsequently be relieved.

> *Tbox: It is important that practitioners make it clear to clients as to the purpose of psychotherapy and what it entails.*

Some Additional Suggestions

REBT and CBT try to impart or adapt functional feelings to clients, as therapeutic goals. This is a book written for academicians, psychotherapists, and people who have met and interacted with therapists, in any capacity, and not a book about sociology. It is intended to help other types of guides, including university and school counselors. It is plain that deep research into this subject is surely the work of psychologists. RE & CBT researchers need to investigate what clients understand about emotions in qualitative studies.

Depression, Sadness, and Hurt

As mentioned previously, sadness and hurt are considered normal in the community. It is hard for clients to make a distinction in their minds as to what 'real' depression and what 'everyday sadness' are. Some people live their entire life in a depressed mood. *DSM-IV* and *DSM-5* say dysthymic disorder, while Middle Easterners may say, 'Life itself!' For many Middle Easterners suffering is inevitable.

Music is a very important part of Turkish life, despite the recent divergence of pop stars. Indeed, the precursor to the violin was the *rabab*, an Arabic instrument that featured two silk strings. A generation of Turks and Arabs, whose depression (a feeling of intense sadness) was influenced by arabesque music culture, are now 40-something years old. The arabesque style is very different to the rock and roll/jazz/pop/punk and so forth culture of the West, but it influences Turkey, Iraq, Syria, Jordan, Israel,* Lebanon (even Greece), and other Middle Eastern countries. Arabesque songs place a lot of emphasis on depression, sadness, and hurt. This is then propagated by adults who may not have recovered from, or grown out of, their own teenage years and who have adopted a mantle of adulthood without really knowing which way they are going to go, nor which way their country is even aiming at. Among the younger, mainly urban, genera-tion, hip-hop and rap music are taking arabesque's place. Gençtarım's survey of the Turkish population found irrational beliefs in discourses in the songs of famous singer Sezen Aksu.[16]

It was observed that painful themes such as separation and deception were generally embraced in arabesque songs (Gençtarım, 2007). In arabesque music, the songs emphasize that external forces, such as a lack of friendship, or economic difficulties, are a contributing factor to painful feelings, and great store is set by them. According to Gençtarım, Turkish arabesque music culture reflects a dys-functional thought system and a dysfunctional attitude towards life.[16] Certainly, people in positions of power do not make it any easier for the young to feel positive about the future, so destiny becomes a self-fulfilling prophecy. Bad tempers and negative moods and feelings are contagious. Arabesque songs do nothing to halt these feelings.

Learned Helplessness

Arabesque music profoundly influenced Turkish culture for about 35 years, from the 1970s to the mid-noughties and is still felt, even now. Many expressions in arabesque music culture show that depression/melancholy is a normal way of life. For example, Orhan Gencebay's famous song 'Let This World Collapse!' is very popular among famous arabesque music singers. Another song by a famous singer, Ibrahim Tatlıses, 'Shoot me down!', is also popular. Some of the lyrics go like this: 'This world is messed up, I'm done and my life is over, kill me, shoot me, you do not love me, so burn me, I will never love anyone again.' There are learned helplessness statements such as 'no way out' or 'nothing I can do' in these songs. Suffering and painful life events are the core ideas. Arabesque music has caused many psychological disturbances, which cannot be ignored, such as depression, anxiety, and hatred. Being depressed may be seen as destiny, rather than a dysfunctional emotion, and thus not a major depression, but a dysthymic disorder, and may not be regarded as a psychological disorder to be treated. This may also be due to socioeconomic reasons, youthful affairs of the heart, and family infighting. It could also be a reflection of the geography (earthquakes, where there is a weak infrastructure, are no fun). In communication with clients in Turkey, in order to give the meaning of depression, some of the words that are used in therapy are listed under the following headings: feel extremely suffocated, ruined, a big nervous breakdown, chronic unhappiness.

Jealousy

Is it unhealthy in the Middle East? Readers should note that jealousy and envy (which are separated in REBT) are indistinguishable in the Turkish language. Jealousy is common to all cultures but hard to explain and define. It would be a mistake to approach the issue as dysfunctional where REBT is applicable. In REBT terms, healthy jealousy is not quite the appropriate term for Middle Eastern culture. Jealousy is not perceived in Middle Eastern society in the same way as it is in Western societies.[17] Jealousy viewed as a pathological discomfort may 'disturb' Middle Eastern clients, since, according to social norms, it is seen as a normal and even a necessary feeling. Jealousy is a concept rather than an emotion and it is not perceived as a feeling. It is a concept of norms and traditions, and a principle, in life. It is not a sentimental but a cognitive process. Jealousy may lead to various unhealthy negative emotions, such as anger, anxiety, and depression, and behavior, such as violence,[18] and even death. Jealousy among couples and within families is a sensitive issue in Turkish culture. In romantic relationships, jealousy is one of the most serious problems encountered.

Perhaps it is necessary to discuss jealousy with clients as a feeling. This does not mean that jealousy should be perceived as it is in Western culture, nor that it should be accepted as a feeling. Put simply, jealousy should be considered as a feeling. It is necessary to point this out before treatment so that a therapist and client view it as a feeling. Robert Leahy criticized Albert Ellis's view on healthy jealousy, indicating that jealousy can never be healthy.[19] If a therapist initiates a discussion about a jealousy problem before tackling an open conversation about feelings and 'jealousy feelings,' the therapeutic relationship with a client (male or a female) will most likely be shaken.[20] The client may feel a challenge to his or her norms and priorities.

> Tbox: Anger (or extreme depression) always accompanies jealousy in the Middle East, so initially working with that would be something to consider and, if necessary, act upon.

An important point, in terms of another cultural adaptation of a Western theory to other cultures, has been touched on here. While theoretically, jealousy is treated as a psychological disorder, it is not possible to treat it as a mere psychological disturbance during the application of this theory in another culture. It needs to be modified to make the theory harmonious with an explanation of different types of jealousy. In a survey conducted about jealousy in Turkey,[17] satisfaction in relationships was shown to go hand in hand with an increase in the level of jealousy. Moreover, according to the findings, as the duration of the relationship increases, the physical, emotional, and cognitive reactions, given in the case of jealousy, decrease.

Shame and Guilt

Although feelings of shame, embarrassment, and guilt in REBT are treated as unhealthy emotions, these emotions may find different responses in Middle Eastern clients. Feelings of shame and guilt in this culture are more intertwined with each other. These emotions are used as an important and necessary state in some families. Children may be motivated by these two emotions—for instance, in their academic lives. Hence, these emotions may not be understood as unhealthy emotions, because they are used to heal a moral condition. On the other hand, whereas guilt in Western society appears to be related to an individual, in many Middle Eastern and Eastern societies it appears to be experienced family-wide. This may not be true in Jewish culture since, although geographically Middle Eastern, there is a sophisticated sense of humor that is valued, despite the hardships.

Guilt affects family honor, and the maintenance of the honor of the family frequently means that the source of guilt must be removed. For instance, a family will act together if they have a criminal family member. It is clear that when transposing guilt to remorse, it may be nigh on impossible for an individual to accomplish it without involving other family members. In Western terms, an individual can develop by herself but an individual from the Middle East needs the approval of others to do that. For sure, this is not possible most of the time. Unconditional self-acceptance can be used only for all the family in such cases.

Issues in Disputing

An advantage of cognitive behavioral therapy is that it is a structured therapy model. The didactic model of CBT is very clear. That is to say, when didactic methods are preferred, rather than Socratic methods, clients react more quickly and willingly in the Middle East. They prefer a method of being active and directional. This illustrates an important cultural difference in perception. For instance, studies reviewed[21,22,23] by researchers noted that, while North Americans and Europeans perceived emotion as an individual expression, regardless of context, Asian individuals were much more likely to pay attention to the context, perceiving an individual as inseparable from other people, and therefore judged emotion based on the entire picture. Studies illustrating the importance of perception, a key element in REBT, were conducted on the cultural differences in the perception of facial emotion between North American and Asian individuals.[21] The researchers found that there was a clear difference in the way North Americans and the Japanese perceived emotion. When shown pictures of cartoon characters clearly expressing different facial emotions, North Americans judged what emotion the character experienced based solely on the character's facial expression, while the Japanese participants were clearly more influenced by the facial emotions displayed by the surrounding characters.[21,22]

Middle Eastern cultures prefer didactic disputing over a Socratic one. They like to hear what to do, what to feel, and what to think. They always like functional disputing. 'What is the benefit of your beliefs?' is a good way to initiate proceedings. On the other hand, they dislike 'logical' disputing. The question: 'Why must they respect you?' may upset them. A session needs to be well prepared and well explained before using logical disputations. Evidence-based disputing ('Do you have any evidence that your irrational belief is a healthy one?') may cause confusion because Turkish clients will find an inexhaustible supply of 'evidence' for their beliefs. There are plenty of examples that even if evidence-based disputation does work, it is only 'for a short time.' Therefore, CBT therapists (not RE & CBT) need to be warned, at this point, that evidence-based disputing may overwhelm you and your client! Using humor and many types of metaphors for disputing is often beneficial for most clients in the Middle East (as demonstrated in Part II of the book).

Tbox: The most frequently occurring disputes in Turkish clients are confrontational, rather than collaborative, and you should take steps to allow time for an atmosphere of calm to dispel any potential physical discomfort or harm.

Additional Supplement: Interviews

Here are some quotes taken from interviews with academics, teachers, students, clients, and foreigners who live in the Middle East, in order to give some hints to readers as to how things are viewed from a Middle Eastern perspective. Some of the contents of these interviews give an idea as to how a Westerner thinks and perceives an Eastern culture, and also how an 'Easterner' thinks and perceives a (Middle) Eastern culture.

What Do You Think About Psychotherapy and Psychological Counseling?

I use transactional analysis and CBT in my applications. I've come across two things: clients and therapists have difficulty understanding these therapies, depending on the level of education; some can't grasp the idea of theoretical models. If a therapist offers a theory symbolically, clients have a hard time to match what we mean theoretically. (A therapist)

Clients with high intellectual levels criticize Western therapies for simplifying problems. They see Western therapies as simply stuck on a cause and effect hypothesis. They sometimes think that human psychology cannot only be explained by a reason-related relationship. (A therapist)

About cognitive therapy . . . our people (Middle Easterners) are very emotional. It takes time to reconstruct the cognitive schemas. Our people need to feel the emotions before they internalize the therapy. They absorb many ideas—including theories—emotionally. They approach things with feelings, not with logic or intellect. If they like a theory, they apply it. If they don't, they refuse to take action, using only theoretical information. (A therapist)

As a language, it is necessary to explain the theory with multiple examples. Theoretically there is no need to transfer using analogy. (A therapist)

When I think of psychological treatment, it means drug treatment and a madhouse. (A member of the public)

When it comes to psychological treatment, my idea is that you get advice from a mentor who will direct you to solve problems in your life, especially when you have relationship problems. (A member of the public)

I used medicine, but I don't believe in psychiatric treatment. I prefer to talk to a psychologist; it seems more natural and more beneficial. (A client)

My friends look in to the distance, if I talk about receiving psychological treatment, they have stereotypes. When I tell them I go to psychologist, they think I'm crazy. (A member of the public)

I think that everyone should get therapy, regardless of whether they are psychologically sick. I think it is always good to consult someone who has knowledge of psychology. (A member of the public)

Using a theory/model of foreign origin, it is difficult for a person (a client) of another culture to internalize this therapy process. I believe that to maximize any gains from a foreign therapy theory the opportunities remain limited. (An academic)

Many people in the Middle East, at least, are still fearful that psychiatry and psychotherapy are the work of the devil. (A foreigner in the Middle East)

Why Can't 'Eastern' People Provide a Scientific Theory That Is Universally Accepted?

Western scientists are open-minded. I guess the core problem in the Middle East is that people do not have an open-minded attitude, as in the West. I am not certain about Westerners, but in the Middle East we do not trust each other in the name of creating a theoretical approach. (An academic)

It is my observation that people in Western countries believe in human potential. Hence, we see that people can be courageous and productive. They are also able to draw on a rich source of material to develop and create psychological theories, which Middle Easterners cannot. This may be for economic reasons as well as political and religious ones. It is also my belief that there are geographical reasons which upset the balance and less an attitude of being work-shy. (An academic)

In my opinion our scientists may add original new concepts and visualizations to existing Western theories, but not necessarily create a whole theory. (An academic)

Not only true for psychology or other sciences but also in other fields, such as in art. . . . Artists suffer from a narrow mind-set of the people and politics in the Middle East. Very rarely do significant art works from the Middle East come up! Such work is not respected, nor is it supported by society. Talented artists and intelligent scientists from the Middle East, therefore, frequently move to the West. Eskisehir and places in Anatolia are full of touristic folk art. (An academic)

There are some obstacles in applying a Western therapy to clients in the Middle East. For example, Eastern people are fascinated by mystical things. We believe more in destiny than in facts. Since we are not accustomed to acting on the basis of thought, it is very difficult to develop a methodology. However, Middle Easterners might create an emotional and maybe a spiritual therapy. (A therapist—Supervisor)

A complete overhaul of the education system is required, but to whose benefit that will be it is impossible to judge. It should be for everyone and it should be modern. New Zealand and Finland may be shown to be good working models for Middle Easterners. (A foreigner in the Middle East)

Eastern people have been caught up in the maelstrom of modern 'Western' thought and action but this in no way restricts the human desire to search for 'more.' (A foreigner in the Middle East)

Scientific institutions are not properly funded here and this is not conducive to the inquiring mind. It is self-evident that many Eastern cultures have advanced, usually after times of geopolitical upheaval. In my experience, Middle Eastern and generally Muslim people are not focused on generating new ideas, as they require a large budget to set up, and maintain, at adequate levels. (A foreigner in the Middle East)

Is There Any Political or Prejudicial Reason for Eastern Scientific Psychotherapeutic Discoveries Not to Become Universal?

In the Middle East, all discoveries are based on a Western model. No work has been done to move things forward for Muslim people on an industrial basis. Would you count Steve Jobs's work as a discovery? He is half-Syrian but he grew up in the US. Middle Eastern ideas are in use everywhere and Jesus was Middle Eastern! Would you count the factories that were established in Atatürk's time? I believe it was his desire that Middle Easterners use a Western approach. (A foreigner in the Middle East)

I don't think Westerners have any prejudices against Middle Easterners about establishing scientific theories. When I have worked with American scientists, I notice they think that Eastern people have a different perspective about science. They respect and trust the potential of Eastern scientists. (An academic)

When I attend international congresses or when reading scientific journals, I witness that most scientists who suggest new ideas are Western. I feel the editors and advisors of congress belittle scientific works belonging to Middle Easterners. (An academic)

Do We (Middle Easterners) Have to Assimilate a Western Understanding of Science?

I think you do. All scientists who work well in Turkey, and those who work abroad, follow the Western version of researching, collating, indexing, archiving, debating, and studying. This type of work does not only mean rote memorizing. There should be a creative element in study and research but this has not been promoted, at least in Turkey, where control by 'superiors' is endemic. (A foreigner in the Middle East)

What Are Your Observations of the Different Ways Turkish People and Western People Look at Science?

I know people in Anatolia who want to use modern science in all its forms, more than they can—not solely for economic reasons, and I know farmers who will simply not listen to reason. It is strange, though, that farmers and other producers, for many reasons, apart from knowing all the tricks of the trade regarding serial, fake, or copycat everything (textiles, technology, pharmaceuticals, agricultural products, auto industry, etc.), will always be happy to follow Western guidelines, when they know how much profit they will make financially. (A foreigner in the Middle East)

Psychology and the study of psychology are very popular among women in Turkey. But then again, so is having a coffee cup read, fortune-telling, and astrology. Although Middle Eastern society seems to be patriarchal, at home the women would appear to rule the roost. (A foreigner in the Middle East)

Some people I have met fully understand the need for psychology. Some of the great work done before and after World War II, set up by predominantly (Jewish?) French-men(?) may be instrumental in an understanding of the general state of mind of Middle Easterners. Education is the root of the problem here, and not just in terms of psychology or taking a look at problems concerning everyday life. (A foreigner in the Middle East)

Note

* Please note that Israel is geographically considered to be in the Middle East, however, the scope of the book is aimed at only Turks, Arabs and people from other Islamic countries, or wherever Middle Eastern people are to be found, throughout the world.

References

1. Hofstede, G. (2010). The GLOBE debate: Back to relevance. *Journal of International Business Studies, 41*(8), 1339–1346.
2. Cosan, D. (2015). The perception of psychotherapy in Turkey. *The European Journal of Social & Behavioural Sciences, 13*(2), 1842.
3. Taskin, E. O. (2007). *Stigma: Ruhsal hastaliklara yonelik tutumlar ve damgalama [Stigma: Attitudes of Mental Diseases and Stigmatization].* Izmir: Meta Basim Matbaacilik.
4. Johnson, W. B., Ridley, C. R., & Nielsen, S. L. (2000). Religiously sensitive rational emotive behavior therapy: Elegant solutions and ethical risks. *Professional Psychology: Research and Practice, 31*(1), 14.
5. Shumway, B., & Waldo, M. (2012). Client's religiosity and expected working alliance with theistic psychotherapists. *Psychology of Religion and Spirituality, 4,* 85–92. doi:10.1037/a0025675
6. Flückiger, C., Del Re, A. C., Wampold, B. E., Znoj, H., Caspar, F., & Jörg, U. (2012). Valuing clients' perspective and the effects on the therapeutic alliance: A randomized controlled study of an adjunctive instruction. *Journal of Counseling Psychology, 59*(1), 18.

7. Johnson, W. B., Digiuseppe, R., & Ulven, J. (1999). Albert Ellis as mentor: National survey results. *Psychotherapy: Theory, Research, Practice, Training, 36*(3), 305.

8. Khurgin-Bott, R., & Farber, B. A. (2011). Patients' disclosures about therapy: Discussing therapy with spouses, significant others, and best friends. *Psychotherapy, 48*(4), 330.

9. Karakoc, B. (2016). *Relationships Between Irrational Beliefs and Anxiety and Depression, and Interaction Between Irrational Beliefs Themselves.'* 'Thesis in Clinical Psychology. Istanbul, Turkey: Istanbul Arel University.

10. Yildirim, R. D. (2016). *Evaluation of Irrational Beliefs on Ontological Well-Being: Demandingness as Suppressor Variable* Master Thesis in Clinical Psychology). Istanbul Arel University.

11. DiGiuseppe, R. A., Doyle, K. A., Dryden, W., & Backx, W. *A Practitioner's Guide to Rational Emotive Behavior Therapy* (3rd ed.). New York: Oxford University Press,

12. Türkler çabuk sinirlenip, ani tepkiler veriyor. (2010). Retrieved from www.haberturk. com/saglik/haber/522430-sabirsiz-turkler

13. Markus, H. R., & Kitayama, S. (1991). Culture and the self: Implications for cognition, emotion, and motivation. *Psychological Review, 98*(2), 224.

14. Kitayama, S. (2002). Culture and basic psychological processes-toward a system view of culture: Comment on Oyserman et al.

15. Dehaene, S., Izard, V., Spelke, E., & Pica, P. (2008). Log or linear? Distinct intuitions of the number scale in Western and Amazonian indigene cultures. *Science, 320*(5880), 1217–1220.

16. Tsai, Y. (2011). Relationship between organizational culture, leadership behavior and job satisfaction. *BMC Health Services Research, 11*(1), 98.

17. Demirtaş, H. A., & Dönmez, A. (2006). Yakın ilişkilerde kıskançlık: Bireysel, ilişkisel ve durumsal değişkenler. *Türk Psikiyatri Dergisi, 17*(3), 181–191.

18. Gençtanırım, D., & Voltan-Acar, N. (2007). Akılcı duygusal davranışçı yaklaşım ve Sezen Aksu şarkıları. *Eğitim ve Bilim Dergisi, 32*(143), 27–40.

19. Leahy, R. L., & Tirch, D. D. (2008). Cognitive behavioral therapy for jealousy. *International Journal of Cognitive Therapy, 1*(1), 18–32.

20. Leahy, R. L. (2008). The therapeutic relationship in cognitive-behavioral therapy. *Behavioural and Cognitive Psychotherapy, 36*(6), 769–777.

21. Fang, X., Sauter, D. A., & Van Kleef, G. A. (2018). Seeing mixed emotions: the specificity of emotion perception from static and dynamic facial expressions across cultures. *Journal of Cross-cultural Psychology, 49*(1), 130–148. doi:10.1177/0022022117736270

22. Masuda, T., Ellsworth, P. C., Mesquita, B., Leu, J., Tanida, S., & Van de Veerdonk, E. (2008). Placing the face in context: Cultural differences in the perception of facial emotion. *Journal of Personality and Social Psychology, 94*(3), 365.

23. Lim N. (2016). Cultural differences in emotion: differences in emotional arousal level between the East and the West. *Integrative Medicine Research, 5*(2), 105–109. doi:10.1016/j.imr.2016.03.004

PART II

Eastern Sources

6

A BRIEF HISTORY OF PSYCHOLOGY IN THE MIDDLE EAST

Yesterday I was clever and I wanted to change the world. Today I am wise, so I am changing myself.
—*Rumi*

Psychology is a study of the field of behavior, emotions, and cognitions. It covers almost all other aspects of behavioral science. It seeks to understand individual and group behavior. REBT and CBT academics and practitioners investigate human intelligence, motivation, perception, attention, affection, personality, brain functioning, other thought processes, and interpersonal relationships.

Psychology has a long history in the Middle East, yet it is not well documented. In this section, some of the Arab thinkers, some of the scientists who lived in Ottoman times, those of the new Turkish Republic, and some from other Middle Eastern countries will be referred to. Contemporary trends will also be discussed in this chapter. Many things seen in the West are replicated in Muslim countries and also throughout Asia. Throughout history, a variety of Islamic thinkers expressed thoughts about human psychology. Rhazes (Al-Razi) (865–925AD), Avicenna (İbn-i-Sina) (980–1037AD), and Jorjani (1042–1137AD) wrote books about medicine, including their use in psychological treatment. Avicenna and Rhazes also suggested methods for psychotherapeutic treatment. The information in these books is still accurate today. Some of their definitions of symptoms of psychological disorders, such as hallucination, delusion, and other affective conditions, can be found in modern psychopathology books. Such ideas and thoughts have, unfortunately, faded away and not reached modern times.

Psychotherapy is not recognized as a treatment for many countries in the Middle East, such as Saudi Arabia and Iraq. For instance, in Saudi Arabia, if anyone is psychologically distressed, she has to go to a psychiatrist to get a prescription.

In Saudi Arabia, psychiatrists are not often native mental health workers, and foreigners fulfill these functions; this in itself has a culturally distancing effect. Some countries like Syria, Qatar, Iran, Israel, and Lebanon are similar to Turkey (where psychotherapy is developed), and where psychotherapy as a psychopathological treatment is recognized and used.

In the Middle East, practitioners have difficulty in explaining what psychotherapy can or cannot do for clients. The latter frequently seek assurance, which may not always be possible. They also frequently make irrational demands of the process of therapy, as well as of therapists: '*Tell me how I am going to solve my problems*,' '*Guide me to change my "self*,"' '*Teach me how to fix my entire life*,' '*Help me to clean up my past failures!*' are phrases all too commonly heard. Clients often seek advice, rather than analyzing their cognitive schemas. When introducing the framework of the B-C connection, which is that our thoughts cause our stress, and not what has happened or what we experienced, therapists often hear clients exclaiming: '*Thinking about what happened (A's) to me, it's pretty hard to believe that my thoughts create my stress. Prove it!*' A scientific psychotherapy approach to psychological difficulties seems 'strange' to some of them. Most of them do not seek out science, but they hunger for a 'cure'—a scientific cure or a non-scientific cure, it doesn't matter! If they visit a practitioner, most of the time they do not question RE & CBT applications; they are willing to do, and trust, whatever the therapist says. The majority of Middle Eastern people are not aware of their own scientific history. Although this may be hard, one thing for a clinician to do is to remind them of their own knowledge of science. Even in a quick search of the history of the Middle East, it is clear that many wise people and their scientific ideas have existed for centuries, including on matters of psychology and well-being. These days therapy seems 'too long' a process, and most clients want quick answers rather than a 'long-lasting cure.' Clients tend to require advice about what they should do about their problems and even want a method to learn the best way to achieve their goals.

There is no magic in *curative* work in psychology. A Middle Eastern person is rarely without prejudice in the field of psychology, and it is as if the lessons of the past, in any scientific field, have been willfully ignored and disregarded. This may be a cultural anomaly or a fault of the education system. Clients frequently visit therapists expecting a miracle solution, some magic touch, or that a therapist will secretly embed in them a specially provided (verbal, herbal, or maybe [for psychiatrists] pharmaceutical!) potion or elixir to 'change' or subvert their mind, in order to answer their preconceived questions (to which they also have the answer on many occasions), or they seek guidance and answers to the 'real truth' about themselves.

Psychology in the Arab World

According to some Islamic thought, the progress of human mental and spiritual development has stages that begin with self-gratification (*nafs-i-am-mareh*) and pass through self-doubt and self-accusation to inner peace, self-assuredness (*nafs-i-mutma'enneh*), and self-acceptance.[1] Arab culture exists from northern Africa to the borders of Iran. Historically, the first examples of psychiatric work exist in Iran, called *ravan-pezeshk*, which was known as what is called psychiatry today. Psychiatric diseases were taught at Jondi Shapur University during the Sassanid dynasty.[2]

The first writings about psychology in the Middle East go back to the sixth century: *'Ilm al-nafs* or the science of the *nafs* (Nafs by Al-Ghazali).[3] *Nafs* describes a broad range of topics, including the *qalb* (heart), the *ruh* (spirit), the *aql* (intellect), and *irada* (will).[4] With the help of the introduction of ancient Greek thought to Arabs (please see Al-Mamun's translations (AD 813–933), Islamic philosophy in Egypt and Syria became popular in the eighth and ninth centuries. Early writings usually mixed Islamic philosophy with diatribes about religion and the soul. In the Middle East, modern terminologies (Western terms) of psychology, and comparisons with the Islamic conceptualizing of the human psyche, are frequently misleading, because they are usually used interchangeably, not cross-culturally. It is hard to call 'psychology,' therefore, a separate field from religion and studies of the soul, until the late twentieth century.

The hadiths play a big role in people's lives and have great power in determining human behavior (especially moral values, social rules, and psychology) in the Middle East. Hadiths are assumed to be the Prophet Muhammed's (s.a.v.) sayings, or anecdotes from his life. However, this is a controversial issue, because some Muslims say every Muslim should depend only on the verses of the Quran and not on the hadiths, due to lack of evidence as to whether the hadiths have degenerated. There are other controversial issues in the sciences and in philosophy throughout Islamic history. A famous one was between Ibn Rushd (Averroes) and Al-Ghazali. Ibn Rushd is known to have taken the side of the Aristotelian and Neoplatonic ideas in his thought, while Al-Ghazali (AD 1058–1111) was concerned that Islamic philosophers were leaning too heavily, and uncritically,[5] on ancient philosophy. Some early Muslim scholars, including bn-i-Sina (Avicenna) and Ibn Rushd, had charges of atheism brought against them. Some Muslims believed that new thoughts (especially philosophic ones) would lead to new perspectives about the Quran and hadiths, and therefore they were haram (a sin/forbidden). Recently, many Islamic scholars have clarified that scientific innovations in Islam do not mean re-evaluating the Quran, nor that the hadiths are a sin, but that it is necessary to study the sciences. Yet other Muslim scholars, such as Faruqi (1982), criticized the secular education system by saying it led to an intellectual crisis among Muslims.[3]

Muslim contributions to psychology are really sparse. Al-Kindi (Latin, Alchendius) is considered to be the first Muslim philosopher who wrote many texts about sleep, dreams, sorrow, and how to tolerate losing.[3] He also suggested cognitive strategies to overcome depression. Al-Tabari (AD 838–870) wrote about the importance of relaxation in psychological well-being and the importance of psychological counseling in general health.[6] Al-Balkhi (AD 850–934) was interested in clearly differentiating between neuroses and psychoses, and he wrote about anxiety, anger, depression, obsessive behavior, and thoughts.[3] Ibn Zakariya Al-Razi/Rhazes (AD 864–932) wrote about psychosomatic illness.[3] Please refer to the Haque article[3] 'Psychology From an Islamic Perspective: Contributions of Early Muslim Scholars and Challenges to Contemporary Muslim Psychologists' for detailed information about other thinkers and scientists who wrote about psychology in the Middle East.

Contemporary Developments

Badrī discussed that blindly accepting Western theory and practice was unsuitable for Middle Easterners, due to the lack of a spiritual aspect in explaining human behavior, which would implicate a loss in meaning for a Middle Easterner.[7] From a prejudiced Middle Eastern perspective, many Western theories about psychology may have roots in Western atheistic philosophies.

An Egyptian psychologist, Yousef Mourad, who returned from France in the 1940s, became a doctor of psychology at Cairo University and, with him, the teaching of psychology began, under the umbrella of philosophy, marking the start of a fresh period in the development of the discipline.[8] In 1945, the first issue of the *Egyptian Journal of Psychology* was published. In 1948, the Egyptian Psychological Research Association was established.[9] Ain Shams University was established in the 1950s, and psychology lectures commenced for students from Egypt and other Arabic countries, and whose courses are highly regarded. The first psychology department was established in 1974 at Cairo University. In 1978,

FIGURE 6.1 The Cairo University (efensko, 123rf.com).

the King Saud University offered a master's program in psychology. In Syria, Lebanon, and some Northern African countries (Morocco, Tunisia, and Algeria), psychology was influenced by the French tradition.[8]

Psychologist Linda Sakr says that 'Psychology in the Arab world has always been a taboo word. Mental health was never spoken about or referred to, except behind closed doors in whispers.'[10] This is rapidly changing as Arabs adapt to different ways of coping in an ever-changing world. People from North Africa, Syria, Jordan, and Lebanon are accustomed to therapy because of traumas endured due to conflict in that region, and since they are also older societies. As for the Gulf, therapy is still relatively new. This is no different to most parts of Turkey, where many psychologists lack the necessary skill and training to adapt to the culture.

Here are some statistics for mental health services in the Arab world: Out of 20 countries (about which information is available), six do not have mental health legislation and two do not have a mental health policy. Lebanon, Kuwait, and Bahrain had 30 psychiatric beds per 100,000 people in 2007, while Sudan and Somalia had less than 5 beds per 100,000. The greatest quantity of psychiatrists is found in Qatar, Bahrain, and Kuwait, while Morocco, Somalia, Sudan, Syria, and Yemen have less than one psychiatrist per 200,000 people.[11] There is no record of how many clinical psychologists and psychological counselors live and work in these countries. Regulations often distinguish between prescription-only and over-the-counter drugs. In most Middle Eastern countries, prescription medicines can easily be accessed without a prescription, resulting in possible misuse and therefore vital risk to clients.

The Middle Eastern world still appears to require more than just an awareness of mental health issues. There is a shortage of mental well-being administrators and experts.[12] In modern times, the emphasis has been on psychoanalysis and phenomenological, psychological theories, rather than quantitative research with psychometric and statistical analyses. There remains an absence of experimental studies.[8]

In the Arab world, researchers in the field of Islamic psychology are divided into two separate groups—arguing that modern psychology forms, concepts, theories, and practices of the West fail to explain the psychological structure of Muslim individuals.[13] Unfortunately, neither Arab nor Turkish scientists and practitioners have been able to offer a new, 'well-recognized,' therapeutic approach, nor a single psychological theory.

Turkish psychologists Muzaffer Sherif and Çiğdem Kağıtçıbaşı's work, which is famous around the world, have never, in fact, posited any theories. Kağıtçıbaşı is known as one of the founders of social psychology as well as Sherif. In 1935, Sherif conducted an experimental study, the goal of which was to demonstrate that individuals conform to group norms when they are in an ambiguous situation. This experiment led to valuable information about group behavior.

Mental health problems are increasingly widespread within the Middle East, not surprisingly. However, these disorders and their conceptualizations, utilized to assess and treat clients within the region, were developed by a fundamentally Anglo-Saxon populace, based within the United States and Western Europe. Ziad Kronfol, a therapist at Weill Cornell Therapeutic College, in Qatar, made a difference to this situation, by organizing a congress to discuss how guidelines within the Middle East can be developed to better handle advancements in the field of psychotherapy.[14]

Currently PTSD is the most common mental health issue globally, as a result of periods of combat, social upheaval, and violence, seen predominantly in many Arab countries and Turkey. This is a major 'unrecognized' problem in the Middle East. Although lifelong PTSD is best predicted by traumatic events, trauma itself can result from violence, recurring memories, displacement, and fear.[15] Imagine how the people in the Middle East feel when they are caught up in war. It is very distressing. Mental health problems are often suppressed for fear for bringing shame and disgrace to society. Due to cultural challenges, Arabs often express psychological problems in physical terms, thus avoiding a mental health stigma and rejecting the few mental health services that may exist. In Tunisia, for example, physical manifestations of trauma have been linked to traumatic experiences.

Any promulgation must be cognizant of these, and other, cultural sensitivities. One method used in Iraq includes 'cognitive behavioral treatment provided entirely on the Internet,' which can cater for the treatment of a wider variety of people in dangerous, or underpopulated areas. This can allow interested parties to address PTSD before conflicts cease.[15] Thus mental health in the Arab world is a taboo topic that few dare to broach openly. A small minority resort to psychotherapy that ensures that it is undertaken in complete privacy and discretion. According to the World Health Organization (WHO), Arab countries are world leaders in terms of rates of depression, due to the levels of violence, the lack of stability, and rapidly increasing urbanization.

As a promising development, there is a growing trend in the number of qualified psychologists in Egypt, equipped with modern methods, to address mental health issues without resorting to medication. At the other end of the spectrum, psychiatric specialists around the Arab world, particularly in countries like Egypt, have a tendency to be all too generous with their drug prescriptions.

The shortage of doctors and psychologists in Iraq has become noticeable following the emergence of Islamic State, and the violent war against it. According to Médecins Sans Frontières (MSF), the shortage has had a clear impact, with many Iraqis suffering from trauma as a result of having to coexist with Islamic State. In a report in March 2017, the WHO stated that 'Emergencies are also opportunities to build better mental health systems for all people in need. Access to mental health care is better in Syria, in 2017, compared to the situation before the war.'[16]

Primitive Psychotherapy Among Turks

Turks are not originally a Middle Eastern nation. They are from a large 'tribe' located over a wide range of Central Asia. The original spiritual belief system of these Turkish 'tribes' was shamanism. Shamanism was one of the very first religions[17] and was also an early attempt to heal people's stress and unhappiness. It was the roots of a primitive method of psychotherapy and may be the very first form of spiritual healing around the world (e.g., Aztecs, American Indians, India, and Nepal). According to some sources, there is evidence of shamanism dating back 30,000 years. (Readers may consider, too, that even Native American Indians are related to Turkish tribes.) Shamanic prayers helped people to feel good about themselves, others, and life. In shamanic practice, the priest really takes advantage of the integrity of the patient to influence her body through consciousness, hypnosis therapy, visualization, a positive approach to reality, psycho-surveillance, personal adjustment of the patient to healing, and psycho-rhythmotherapy.[17]

Nowadays, integrating *shamanic methods* into psychotherapy is still applicable for some practitioners[18] even if it is not scientifically proven. A shamanic journey is one of the common methods to enter a state of consciousness.[18] Hammerman claims that suffering from depression is related to a sense of emptiness, or of not being all there and that shamanic interventions are beneficial to clients.[18] According to him, certain unhealthy negative emotions (UNEs), such as shame, can be treated by applying a shamanic journey during a session, by stabilizing the self. He says, '*My initial therapy with him focused on helping him to tolerate and manage his emotional swings on a daily basis.*'[18] While shamans (in a trance, much like the dancing Sufis) contact evil and good spirits, psychotherapists work with negative issues, as well as the resources of the person.[19]

Shamanic interventions may be similar to yoga; however, there are different purposes, such as healing in peace (yoga) versus healing in dancing and music. Unlike yoga, or other forms of meditation, a shamanic journey tends to be practiced more for religious purposes, rather than for use as psychological treatment. This may also endorse why people involved in the creative arts are also frequently seen to be 'possessed.' Shamanic healing is found in many areas of the world, such as Peru and Nepal, and it is unfortunate that the media show an interest only in the more extreme parts of this, such as imbibing ayahuasca.

When considering the Turkish roots of shamanism, they are to be found in Middle Asia mostly (Turkmenistan, Kazakhstan, etc.), the point being that Turks migrated to Arabic lands from Central Asia and encountered Islam there. A shaman 'priest' employs his soul to give orders concerning the client's thoughts, emotions, and behavior, whereas a modern psychotherapist assists a client in evaluating her life circumstances and cognitive distortions and in discovering strategies to restructure cognitive schemas (e.g., irrational beliefs and negative automatic thoughts). The psychotherapist may use different tools to guide clients, including reference to folk sayings, parables, and spiritual statements, in order to refine the wisdom of the individual, before shamanic interventions. Spirituality is used as a treatment aspect in many psychotherapy approaches—for instance, dialectic behavior therapy, Jungian therapy, and client-centered therapy.

FIGURE 6.2 A Shamanic healing practice (Feije Riemersma @123rf.com).

Islamic and shamanistic beliefs are somewhat similar to each other. They both believe in 'one' God. This is neither a history nor an anthropology book, nor is it a religious discourse. Therefore, these examples are cited from a psychological point of view and this is the reason they are included in this chapter.

Asklepion

Anatolia and some parts of Syria contain ancient ruins that 'possibly' affected later work on psychology and medical science in this part of the world. Among these ancient buildings, there are structures and figures related to medical and psychological treatments. The Ottomans' interest in mental health may have begun when they encountered these structures in Anatolia.

The most interesting building complex in ancient times was built for the treatment of snake phobia in Asklepion. Asklepion is an ancient healing complex and temple found on the Pergamum acropolis in Turkey, built in honor of Asklepios, an ancient Greek god of healing. This is a popular tourist destination and thousands of people still visit every year in the hope of a cure. Tradition says that therapies, even centuries ago, based on both psychological and physical treatment, were beneficial in restoring health. The

FIGURE 6.3 Asklepion (Zwiebackesser, iStock/Getty Images).

treatments employed at Pergamum have been used for centuries and were believed to cure all illnesses, including phobias and other psychological disorders. It is near a sacred source of water that was later discovered to have radioactive properties. There were also snake massage treatments at that time, and there are recent news reports that therapy featuring snake massages is growing in popularity today.

Islamic Thinkers

As mentioned, several significant Islamic thinkers in history wrote books about medical science and human psychology, especially during the rise of Islam (from AD 700 onwards), but, because these thoughts have not been developed they have been forgotten and are now largely a footnote in history. Islamic thinkers tended to be interested in social life and social rules rather than individual development. These thinkers tried to synthesize the perspectives of the Greek philosophers with Islamic rhetoric. In the Islamic world, thoughts have not been transformed into individual psychological guidance approaches, or any kind of wisdom, and invariably end up in negative judgement. Since the importance of scientific knowledge is less valued in Middle Eastern cultures, compared to Western cultures, it is hoped the balance will be redressed with this book. A lot of Middle Eastern thinkers focus on the *nefs* or *nafs*, as previously mentioned. *Nefs* are defined as desires and extreme wishes, as in REBT's irrational demandingness beliefs. A pure soul can be achieved using the mind and heart (faith) together with *non-demandingness*. Interestingly, the first Islamic thinkers were not only believers of Islam but also leaders of an approach that emphasizes the importance of thinking and logic.

Al-Farabi was one the first Islamic intellectuals who was instrumental in giving instruction about Plato and Aristotle to the Muslim world. He also influenced later Islamic philosophers, such as Avicenna (İbn-i-Sina), who is recognized as one of the world's first great surgeons. Farabi (870–950) conducted ideas on the concepts of soul and dignity (Kırklaroğlu). According to Farabi, the soul and the divine are divided into two, and if the soul is *pure*, as a source of well-being, it is under the control of the emotions and demands.[20] As we see from a glance at Farabi, for instance, demandingness and dysfunctional emotions were not new things for Islam.

Avicenna (İbn-I-Sina)

İbn-i-Sina was one of the first thinkers interested in psychological disorders. He was the first doctor to treat hysteria and depression.[13] He thought that psychological factors were important for health, and crucial for children. He argued that a person who is not mentally healthy cannot be physically healthy, and, likewise, that a person who is not physically healthy cannot be mentally healthy.[1]

FIGURE 6.4 Avicenna ([İbn-i-Sinaibn-i-Sina)] (Oleksandr Pakhay @ 123rf.com).

Ultimately mental health is affected by everything that affects the body. He emphasized the importance of relaxation for mental health and according to him rest should be personalized. In addition, he recommended that play, sleep, and relaxation were particularly important for children.[2] İbn-i-Sina ascertained that sleep and alertness create opposite effects. He wrote that long-time sleeplessness creates confusion and stress in the mind; too much sleep leads to drowsiness and mental activity slows.

Institutions in Ottoman Times

Recently, music and art therapy have been gaining ground in the field of psychological treatment and the improvement of learning in all fields. Music therapy has been known in the Islamic world for a long time. Music was used as a treatment method in the Seljuk (the first settled Turkish empire in Anatolia) and Ottoman *Dârüşşifa*.[21] Most Islamic philosophers, such as Zachariah-al-Razi, al-Farabi, and İbn-i-Sina, were also musicologists. The Ottomans established mental health facilities called 'Darüşşifa' (mental health hospitals), and patients who were suffering from depression, anxiety, and psychotic disorders were treated, using music and the sound of water. Patients respond well to music and dance, as part of the merry-go-round of life, and also to therapy. One of the goals of therapy was to obtain 'peace.' It is obvious that music has a huge power to instill this state in people. Likewise, creating a trance-like atmosphere is crucial in mental health.

According to İbn-i-Sina, the best treatment was 'to increase the patient's mental and spiritual powers, to give her the courage to fight better with the disease and to have her listen to the best music.'[22] He sought to treat mental illness with music at the Nurettin hospital in Damascus, Syria.[22] He felt that ill health was not just a disease and disability but that good health 'must be a state of physical, mental and social well-being.' According to him, the best exercise to protect and maintain good health was to sing.[21] His books included information about the interaction between the body and soul.

Al-Muhasabi (AD 781–857) established the concept of self-reliance using a scientific-psychological approach, but they were mostly his own ideas and were not developed by subsequent generations. He emphasized, from the ontological point of view, that controlling the *nefs* fully is almost impossible, as is an understanding of mysticism (or Sufism).[20] Al-Muhasabi seeks to suggest that what is useful to man should be treated in the spirit, *nefs*, and body trilogy. It could be argued that al-Muhasabi's ideas are the basic concept of what can now be called psychology or pastoral counseling, but we can see, in the incantations of the Buddhists and the choral singing of churches throughout the world, that this science was not enacted upon and embellished.

The Historical 'Darüşşifa'

The authentic 'Darüşşifa' social complex in Edirne in northeastern Turkey was popular for elective treatment strategies from the fifteenth to the nineteenth centuries. Pediatricians utilized music to treat patients and nearby water, sound, and 'fragrance' treatments also took place. A monk named Çelebi[23] recorded the number of specialists working there, how much they earned, and which *makams* (classical Islamic chant/music frameworks) were suitable for treating certain sicknesses, in addition to common therapeutic medicines, such as cauterization. As a reminder, music is broadcast on certain days at the clinic, which became a well-being exhibition hall in 1993.

FIGURE 6.5 The historical 'Darussifa' ([mental health hospital in Ottomans)] (Konstantinos Michail @ 123rf.com).

Within the clinic, which was built by Sultan Bayezid II (AD 1447–1512), three vocalists, a *ney* (reed woodwind) player, a violinist, a *miskal* (skillet woodwind) player, a *santur* player, a *çeng* (hassock harp) player, an artist, and a lute player gave concerts to patients to remedy them. Certain *makams*, such as Neva, Rast, Dügah, Segah Çargah, and Suzinak, are great, particularly for rationally sick patients. Other *makams*, including the Zengüle, Buselik, and Rast, offered assistance to all patients. The music treatment section is one of the most striking parts of the historical center.[24]

This may seem primitive by today's standards, but the buildings that were created for treatment and cures show the importance placed on health by successive rulers and governments or governing bodies. Turkey is full of spas, baths, and natural springs for natural healing treatments, and now that this kind of treatment has become a tourism business, the future is bright.

Modern Turkey

Times change. Life ebbs and flows. At the end of the 1800s, the first psychology books were published by citizens of the Ottoman Empire. These books were generally written in the name of psychology, or psychology as a subdivision of philosophy, and made suggestions about mental health. The first three books written about psychology in Ottoman times were Hoca Tahsin Efendi's *Psikoloji or İlm-I Ruh* (Psychology or the science of the psyche), Yusuf Kemal Bey's

Gâyetü'l-Beyan fî Hakikati'l İnsan (A declaration of human reality), and Mehmed Emin's *Ilm-i Ahvâl-i Ruh* (The science of circumstances of the psyche). Psychology lectures were first introduced at Istanbul University in 1915, conducted or aided by German professors. They had come from Germany to the Ottoman Empire before the First World War. A Turkish professor, Şekip Tunç, was interested in

FIGURE 6.6 Mustafa Kemal Atatürk (Halil ERDOGAN @ 123rf.com).

William James's and Sigmund Freud's work and published articles in newspapers[25] starting in 1919. In 1925 the Faculty of Medicine at Istanbul University performed some psychological research. One of the studies was about suicide in Istanbul in 1928.[26] After the Ottoman Empire collapsed, Mustafa Kemal Atatürk announced a new republic called Turkey. It is a republic using a democratic system. Atatürk and his colleagues placed great importance on all kinds of science.

Atatürk, the founder of the Turkish Republic (1923), who continues to have a great influence on Turkish people, is also quoted as saying, 'There are no hopeless situations, only hopeless people. I've never given up hope, even under attack from all sides. If one day you find yourself without a savior, don't expect one to come along. Save yourself.' He was a leader that supported all kinds of scientific innovation and institutions that would further the cause of science in Turkey.

Further Development

In 1933, after emigrating from Nazi Germany, many German professors settled at Istanbul University. Lectures and talks were given, and courses on experimental methods were taught. Many studies were conducted and doctoral theses were presented. Not only in Istanbul but also in Ankara there were some scientists who were interested in psychology. The world-famous Turkish psychologist Muzaffer Sherif from Ankara University moved to the United States and conducted leading research in social psychology. Professor Mümtaz Turhan is another social psychologist who pioneered work on culture and psychology.

This is the very first, real scientific work of the Turks. Istanbul University, with the preparation of various publications, journals, and articles, also established psychology laboratories that laid the foundations for the formation of the science of psychology in Turkey in the 1950s and 1960s. Slightly later, the Binet-Simon Test of Intelligence was translated into Turkish.[27] The well-recognized Psychology Ordinarius Professor Wilhelm Peters from Jena University, and a former student of Wundt, made significant contributions in developing the work of psychology in Turkey.[25]

Besides the scientists, there are a couple of important practitioners who contributed to the development of the mental health field in Turkey. One of them was Prof. Dr. Mazhar Osman, who is also known as the founder of modern psychiatry in Turkey. He trained in neurology and psychology in Berlin and Munich. He made major contributions in the field of psychology and psychiatry. His work was fully recognized in 1926 when a mental hospital was established in his name and is now Turkey's largest mental health hospital in Istanbul.

Apart from this scientific development, it must be stated that, even recently, Islamic 'understanding' has begun to influence psychological treatment in the Middle East. In Turkey, a trend has begun to integrate Islam into psychological counseling, similar, but not equivalent, to pastoral counseling in church-related institutions. Recently some mental health departments at universities in Turkey have placed 'Islamic Counseling' on their timetable. Some books, such as *Counseling*

Muslims,[28] have been published to introduce the idea of how Islamic statements and understanding of psychological treatments can be used. Islamic belief in the bio-psychosocial model for the managing of psychiatric disorders, including focusing on the alteration of psychotherapeutic procedures as cognitive restructuring,[29] is fashionable nowadays.

There is no well-developed scientific taxonomy in the Middle East. There are, however, a variety of teachings that psychology and psychotherapy derive from—for example, the teachings of Sufism. Most people in the world who are interested in psychology are curious about the teachings of Sufism. Sufism focuses on a love of God and God's creatures which brings about human happiness, and therefore peace and joy, and was the first psychological initiative, influenced especially by Aristotle and Plotinus. According to Plotinus, everything is 'out of one' and it is emphasized that the main purpose of life is to reach this 'one.' 'Love' moves *everyone* and is a great motivator, but it is better to keep up with and follow scientific facts, when historical and religious or pseudo quasi-religious sources, such as shamanism, or any other interventions, are still being used.

As set out in this chapter, Turkey has a history of trying to define itself in more Western terms. Since Islamic countries, especially, view Turkey as the heart of the Islamic world, it is to be hoped that they will follow suit. This book is not about religious practices in psychological treatment, but it is easy to see that Turkey is far in advance of most Islamic countries in terms of modern psychological counseling. Atatürk's ideas of attempting a more Western vision of the future can be achieved, not only with the parallel of Sufism and scientific approaches but also with a greater understanding of the importance of education and critical thinking methods.

References

1. Mohit, A. (2001). Mental health and psychiatry in the Middle East: Historical development. *La Revue de Sante de la Mediterranee orientale*, 7(3).
2. Elgood, C. (1951). *A Medical History of Persia*. Cambridge: Cambridge University Press.
3. Haque, A. (2004). Psychology from Islamic perspective: Contributions of early Muslim scholars and challenges to contemporary Muslim psychologists. *Journal of Religion and Health*, 43(4), 357–377.
4. Achoui, M. (1998). Human nature from a comparative psychological perspective. *American Journal of Islamic Social Sciences*, 15(4), 71–95.
5. Jeanine, D., & Asa, K. (2012). *Models of God and Alternative Ultimate Realities*. Dordrecht, Heidelberg and New York: Springer.
6. Hamarneh, S. K. (1984). In M. A. Anees (Ed.), *Health Sciences in Early Islam: Collected Papers* (Vol. 2, p. 353). Blanco, TX: Zahra Publications. https://archive.org/stream/ArabPainting/arab%20painting_djvu.txt

7. Badrī, M. (1979). *The Dilemma of Muslim Psychologists*, London: MWH London.
8. Ibrahim, A. S. (2011). Arab world psychology. *Cross-Cultural Psychology*, *1*. https://doi.org/10.1002/9781118339893.wbeccp032
9. Abou-Hatab, F. A.-L. H. (1997). Psychology from Egyptian, Arab, and Islamic perspectives: Unfulfilled hopes and hopeful fulfillment. *European Psychologist*, *2*(4), 356–365.
10. Arij Baidas. (n.d.) Interview with Psychologist Linda Sakr in Duba (n.d.). Retrieved from https://thepsychologist.bps.org.uk/volume-25/edition-6/interview-psychology-arab-world
11. Okasha, A., Karam, E., & Okasha, T. (2012). Mental health services in the Arab world. *World Psychiatry*, *11*(1), 52–54.
12. Al-Krenawi, A. (2005). Mental health practice in Arab countries. *Current Opinion in Psychiatry*, *18*(5), 560–564.
13. Ayten, A. (2012). Arap Ülkelerinde İslâmî Psikoloji ve Din Psikolojisi Çalışmaları. *Çukurova Üniversitesi İlahiyat Fakültesi Dergisi*, *12*(2).
14. Yahia, M. (2012). Dealing with mental illness in the Middle East. Retrieved from: https://www.natureasia.com/en/nmiddleeast/article/10.1038/nmiddleast.2012.103.
15. Mental Health as Foreign Policy: Trauma in the Arab World. (2016). Retrieved from www.fairobserver.com/region/middle_east_north_africa/mental-health-ptsd-middle-east-health-news-78002/
16. The Quest for Mental Health Awareness in the Arab World. (2017). Retrieved from https://raseef22.com/en/life/2017/05/22/quest-mental-health-awareness-arab-world/
17. Anjiganova, L., & Katanov, N. F. (2007). *Yaşayan Eski Türk İnançları Bilgi Şöleni: Bildiriler*. Hakas Devlet Üniversitesi. Geleneksel Ve Çağdaş Hakas Kamliği* Hacettepe Üniversitesi, Türkiyat Araştırmaları Enstitüsü. Hacettepe Üniversitesi Sıhhiye Yerleşkesi, 16–17 Nisan.
18. Hammerman, D. (n.d.). Integrating Shamanic Methods into Psychotherapy. Retrieved from www.hammerman.net/Integrating.pdf
19. Thalhamer, A. (2015). *Where Shamanism and Psychotherapy Meet the Shaman's Art to Heal in the Light of Western Psychology*. Conference Presentation: Science and/or Religion: A Debate of the 21st Century, At Vienna.
20. Kırklaroğlu, H. Bilim Tarihi Açısından Psikoloji Ve Bilimselliği Üzerine Tartışma, Yıl. (2018). Cilt 5, Sayı 13, Sayfalar 194–210. Gazi Üniversitesi *Sosyal Bilimler Dergisi*, Arşiv Cilt 5, Sayı 13.
21. Miri, S. M. (2014). The many masters of Ottoman hospitals. *Turkish Historical Review*, *5*, 94–114. doi:10.1163/18775462-00501010
22. Hatunoğlu, A. (2014). Psikoloji Biliminin Oluşum ve Gelişimine Katkıda Bulunan Doğu İslam Medeniyeti. *Akademik Sosyal Araştırmalar Dergisi, Yıl, 2*, 272–279.
23. 'Evliya Çelebi'. (n.d.). Retrieved from https://en.wikipedia.org/wiki/Evliya_%C3%87elebi
24. Healing in Ottoman Times. (2014). Retrieved from www.dailysabah.com/music/2014/10/09/music-as-a-method-of-healing-in-ottoman-times
25. Toğrol, B. B. (n.d.). *History of Turkish Psychology*. Istanbul, Turkey: Istanbul University.
26. Magnarella, P. J., Turkdogan, O., Zahra, N. A., Eberhard, W., Erdentug, N., Guvenc, B., & Yasa, I. (1976). The development of Turkish social anthropology [and comments and reply]. *Current Anthropology*, *17*(2), 263–274.

27. Tan, H. (1972). Development of psychology and mental testing in Turkey. In L. J. Cronbach & P. J. D. Drenth (Eds.), *Mental Tests and Cultural Adaptation* (pp. 3–12). The Hague: Mouton.

28. Ahmed, S., & Amer, M. M. (Eds.). (2013). *Counseling Muslims: Handbook of Mental Health Issues and Interventions*. Abingdon, UK: Routledge.

29. Sabry, W. M., & Vohra, A. (2013). Role of Islam in the management of psychiatric disorders. *Indian Journal of Psychiatry*, *55*(Suppl 2), S205.

7

UNCONDITIONAL ACCEPTANCE AND SUFISM

Your task is not to seek for love, but merely to seek and find all the barriers, within yourself, that you have built against it.[1]

—*Rumi*

What is Sufism? It is not a glossy show of dancers with strange hats that can be seen in the posters advertising the Mevlânâ in Konya-Turkey. It is not very well known. It has been labeled 'mysticism'—a kind of exotic 'take' on life. Some of this chapter may be seen as an Islamic perspective. It would, however, be incorrect to form any opinion about cognitions without a closer understanding of other religious teachings and how not just Middle Eastern but also other cultures respond to daily life.

In no way is this to be seen as an excuse, but you, the reader, may have many questions about the style, flow, and contents of this chapter, and whether it goes with the rest of the book, and whether it is a standalone or intrinsic work that will hold up to scientific and possibly religious scrutiny, and also whether it will be possible for people to use in their lives in a practical way, which is one of the main aims of this book. It is truly hoped, in this chapter, to attempt to summarize more than a passing understanding of Sufism, and how it can be used in therapy—though it bows to the wisdom of the truly great masters—and explains its relevance to unconditional self-acceptance (USA), unconditional other acceptance (UOA), and unconditional life acceptance (ULA). Psychology has endeavored to become a science, but there is also an undoubted spirituality in clinical practice.

'Sufism' has no original meaning in English. It connotes self-purification and the study and practice of Islam.[2] For some of the more esoteric parts, which require a deeper knowledge of Arabic words, relating to rituals and observances,

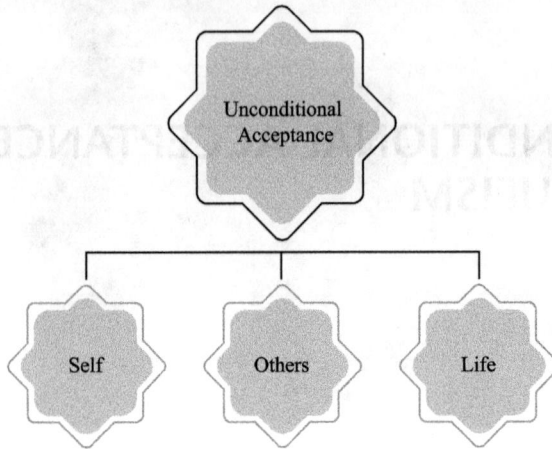

FIGURE 7.1 Ellis's proposed three types of acceptance.

readers may refer to a variety of sources! This chapter is not intended to be a religious exposition but vaingloriously seeks to address some ideas to be used in parallel with RE & CBT theory. Simultaneously, however, not to mention some things about comparative religions would also be aberrant.

Life is sometimes complex, chaotic, and stressful for most of us. Many people look for peace and happiness in their lives. Through which source can we reach inner peace? Does the answer lie within religions, diets, fads, or ways of (self-)actualization? It can be assumed that psychotherapy is a scientific way to provide peace, meaning, and happiness in life. RE & CBT may have some answers that can be beneficial to different people, worldwide, as a means to psychological well-being. They analyze both positive human attributes and shortcomings, as we go about our daily routine. REBT and CBT are a way of tapping into getting on better with peers, colleagues, and family constructs. In REBT, self-acceptance refers to unconditional acceptance.

One of REBT's important contributions to psychotherapy is conceptualizing the notions of the rational beliefs of USA, UOA, and ULA. These rational beliefs help clients to deal with stressful events, maintain healthy functional emotions, and support clients to live rationally over the long term. However, understanding USA, UOA, and ULA is sometimes difficult to grasp because Ellis was influenced by deep philosophical questions, including the core of Eastern religious teachings, to create his theories. Clients usually want extra resources to better understand them. Since unconditional acceptance is hard to conceive, Ellis's contribution must be developed further, in order to help clients and support mental health workers, cross-culturally speaking.

The core of Sufism contains concepts very similar to USA, UOA, and ULA, which have their roots in old scripture, sacred texts, and ancient philosophical and spiritual ideas. How can the basic tenets of Sufism serve as useful metaphors for *unconditional acceptance*? The aim of any religion is to offer a method (direction) and catalyst (teacher) for alchemy (the spiritual alteration of the student); a transformation of lead (the childish ego) into gold (the profoundly responsible adult).[3] All teaching must provide formulas, but without the alchemist or teacher to act as guide, these equations are without reality—meaningless and ineffective.[3] This is where psychotherapists come in. They act as a guide towards an understanding of such concepts, and make them useful practically.

Self/Others/Life Depreciation

Individuals who have global rating irrational beliefs (IrBels) take one negative point in a situation and place blame on themselves and conclude, 'I am a bad person' or evaluate the situation as if nothing will ever be better. Self/others/life downing irrational beliefs[4] have also been called global evaluation beliefs, self/others/life depreciation or condemnation beliefs[5] in REBT literature. Self/others/life depreciation is described as an irrational belief of rating oneself, others, or life, in 'a single' light.

Examples of depreciation beliefs:

* Life is totally bad.
* I am worthless.
* I am inadequate.
* I am incapable.
* Other people are worthless.
* They are all stupid.
* Life is not worth living.

From a CBT point of view (not REBT), self/others/life depreciation IrBels may be listed as several cognitive distortions: labeling, discounting positive, jumping to negative conclusions, and blaming.

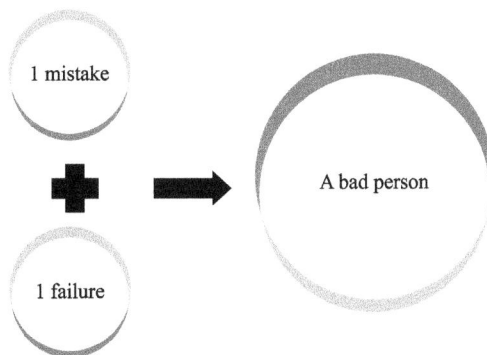

FIGURE 7.2 This is the mind-set of the people who rate themselves globally.

The opposite of unconditional acceptance is conditional acceptance, which consists of many scales, measurements, degrees, rates, levels, and other modalities. Thus, it is better to look for demandingness IrBels when someone has self/others/ life depreciation beliefs. They are related to global rating beliefs. Irrational demands may lead to self/others/life depreciation beliefs.

Unconditionality

USA, UOA, and ULA are rational beliefs and their opposites are irrational self/ others/life depreciation beliefs. In REBT, self-acceptance is defined as accepting oneself properly, genuinely, and competently, regardless of other individuals and whether others are likely to state appreciation or admiration.[6,7] People make mistakes, or they may not be skilled at certain things; however, this does not make them a 'totally bad' person. Using a spiritual with a scientific explanation, REBT emphasizes a client's own self-acceptance. According to Ellis, being a human is enough to be worthy and valuable,[8] and REBT is keen to stress this as a unique creation—the 'self' is free from many degrees, labels, categorizations, or quantitative numbers. Thus, you can evaluate, analyze, and judge behavior, acts, and performance as good or bad, or any other variation, but not the 'self.' To illustrate this, imagine, if you will, the idea of measuring or grading a fish at its ability to climb a tree. Thus, you can be satisfied or dissatisfied with your performance, or anyone else's. You are free to understand, rather than just take on faith, that there are no bad people, only bad acts/behaviors. For instance, you can judge some behavior as horrific. Self-evaluations are replaced with what Ellis called unconditional self-acceptance (USA).[4]

Sufism represents a journey into the self but there is no universally acceptable definition of 'self' (see the Sufi Enneagram). Many philosophers, writers, and therapists, from Descartes and Kant to Heidegger, have put forward ideas about the self. Anyone can define her or his 'self' in any way, so the 'self' concept is malleable and cannot be rated as good or bad. Philosophy and theology are two disciplines that compete with each other in their method and nature. It is true that theology can easily turn to fanaticism and ideological monomania. Enlightenment is the period through representations, without philosophy. On the other hand, philosophy has the potential to redefine the relationship between psychology and theology.[9] Religious approaches also suggest many ideas about 'self.' In Islam, Christianity, Judaism, Buddhism, and other religious beliefs, followers are always being suggested to accept themselves, life, and others, unconditionally. For instance, in Christianity it is a fundamental tenet: Love your neighbor as you love yourself. As Mahatma Gandhi said, Hate the sin, but love the sinner.' Buddhism, in essence, dramatically rejects the self.

This book, notably this chapter, is an exposition about unconditional self and other acceptance, and *NOT* self and other *abuse* because (especially when considering family, partner, business/work colleague, and friendship relationship issues), when one person has true UOA and the other does not, there is a risk of unfairness. To prevent this some points need to be clarified. Korzybski's position on E-Prime greatly influenced Ellis's identification of the irrationality of global evaluations of human worth and his notion of unconditional self-acceptance.[4] Instead of saying, 'She is a failure,' one would say, 'She failed at [enter the specific task.]'

Ellis carried over some of the concepts of certain philosophical statements to his therapeutic approach, and thus REBT has its roots in philosophy, but his was not a new-fangled attempt to understand the mind. According to Ellis, no matter how many mistakes a person makes, or how big the mistakes, a person is considered a 'human being' and as a human being she or he is 'worthy.' Besides philosophy and Buddhism, Ellis may have been influenced, too, by the Anglican Christian humble prayer to access.[10]

Much research supports the idea of USA, UOA, and UOA.[11] It has been found that unconditional self-acceptance correlates negatively with depression. So, whoever accepts herself unconditionally is less likely to get depressive moods, because she will not compare herself with others in the first place. She will not take one negative side of herself and treat it as a big problem (globally rated as totally bad); she will still remain hopeful about life, thinking, 'Life is still worth living.'

Cbox: *An understanding of unconditional self, others, and life acceptance takes time. It does not happen overnight. Trained therapists believe gentle guidance can help you. Since the beginning of time self-respect and the uniqueness of an individual have arguably been among the biggest problems for our species.*

A Long Road to Discovery

Self-acceptance takes extensive work and considerable dedication. It involves a modicum of creativity. It is a major reason for clients to seek out a psychologist. Confronting how you live, and the things you can accomplish, is an intrinsic part of learning how to love and treat yourself well.

Unconditional love of self/others/life may take even longer than unconditional self/others/life acceptance. Even accepting our shortcomings, mistakes, failures, and weaknesses and doing nothing to improve them is not the right kind of self-acceptance. It does not contribute to real progress and betterment. We can all find a myriad of genuine excuses not to make the effort. Does it mean accepting our behavior, manner, and harmful life style, and not doing anything to heal and improve? It may seem so simple to give in to laziness and find excuses for leaving everything as it is.[12]

An attempt to realize your worthy and base qualities, where you can try to reduce feelings of guilt, lack of self-regard, and sadness, is an active process. USA does not mean that you accept what you are, your fate, and life as it is, and do nothing. Not being scared of looking at yourself rationally and realistically, and an awareness of your bad, harmful behaviors and attitudes, is the first task to accept and love yourself/life and others. 'Knowing yourself' and 'being yourself' give you an opportunity to change. They allow you to see what you can do to improve yourself and your life. Accepting yourself as you are is the first step to enlightenment. This is a challenge and you may be fearful along the way. However, the culturally redefined RE & CBT proposed in this book may unlock some doors in the search for 'knowing oneself.'

Self-Esteem or Self-Acceptance

Before going further into the topic of self-acceptance, a close look at the issue of self-respect and self-worth needs to be made concerning unconditional self-acceptance. The concept of unconditional self-acceptance is an attempt to replace the term 'self-esteem.' Dr. Ellis discriminated between self-esteem and unconditional self-acceptance. 'Ellis argued that the concept of self-esteem is limitative, because it fails to take into account the fact that people are a process, and calls it perhaps the greatest emotional sickness known to humans.'[8] In so doing, Ellis brought to psychology a similar concept to Carl Rogers's unconditional positive regard.[13] However, according to Ellis, unconditional positive regard is a very soft idea in dealing with heavy pathological problems and it is also related to self-esteem, not self-worth.

Why Ellis called self-esteem the *greatest sickness* is because self-esteem requires 'doing something good,' or, 'achieving/obtaining good things in life,' such as money, status, and good exam scores, and in this way a person feels good about herself and maintains self-esteem. This would also mean that our value of ourselves depends on what we have achieved and/or not achieved. On the other hand, if someone makes a mistake, it brings her self-esteem down and so the concept of self-esteem becomes like a roller coaster. We will have a poor life if we depend on our self-esteem. Our life cannot be tied to our successes and failures. This kind of attitude creates a life of *conditional acceptance*. Instead, we walk towards our goals in life knowing that 'we are a worthy person,' regardless of whether we achieve those

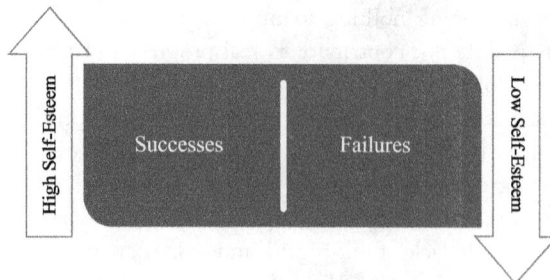

FIGURE 7.3 How self-esteem works.

goals. In therapy, increasing a client's self-esteem is equal to taking risks. What will clients do if they really do become unsuccessful in their tasks or life?

> Tbox: If a client asks you whether we measure ourselves by what we achieve, then your answer may include this clear message: Certainly, we measure the level of our achievements, but we do not measure ourselves as human beings. We are human and worthy, regardless of how we rate our achievements.

Şark (Shark) Culture

Islam claims to be a spiritually, personally, and socially transformative affect and the Sufic way is known as an alchemy for this spiritual transformation.[14] Sufism is full of Eastern philosophy, which Middle Eastern people come into contact with from a very early age. It is also suffused with politics, geography, and Şark (pronounced 'shark') (note: its not totally satisfactory meaning: Eastern) culture too. All of this can be seen in primary, middle, and high school life in the Middle East. Children are nominally taught some of the precepts of Western philosophy, but by dint of their location they absorb a Muslim culture readily. In the West, celebrities, for instance, have sought out a pattern of life that is not well documented nor understood, even in scholarly arenas, from a modern Western point of view—notwithstanding the peerless work available at various Western institutions—in what may be a quest for a religious path, or to quench a longing for an alternative route to inner peace. Philosophy may criticize, whereas theology accepts without criticism. Thus, they are inextricably linked.

The Core of Sufism

The birth of Sufism lasted until the seventh century in the Islamic world. Rumi (Mevlânâ) devoted himself to praying and surrendered to God through Islam. He believed that music, poetry, and dance can be a path to reach God. He was a kind of saint but more like one of the greatest monks in Islam. Sufism is interested in the (1) *Nafs* (self, ego, or psyche), (2) the *Qalb* (heart), and (3) the *Ruh* (spirit),[15] which are very close concepts to psychology terms, and therefore need to be carefully investigated. Sufism is defined as a mystical belief and practice based on Islam, in which one seeks to find divine love.[16] It has its own history, literature, and devotional practices.

Sufism can teach us 'truly' and 'unconditionally' to accept and love ourselves, others, and life. The practice of the 'whirling' dervishes grew into a ritual form from these ideas. Rumi's concept of *tawhid* (the indivisible oneness concept of monotheism in Islam), similar to work by other poets in Persian literature, is essentially the union with her beloved (the primal root) from which she has become estranged—and her desire to restore it. *The Masnavi* (Rumi's masterpiece)

FIGURE 7.4 Whirling dervish in Nasir Al-Mulk Mosque/Pink Mosque, Iran.

is arranged into a vast and intricate mosaic of fables, anecdotes from everyday life, Quranic revelations and exegesis, and mysticism. This became the basis for the Mevlevi, which Rumi's son, Sultan Walad, organized.

The Sufic Way

Sufism, based on the Quran and the teachings of the Prophet Muhammad (born AD 570), was influenced in its formation by Christian asceticism and Hinduism.[2] Its origins are disputed but traced to the eighth and ninth centuries. Besides Rumi there are several significant people who are interested in Sufism. One of them is Idries Shah. While no work about Sufism can be complete without a good understanding of work expounded by Idries Shah, if we delve further into his ideas, it is possible to see the humor, not least by noting his amusement at an Eastern saying: 'However useful a garment, it is not for eating.' There is a joke in the East, which highlights how the decline in religion is because of incompetence, and sometimes worse. A spiritual teacher (frequently revered in the community in Middle Eastern culture because, among other things, he leads the prayers, following the call to prayer) said, 'My first disciple was so weak that the exercises killed him. My second was overzealous in his meditations. My third pupil became dulled by contemplation. But the fourth is completely normal.' Someone asked, 'Why?' 'It could be,' said the guru, 'because he refuses to do the exercises.'[17]

The Sufic path is a way of seeking truths concerning the nature of one's relationship with *Being*. A spiritual guide can teach you about yourself, life, and the nature of your relationship with *Being*. Struggling to establish the truth is of fundamental importance to any mystical pursuit. However, without character, the search for truth tends to become dysfunctional, and therefore, those who have aspirations concerning the mystical path (whether Sufi or otherwise) come to understand the importance of seeking to acquire qualities of: *honesty, fairness, patience, tolerance, nobility, courage, humility, gratitude, generosity, perseverance, self-sacrifice, equanimity, forgiveness, friendship, love, and compassion*. To what extent these qualities will help to develop truths and realize a client's own character is a more difficult issue to assess. Did Shakespeare not say, 'To be, or not to be. That is the question'?

Mevlânâ

Rumi's full name was Mevlânâ Celâleddin Mehmed Rumi (AD 1207–1273). He is one of the most famous masters in the history of Islam. He was a Sufist scholar, writer, and poet. Rumi was born in Afghanistan but lived and died in Konya-Turkey,

FIGURE 7.5 Rumi's tomb in Konya (Boris Strouko @123rf.com).

which is still the center of the *dervish* movement. A dervish is (similar to a monk) someone who devotes himself to God and lives without any form of materialism. Rumi's tomb is popular with tourists and locals alike. Middle Eastern readers of the next chapter, especially, will also be pleased to find that the tomb of a cutting-edge, great mind in the field of medicine is also popular.

His poetry is renowned and his teachings are inspiring and far-reaching. He teaches *patience, love, compassion, and benevolence, as well as unconditional acceptance and tolerance, similar to REBT*. His famous 'seven suggestions' (or pieces of advice) are still very much revered in the present time.

The seven suggestions characterize the highest inclinations of humanity, transcend religious boundaries, and constitute the common ideals of all religions:

1. In helping others: *Be like the river.*
2. In sympathy and grace: *Be like the sun.*
3. On circumspection: *Be like the night.*
4. In hatred and anger: *Be like the dead.*
5. In simplicity: *Be like the soil.*
6. In endurance: *Be like the ocean.*
7. Appear as you are or, be as you appear.

The final suggestion in this list is used by all Turkish people and frequently found posted on the walls of educational establishments. However, as in all faiths, knowledge without practice is pointless.

Rumi is in fashion, and has become a best-selling poet in United States, with admirers that include Madonna. Sufism involves rebellion, an antidote to many things in our age. Rumi's non-traditionalism, his anti-dogmatism, gentle icono-clasm, and romanticism[18] have influenced many famous artists throughout the world. Exoticism, and the luxury of distance, releases us—and maybe Madonna, from small-mindedness.[19]

> *Today, like every other day,*
> *We wake up empty and frightened.*
> *Don't open the door to the study*
> *And start reading.*
> *Take down the dulcimer.*
> *Let the beauty we love*
> *Be what we do.*
> *There are hundreds of ways*
> *To kneel and kiss the ground.*

Rumi instructs us that our kindness and aid to others should be similar to a flowing river. Rumi, like Jesus, teaches that we have to forgive others' wrongdoings. Anger and hatred arise from not accepting others and their apparent wrongdoings. Human beings can be truly liberated from anxiousness and hindrances by foregoing anger, hatred, and enmity, and thus there is no absolute yardstick for wrongdoings, but there are men's prejudices. Rumi teaches us to be as humble as the earth and tolerant—like the sea.

Cbox: Today, keep in your mind Rumi's statement 'In the same way, all rivers end in the ocean, and the ocean greets all equally.' And please write down your ideas about this on a piece of paper.

It should be noted that Sufism seeks to address the problem of the acceptance of others. Could this inability be a reason for so much warring—namely, that we do *not* accept each other? Meanwhile REBT, in particular, seeks to comprehend a way to discover self-acceptance, with life-affirming attributes, concentrating on the four major analytical points of frustration: intolerance, demandingness, self-depreciation, and catastrophizing.

The 'similarity' of Sufism, which came to be identified as the inner wisdom of Islam, to Western psychology and the derivation of its claim to the title 'Islamic psychology' are made because the study and application of the expurgation process—including its practices, analysis, and documentation—became the domain of the Sufics.[20,21]

Love

Please remember three things that have been mentioned in previous chapters: (1) love is one of the ultimate goals of the therapy, (2) psychotherapy involves not only scientific knowledge but also art and experience, and (3) Ellis's unconditional acceptance is better redefined as unconditional love of self/others and life for Middle Easterners.

Love, a central tenet of Sufism, is fundamental to bringing commitment and fervor to inspire, whether it is for a loved one or whatever one seeks. Rumi expresses the significance of 'love' beautifully:

> *Love makes the bitter sweet,*
> *Love turns pain into healing.*[22]

Rumi understands *love* as a universal message. Love is the scale with which to measure the position of a celestial body or, in this case, God's mysteries. Rumi believed God is Man's ultimate goal. Rumi lived hundreds of years before Darwin and did not deal with biological evolution at all. He was interested in Man's spiritual evolution but Darwin was interested biological evolution: True consciousness makes him divine but she needs to travel through the various spheres of being.

Centuries-old Sufic philosophy, in spite of the fact that it is based in religion, still offers us several experiences involving the artistic process. Borrowing Sufic allegories, originality may be seen as the development of lifting veils to uncover sincere knowledge. This can be likened to the peeling of an onion or pulling back the curtain to reveal new delights as well as horrors. It can most frequently be found in the transformative effect of good theater, where we seek to see ourselves, warts and all. Sufism's principles are delineated by a rejection of personal and religious doctrines. These are ways to actual knowledge. Sufis are known for a rich tradition of literature, poetry, storytelling, and clever metaphors in stories, music, and dance. What is it about Sufism, a mystical tradition in Islam, that helped Sufis to be creative? While the Sufis' search focused on finding the divine essence, their approach to this quest was probably instrumental in stimulating their creativity in art, music, dance, and literature.[23] Sufism regards love, faith, experience, and knowledge as central concepts in resolving our existential dilemma to ultimately understand and experience the divinity in oneself, or the union of self, with the Supreme, through a process of a progressive lifting of veils, which hide true beauty and knowledge. This love is unconditional and without regard for any personal gains in wealth, fame, or power; a Sufi's principal goal is to experience the divine within and be united with life's essence.

Rumi regarded love as the 'creative force in nature,'[21] and thus love is the basis for all creation and creativity. For Sufis, the Supreme is their beloved and this forms a central basis for their search. Fromm observed that 'Love is the only way to knowledge.'[24] Love, combined with faith and denial of dogma, is critical in providing inspiration, perseverance, and directness in our search for actual knowledge from differing viewpoints—and that includes a deeper understanding of ourselves, which is one of the fundamental aims of psychotherapy.

Other Eastern Sources

Several scholars of religion and psychotherapy claim that those who see a 'caring God' model as a collaborator who works with them to solve their issues are less anxious and take greater advantage of rational systems of psychotherapy, than nonreligious people who have a more negative regard of God. Some authors indicate that REBT includes many sacred philosophies. Within this book, an explanation of the philosophy of REBT is endeavored, and ideally shows how it is analogous to those of many religious people in regard to USA, high frustration tolerance, UOA and the longing, instead of the need, for accomplishment and appreciation, and other mental well-being objectives. It shows how REBT is compatible with some significant religious views, and can be used efficiently with numerous clients who have unquestionable beliefs about God and faith.

The Dali Lama stated,

> If we possess an optimistic mental attitude even when faced with inhospitability, we should not lack inner peace. On the other hand, if our mental

outlook is negative, impacted by fear, mistrust or self-loathing, then, when surrounded by our finest companions, in apleasant environment and comfortable surroundings, we shall not be content. So, mental attitude is critical: it makes a real difference to our state of happiness.

(p. 11)[25]

RE & CBT both set down practices that encourage influence over the psyche and feelings through augmented concentration attention and scrutiny of contemplation forms. All of this leads to an *inner calm*. The practitioner might more fully incorporate CBT's reflective reaction as a method to trim down idle and self-harming cognitive schemas.

Benson found that, with some Tibetan monks he studied, contemplation can create a rational and real state of deep relaxation, so as to assist and amplify the aptitude to organize thoughts and behavior, and can enhance the human resilience and inner strength that REBT endeavors to promote.[26] Consequently, CBT's contemplative methods can increase the viability of REBT, by helping individuals to boost self-control and self-belief. CBT's objective is to promote contentment, spiritual growth, and inner peace. CBT might find a favorable reception, in both the Western and the Eastern worlds, if its methods appeared to be compatible with, and advanced by, recognized healing frameworks.

Understanding the human psychological condition based on a consideration of troubled and good mental well-being, and the way of advancing from one to the other, can advance the aim of achieving inner peace. Moreover, if everybody were reconciled with themselves, then it would augment the likelihood of outer peace and even, dare one say it, world peace—which is something CBT endorses.[25]

From Sufism to the West

There are, of course, clear and evident contrasts purposefully connecting Sufism to Western psychology. It is an element of the aspiration and toil of the Sufis, as Western psychologists carry out their research into the religious conventions of other societies, that they will also be able to utilize the intentions and objectives of the majority of mystical and mythical instructors. Sufis do not claim their practice to be the only way (as it is self-evident that countless successful systems have come before it), but it is claimed that Islamic Sufism is the most modern and complete materialization of the main beliefs of mystical liberation. If only it were maintained in practice. A Sufi maxim states, 'Call no man master lest he set you free.'

It does not take much work to notice that many prized Western traditions are derived from the Middle East. Culturally different in every way, while Judaism and Christianity focus on the idea that we are born sinners, the Islamic way—which has its roots in Sufism, which in the West is more readily known as mysticism—believes that humans are born pure and become soiled. It is these viewpoints that strike at the heart of the CBT approach, since the two ideas—we are born pure but we become dirty, and we are born a sinner but can at least become righteous—are going to find problems in any psychological debate. This has ramifications for an approach to work in non-Western cultures on rational emotive behavior therapy (REBT), which is one of a number of cognitive behavior therapies (CBTs) now reaching a wider audience, thanks to its originator, Dr. Ellis. So, *how can we accept our self or others, if born a sinner?*

There is a Turkish idiom that *you are in debt to your teacher—for 40 years.* It can be seen from a reading of Sufic history that Sufis were rebellious and espoused many art forms, and this may be a reason that many modern artists find a kind of solace in artistic, musical, and dance forms, as well as in the spiritual. In psychological parlance, seeking knowledge (of oneself) can be described as progressive problem-solving, to reveal the 'hidden treasure' behind veils—true knowledge in the form of unity with essence. Derived from unconditional love, this search is intrinsically motivated. Many regard *intrinsic motivation* (as in self-determination theory; see Chapter 4 for more information) and the love of search as critical to the creative process. Erich Fromm argues that creative work involves seeking unity with the material one works with, a world outside of one self, to make it his or her own.

It has been noted that 'Sufis were the rebels of their time.' Consistent with their religious teachings, they stood up for the oppressed and wrote poetry that challenged oppression by the orthodox clergy, landlords, and emperors. They also demanded equality and an end to all oppression. The creative process often requires taking risks to challenge extant ideas, theories, and practices, relying on one's own experiences and intuition, yet being open to diverse viewpoints. This openness to diverse viewpoints, from other cultures, possibly helped the early Sufis to incorporate new ideas into their thoughts and practices, and stimulated their creativity in the arts and literature. The majority of the world's workers are troubled by the pressure of targets and deadlines that the modern boss puts on an employee, so subsequently how do those employees interact in a search for a method of learning independence or *Being*?

Denying the Past

Very similar to Albert Ellis, Sufis suggest discarding personal and religious dogmas, past experiences, and cultural trappings, to lift the veils in pursuit of truth. Rumi advises, 'Limit the worldly I and be yourself, the former restricts you.'[23]

Blind acceptance of authority is supposed to prevent the lifting of veils, so seekers must utilize their instinct and experience to seek real wisdom. Sufis attach importance to learning by experience, under the mentorship of an individual who has traveled the way. Sufis reject the dogma of a single path to salvation. They believe in using such strategies as breathing, meditation, music, and dance, which are often rejected by the more fundamental religious groups, to enhance their research. Sufistic ideals of pursuing the idea that there is no single path to the Supreme has enormous implications for the current-day conflict-ridden world, where religious ideologies prevent acceptance and appreciation of diverse religious views. A culture dominated by rigid ideologies channels its energies to preserve and disseminate them, in turn limiting individuality of expression and creativity. This cultural incongruity of rejecting dogmas possibly played a central role in the Sufis' creative accomplishments, as it allowed them to take risks they normally would not have taken.

Unconditional Love

Human existence comprises joy and anguish. Love, compassion, care, and assistance are the major components that help people to endure—though governments and big business seem to have a difficult time understanding this. Man relies on love and help, or cooperation and collaboration, to survive and thrive (in the face of disaster). It is assumed that neuroscience, religion, and spirituality do not mix, but Art precedes science and imagination precedes physical truth. Although they all aid in the healing process something is missing. Nonjudgemental acceptance of the here and now is vital to gain a metacognitive awareness. It is vital in sense memory for an actor. Thoughts and feelings as passing events, rather than inherent aspects of the self or reality, are achievable as fleeting moments—with REBT. Acceptance of internal experiences instead of avoidance or control, otherwise known as cognitive diffusion, can help in learning to live a valued life.[27]

Here are some suggestions to accept and love yourself unconditionally:

1. Place no condition on yourself to be lovable person.
2. Consider you are loved.
3. Do not use 'if—then' clauses in establishing conditions for accepting and loving yourself.
4. Accept and love yourself for the fact that you exist rather than for what you do.
5. Practice 'enjoying yourself,' as when eating or driving. You do not need to be skillful to do something ordinary.
6. Remind yourself you have value and worth, without seeking evidence.
7. Repeat to yourself: 'I am okay,' 'Others are okay,' and 'Life is okay.'

Inner Peace

Cognitions underlie feelings and behavior, which are under our voluntary control, and can be changed. It is claimed that Islam is a powerful instrument for cognitive realignment. So what may work for Muslim clients is culturally redefined RE & CBT. It also works for other faiths, such as Christianity.[28] Muslims adhere to religious schema above all other competing schema (e.g., familial, traditional, cultural). This is not a long way from Ellis's prescription.

Contemplation and the remembrance of Allah (*SWT*) are allegedly the key to inner peace and well-being in Islam. There is a highly detailed Islamic belief/schematic system. Islamic teaching and practice embody potent cognitive and behavioral prescriptions that may decrease physiological arousal (anxiety) and enhance emotional functioning (mood management). Islamic psychology uses RE & CBT, offering a key to unlock/access/modify schema for advanced well-being outcomes.

The concept of mindfulness is identical to Islamic contemplation and Sufism. There are many similar methods—especially yoga (an advanced physical and mental practice), for contemplation and breathing; and we all know this has become a huge industry. The RE & CBT notion of unconditional acceptance of the here and now is akin to a concept of total submission and trust in Allah (*SWT*), but also a prerequisite for an actor immersed in his craft—living in the moment. Although Rumi teaches acceptance of others, RE & CBT works towards unconditional self-acceptance, but in some way it is genetically built in to humans to try to control each other. It is important to assess the suitability and willingness of the client to answer some questions, if she is requiring a spiritual assessment. There are many questions that may arise for a therapist to confront and this is a sensitive topic in the West, not encroached upon in Muslim countries since it is assumed.

Practicing Sufism

Although it would be great, you do not have to come to Konya-Turkey to learn Sufism. The following section requires a leap that many in the West may consider unacceptable, but for Middle Easterners would not be considered out of the ordinary, in that the following questions are frequently asked in everyday life, without giving much thought. What religion are you? Are you spiritual? Where do you believe we came from? What are your beliefs about the nature of man? What do you think drives our mind and body? What do you see as the purpose of life? Why are we faced with adversity? What happens when we die? What does your faith say about acceptance? These are a small selection of questions that a therapist may pose. REBT & CBT-based therapies are suitable for all religious clients, including Muslims.

The concept of unconditional self and other acceptance in REBT says that one may rate or criticize another's wrongdoing but not her personality. That is to say, everyone is valuable—as an individual. Everyone can and does make mistakes, but this 'value' should not be questioned. Thus, everyone has an equal value as a human being. Of course, it is hard to apply this idea when considering rapists, serial killers, animal abusers, and so forth. However, Ellis's point of view was strict on the issue that everyone is a human being and has worth. Ellis proposed that people take the preamble to the US Constitution and the Judeo-Christian religious tradition seriously, both of which state that all persons are created equal, the former by government and the latter by God. REBT tries to teach people to rate their deeds and not themselves.

Here are some principles to practice Sufism and culturally redefined RE & CBT:

1. Acceptance and surrender are a great source of peace, motivation, and meaning in life.
2. Exert yourself to accepting yourself completely. All of you.
3. Unconditional acceptance doesn't mean giving up or waving a white flag—that's quitting.
4. Acceptance means that we let go of who we think we should be and fall in love with who we are right now.
5. Understand that no matter how bad our act, we cannot be a 'bad person,' or 'a failure.' Likewise, if we perform well, that does not make us a 'good person' or 'a success.' Be content with a good performance and dissatisfied with a deficient one, but don't think that it influences your 'self.'
6. Try to avoid focusing on 'self'; instead focus on the beautiful things in life. What is beautiful? 'Everything!'
7. In order to comprehend and practice USA, UOA, and ULA or love of self/others/life the contrasts between self-esteem and self-acceptance must be clarified. Self-acceptance is not the same as self-esteem. Where self-esteem refers expressly to how valuable, or worthwhile, we see ourselves, self-acceptance implies a far more global confirmation of self. When we are self-accepting, we are able to accept all aspects of ourselves—not just the affirmative, more 'admirable' parts. As such, self-acceptance is unqualified, free of any restriction.
8. We can recognize our shortcomings, boundaries, and flaws, but this knowledge in no way interferes with our talent to fully accept ourselves.
9. If you sincerely want to develop self-esteem, you need to investigate what part of yourselves you are not yet able to acknowledge and approve, and it is exactly because self-acceptance involves far more than self-esteem that it demonstrates that eventually, getting on better terms with yourself has chiefly to do with self-acceptance.
10. After we stop judging and being harsh on ourselves, we acquire a more optimistic sense of who we are, which is why self-esteem is critical to our contentment and state of well-being.
11. With REBT and general semantics, separating out behavior from self is valid, because language purveying such notions as a good or a bad person and the myriad variations are purely semantics.
12. Do not insist or be stubborn about your irrational demandingness. The more strictly you demand, the more you do not accept 'life.'
13. Do you want to replace your negative automatic thoughts? If so, then a very good automatic thought to repeat to yourself is 'as is.' With this repetition you will get used to unconditional life acceptance.

Repeat the following affirmations during your daily activities, including times of stress:

14. The more I accept and love who I truly am, the more I shine.
15. It's okay to accept yourself unconditionally.
16. I love and accept myself the way I am.
17. I will stop to being hard on myself. I am going to try to be at peace with my life.
18. Christians say, 'Love the sinner and hate the sin,' which reminds us of Gandhi that we should judge behavior and not self. This is fundamental to RE & CBT, and can be aligned with Christianity, 'hippiedom,' 'New Ageism,' and the great Asian religious traditions.

Apart from you, the world and others are okay too. There is no need to wear a mask or to act, in any way, just to please others. You need to open up your feelings, with no fear of rejection or non-approval, and seek an honest relationships with others, rather than 'beneficial relationships.' Clients sometimes think of relationships as a trade: 'If I do something for others, in return, they need to do something for me.' Pragmatically this is true in work life; however, personal relationships are built 'not on trading' but in 'sharing life and doing activities together.' As Robert Holden puts it in his book *Happiness Now!*, 'The more self-acceptance you engage in, the more contentment you'll permit yourself to consent to, receive and benefit from. In other words, you can take pleasure in as much joy as you deem you're worthy of.[29]

IrBels

Dr. Ellis created the concept of frustration intolerance IrBels. This is one of the four irrational beliefs in REBT. It is hardly a complicated matter for anyone to grasp! People are involved in psychological discomfort because they cannot tolerate being disturbed. ULA can be used to solve frustration intolerance IrBels, in that accepting 'difficulties' in life may be the first step towards frustration tolerance. In practicing unconditional life acceptance in the disputation of awfulizing, irrational beliefs are also possible. Whatever we fear, we need to learn that life can sometimes bring us fearful situations. We need to accept the fact and act accordingly. This is a relatively new term but easy to comprehend. For instance, 'Your presentation was terrible, and you must never act terribly!' misses the point in significant ways:

1. It would be hard to conceive of a presentation that was pitiable, even though many aspects of that presentation could use improvement,
2. Clearly, although you performed badly, there is nothing to say that you must not do so, and also, it is unreasonable to expect that you will always function well and never have a 'bad night.' Still, even the most awful verdict linked to behavior is

superior to judging the self, which is not only destructive and harmful but also nonsense! Think 'task rating,' if you must, but stay away from 'people rating.'[30]

Parents and Children

The role of parents in the Middle East is to provide unconditional love and acceptance of children, where parenting rules are specified. This is a complicated topic because it is mixed with the temperament of the people, the geography of the land, the climate, those peoples' own upbringing and (lack of) education, the socioeconomic status within a certain community, and whether it is a democratic society.

Cbox: A suggestion to parents: 'Raise your words, not your voice. It is rain that grows flowers, not thunder.'

—Rumi

If our guardians were not capable, or disinclined, to communicate the message that we were completely good enough—sovereign, that is, of our hard-to-control, from time to time wayward behavior—we fell into the trap of seeing ourselves, at the outset, in terms of how we were measured or rated. By developing self-compassion, we need to learn how to love ourselves, letting go of guilt, and learning to pardon ourselves. Independently confirming ourselves has nothing to do with becoming complacent—but we are required to develop more, rather than continuing or reverting to our custom of relentlessly judging ourselves. If deep inside us we are ever to encounter individual fulfillment and peace of mind, we must first rise to the challenge of complete, unqualified self-acceptance.[31]

Self-Pardon!

To steadily progress to a state of unconditional self-acceptance, it is vital that we espouse a mind-set of 'self-pardon' for our transgressions (regardless of whether real). We may even come to realize that there is nothing to pardon. In spite of what we may have done previously, we were always innocent, in a sense—doing the best we could, given (1) what was instinctive in us, (2) how compelling our needs (and feelings) were at that point in time, and (3) what, back then, we believed about ourselves.[29]

What determines most tricky behavior is connected to common psychological defenses. It almost borders on the pitiless for us to reproach ourselves—or hold ourselves in disdain—for acting in ways that, at that moment in time, we thought we had to, in order to defend ourselves from disgrace and emotional suffering generally.

> *Cbox:* Watch your child and how often she/he is smiling: *'To me nothing in the world is as precious as a genuine smile, especially from a child.'*
>
> —*Rumi*

A Supplementary 'Codicil'

Self-acceptance is here-and-now oriented—not future oriented, as in: 'I'll be fine when . . . ' or 'As soon as I achieve . . . I'll be okay.' It is about—as of now—being okay, with no qualifications. We cannot ignore or deny our faults or frailties, but they can be viewed as irrelevant to our basic acceptability. It is possible to be fond of ourselves and still be committed to a lifetime of individual growth. This self-acceptance is not really tied to such modifications. Even scoring an A+ in no matter what, whatever method we are utilizing to measure ourselves, can offer us transitory breathing space from our striving. The continuous task of accepting ourselves can rarely be completed. We can never ultimately 'arrive' at a position of self-acceptance, because we have unintentionally defined our mission for such acknowledgment as perpetual.

Lastly, it is you, single-handedly, that sets the guidelines for your self-acceptance. Once you make a decision to end grading yourself, or keeping count, you can take on an approach of non-evaluative exoneration. In fact, once you desist from a deep-rooted addiction of evaluating and reassessing yourself—endeavoring rather to compassionately understand your past behavior—then you will find that there really is not much to excuse. You can promise to do better in the future, but you can nevertheless accept yourself as you really are, at that moment, regardless of deficiencies.

Only after we are capable of giving ourselves definite authorization—by creating better self-compassion and centering a good deal more on our positives than negatives—can we finally pardon ourselves for our flaws, as well as surrender our requirement for others' endorsement. No doubt we have made errors. But then again, so has everyone else. In any case, our uniqueness is hardly the equivalent of our failures. At the end of the day, there is no basis for not deciding, right now, to alter our underlying sense of who we are, and we may need to remind ourselves that our numerous shortcomings are an element of what makes us human. If all our deficiencies and failings abruptly ceased to exist, the theory is that we would vanish.

In the pursuit of unconditional self/others/life acceptance or love of self/others/life we might want to take satisfaction in our/others'/life's defects. After all, were we beyond condemnation to begin with, we would never have the chance to rise to this astonishing human challenge.

Addendum

To enlighten readers as to how Dr. Ellis was preceded by Rumi, concerning all matters of self/life and others depreciation, frustration intolerance, awfulizing, and demandingness, the final part of this chapter quotes loosely from the

Masnavi (the main Sufic text): 'Although your words appear uniform and in harmony, they are the source of contention and anger in their effect.'

Suggested Activities

Activity 1

Write yourself a 400-word letter with the heading:

> **'I am neither a totally bad person or good person because . . . '**
> *Please continue your letter here.*

Now write another letter thinking about other people:

> **'They are neither a totally bad nor good person because . . . '**

Now write one more letter thinking about life/things and life/events:

> **'Life is neither totally bad nor good because . . . '**

Activity 2

TABLE 7.1 A workout to make a plan to develop your skills

	My strengths	My weaknesses that I want to develop	My unchangeable weaknesses that I may need to accept
1			
2			
3			
4			
5			
6			

Activity 3

Fill these sentences in every day (during your week):

- Today, what I accept about myself is . . .
- Today, I accept . . . in others.
- Today, life is . . . and I accept this as it is.

Activity 4

Please repeat these quotations to yourself when you meditate:

- *I am whole and harmonious, regardless of my mistakes and failures.* (Dr. Artıran)
- *All you really need to do is accept this moment fully. You are then at ease, in the here and now, and at ease with yourself.* (Eckhart Tolle)
- *When you live in complete acceptance of what is, that is the end of all drama in your life.* (Eckhart Tolle)
- *Acceptance of the unacceptable is the greatest source of grace in this world.* (Eckhart Tolle)

Activity 5

Suggested readings on Sufism and Mevlânâ.★

- *The Masnavi I Ma'navi of Rumi: Complete 6 Books*, by Maulana Jalalu-'d-din Muhammad Rumi
- *The Essential Rumi* (New Expanded Edition), by Jalal al-Din Rumi (Author), Coleman Barks (Translator)
- *Love Poems From God: Twelve Sacred Voices From the East and West*, Daniel Ladinsky, Translator
- *The Places That Scare You*, by Pema Chodron
- *The Art of Mysticism: Practical Guide to Mysticism and Spiritual Meditations*, by Gabriyell Sarom
- *What Would a Muslim Say: Conversations, Questions, and Answers About Islam*, by Ahmed Lotfy Rashed

References

1. Rumi Quotations. (n.d.). Retrieved from www.goodreads.com/quotes/9726-your-task-is-not-to-seek-for-love-but-merely
2. Nizamie, S. H., Katshu, M. Z. U. H., & Uvais, N. A. (2013). Sufism and mental health. *Indian Journal of Psychiatry*, *55*(Suppl 2), S215–S223. doi:10.4103/0019-5545.105535
3. Ansari, A. (1999). Principles of Sufi Healing. Retrieved from www.communityconnexion.com/article/09-99/principles.html
4. DiGiuseppe, R. A., Doyle, K. A., Dryden, W., & Backx, W. (2014). *A Practitioner's Guide to Rational Emotive Behavior Therapy* (3rd ed.). New York: Oxford University Press.
5. DiGiuseppe, R., Leaf, R., Gorman, B., & Robin, M. W. (2018). The development of a measure of irrational/rational beliefs. *Journal of Rational-Emotive & Cognitive-Behaviour Therapy*, *36*(1), 47–79.
6. Davies, M. F. (2008). Irrational beliefs and unconditional self-acceptance: II. Experimental evidence for a causal link between two key features of REBT. *Journal of Rational Emotive Cognitive Behavior Therapy*, *26*, 89–101.
7. Ellis, A., & Dryden, W. (1997). *The Practice of Rational Emotive Behavior Therapy* (2nd ed.). New York: Springer.

8. Ellis, A. (1996). How I learned to help clients feel better and get better. *Psychotherapy*, *22*(1), 149–151.
9. Ural, Ş. (2013). Felsefe ve Teoloji. *Review of the Faculty of Divinity, University of Süleyman Demirel*, *1*(30).
10. The Anglican Prayer of Humble Access. (2009). Retrieved from https://churchmousec. wordpress.com/2009/03/19/the-anglican-prayer-of-humble-access/
11. Chamberlain, J. M., & Haaga, D. A. (2001). Unconditional self-acceptance and psychological health. *Journal of Rational-Emotive and Cognitive-Behavior Therapy*, *19*(3), 163–176.
12. Sasson, R. (n.d.). Self-Acceptance: What Is It? Retrieved from www.successconsciousness. com/self-acceptance.htm
13. Rogers, A. (1996). *Teaching Adults* (2nd ed.). Buckingham: Open University Press.
14. Sufism: The Science of Perfecting Awareness. (n.d.). Retrieved from www.surrenderworks. com/library/esoterics/threesteps.html
15. Sufi Psychology. (n.d.). Retrieved from https://en.wikipedia.org/wiki/Sufi_psychology
16. Sufism. (n.d.). Retrieved from www.britannica.com/topic/Sufism
17. Shah, I. (1978). *Learning to Learn*. New York: Octagon Press.
18. Jones, J. (2015). The Mystical Poetry of Rumi Read by Tilda Swinton, Madonna, Robert Bly & Coleman Barks. Retrieved from http://jonathandunnemann.blogspot. com/2015/06/the-mystical-poetry-of-rumi-read-by.html
19. Poems of Rumi. (n.d.). Retrieved from https://sufism.org/origins/rumi/rumi-excerpts/poems-of-rumi-tr-by-coleman-barks-published-by-threshold-books-2
20. Taghavi, A. R. (2017). 4 Things I Learned or Confirmed on a Sunday with Coleman Barks' Rumi. Retrieved from https://medium.com/@ARTaghavi/4-things-i-learned-on-a-sunday-with-coleman-barks-rumi-9f7125987bff
21. Kumar, V. K. (2014). Creativity: A Perspective From Sufism. Retrieved from www. psychologytoday.com/us/blog/psychology-masala/201405/creativity-perspective-sufism
22. Chittick, W. (2008). *Sufism: A Beginner's Guide*. Oxford, UK: One World.
23. Arasteh, S. R. (1965). *Rumi the Persian: Rebirth in Creativity and Love*. Lahore, Pakistan: Routledge, p. 10.
24. Fromm, E. (1956). *The Art of Loving*. New York: Harper & Brothers Publishers, p. 31.
25. Holt, S. A., & Austad, C. S. (2013). A comparison of rational emotive therapy and Tibetan Buddhism: Albert Ellis and Dalai Lama. *International Journal of Behavioral Consultation and Therapy*, *7*(4).
26. Benson, H. (2000). *The Relaxation Response* (Rev. ed.). New York: Harper & Row.
27. Yusaf, S. (n.d.). Spirituality in Clinical Practice: An Islamic Perspective. Retrieved from www.theauroraaustralis.net/25-life-changing-lessons-to-learn-from-rumi-luminita-saviuc/
28. Ellis, A. (2000). Can rational emotive behavior therapy (REBT) be effectively used with people who have devout beliefs in God and religion? *Professional Psychology Research and Practice*, *31*(1), 29–33.
29. Holden, R. (2007). *Happiness Now! Timeless Wisdom for Feeling Good FAST*. London, UK: Hay House.
30. Alexander, R. (2018). Will Unconditional Self-Acceptance Make Me Lose My Edge? Retrieved from https://rebtinfo.com/will-unconditional-self-acceptance-make-me-lose-my-edge/
31. Seltzer, L. F. (2008). The Path to Unconditional Self-Acceptance. Retrieved from www.psychologytoday.com/intl/blog/evolution-the-self/200809/the-path-unconditional-self-acceptance

8

MIDDLE EASTERN METAPHORS

Before you start reading this chapter, would you like a glass of tea?

The APA (American Psychology Association) says over 1,000 psychotherapy approaches exist, which are generally called 'talk therapies.' In talk therapies, we obviously mostly use verbal tools during sessions. Other therapies also exist, such as art, play, mindfulness, sand, and music therapy, where verbal communication is less applied. Unavoidably, any talk therapy contains many metaphors that are used consciously or unconsciously. In this chapter reference is mostly made to consciously (purposefully) made metaphors.

Ernest Hemingway said it is possible that for most fiction authors (e.g. Ernest Hemingway) the human brain was structured as a metaphor-making machine. Metaphors have been an important aspect of human beings' verbal communication throughout history. As mentioned before, the general semantics theory, which inspired Ellis and his REBT theory, suggests that by expanding our vocabulary we can entertain clearer thinking about ourselves and others, and increase our understanding of ourselves and our relationships in the world we live in. One way of doing this is to use metaphors in communication.

Studies have been carried out suggesting that metaphors are influential on brain activity. It is claimed that metaphors have mobilized key areas in the brain. The left dorsolateral prefrontal cortex and temporal pole and cingulate gyrus regions are mobilized[1,2] when metaphors are used or practiced for therapeutic purposes, which supports the hypothesis that metaphor processing is the most important cognitive process, especially for functioning memory and comprehension functions. The aim here is to stimulate hot cognitions rather than cold cognitions and to make clients (and all readers) internalize rational beliefs.

Some research studied the neurobiological influences of metaphors and they indicated two findings: a fine versus coarse hypothesis[3] and a graded salience hypothesis.[4] The former indicates that both hemispheres take part in the semantic access, incorporation, and determination process. When a person hears simple language, the left hemisphere works, because the concrete meaning is dominant and contextually related, but when a person uses or hears metaphoric language, the right hemisphere works. One can show that, if the meaning of a phrase or term can be accessed from the mind from all kinds of sources, such as pictures, graphics, and especially word references, then later the meaning of that word is obvious. However, the meaning of the word is not evident, if it requires the understanding and analysis processes. Significant meaning is handled before the nonspecific meaning and the main left brain is in charge. The fundamental part of the brain responsible for the processing of unspecified meaning is the right brain. According to this hypothesis, the meaning in the right hemisphere is not figurative but rather the expression.[5]

Metaphors are analogies that allow us to map experiences tied to the past or other experiences, and thus to collect an understanding of complicated topics or new experiences.[6] Metaphors are context-sensitive and reflect social and cultural processes that influence individual characteristics, but they are also sym-bolistic models of real life, much like schemas in cognition.

Metaphors influence cognitive processing: they help in communication and reflec-tion.[7] They help with self-reflection, anticipation, and communication; they also influence cognitive schemas of the self and the world.[8,9] They allow psycho-therapists and clients to summarize a complex idea that is developed slowly. They are a tool for making ideas in a text memorable and of visualization. Metaphors also serve to explain complex emotional states or to describe some-thing attractively. They assist us in transcending literal meanings. They reach into our knowledge and experience. A metaphor is like a shortcut to a large set of associations, such as sensory and emotional perceptions, logical relations, and usages. The brain loves to make associations, which makes metaphors stimulating and enjoyable.[10]

Linguistic Arguments

Because metaphors frequently occur, they can be a valuable tool for interventions in research into organizational and occupational psychology. Lakoff and Johnson, in *Metaphors We Live By*, suggest that metaphors are an expression of the structure of beliefs and thoughts.[11] Some research focuses on the role of metaphors as symbols of any kind of psychological aspect and also predictors of a therapist-client therapeutic relationship. While clinical studies are individualistic in ori-entation, cognitive approaches are highly sophisticated. They aim to study human behavior overall, regardless of culture. Many Western approaches tend to ignore the culture-cognition link, which is part of metaphorical language[12] and so, culturally, they do not fill the gap between qualitative and quantitative research in psychology.

Conventional metaphors are learned in social interaction as part of language competence. Once learned, conventional metaphors become subconscious and are used automatically.[12] Only conscious effort can help to change automated language behavior. Therefore, it can be assumed that the use of metaphors is reasonably free of self-presentation strategies, which is a significant aspect for psychological research topics. Research stated that automated processes are effective in action regulation, and responsible for the automated and subconscious activation of goals and motives.[13,14]

Metaphors in Psychotherapy

The metaphors used in psychotherapy can be categorized in five ways:[15] (1) They are objects used to represent something different in therapy; drawing, painting, toys, and so forth, (2) for identifying certain points, (3) for relationship metaphors—that is, people, certain objects, animals, such things as when a relationship problem arises, (4) for long and complex stories, and (5) for anecdotes and short stories.

The *lct* Technique

From a concrete level of understanding, to improve abstract learning, a client may need to use metaphors for disputation and rehearsals of rational beliefs. Metaphors are bridges between the verbal to the imagined, orally, kinesthetically, aurally, and visually. The metaphor may provide a tool that supports a quick and deeper conceptualization, rather than a boring explanation. This is especially true for RE & CB therapies because the basic concepts of the theory are actually 'very clear' and 'very easy' to understand; however, application or conceptualization may be difficult initially. This is termed 'a ladder climbing technique (lct)' in disputation. When using *lct*, begin from a concrete level of understanding to eventually reach an abstract level of comprehension. The right brain's skill is used for imagining and the left brain's ability is used for logical and concrete rationalization. The basic application of *lct* is as follows:

Step 1: Identify the clients' irrational beliefs or any other cognitive distortions.
Step 2: Work with the client and come up with alternative rational beliefs or any other functional thoughts.
Step 3: Choose one of the 'rational' metaphors and write it down.
Step 4: The concrete meaning of the metaphor must be comprehensively explained by the therapist. Additionally, the purpose of the task must be discussed with clients at this stage.
Step 5: Other possible abstract meanings need to be evaluated when necessary.
Step 6: Use your imagination when repeating the metaphors as vividly as possible.

Step 7: Whatever causes you to feel stressed, remember the metaphor *before, during, and after* the session.

Metaphors, in the Turkish and Arabic languages, can be one word, one sentence, or a form of stories (short or long ones). Some already exist and some are created. Metaphors in psychotherapy can also be used as words and phrases. Animals, like horse, dog, wolf, donkey, and sheep, or things in nature, like mountains, rivers, and trees, are simple enough to create metaphors with. For instance, any stories in the news or documentary movies about horses or dogs are good examples of rational living. A volcano can be used in giving examples for 'anger.' Metaphors can be constructed by the therapist and the client. Different types of metaphors are possible but their true importance is applicability and mode. For instance, even the sound 'oh!' or 'ah!' can be a metaphor when used at the appropriate time. In fact, 'ready' metaphors can also be used in therapy. In this chapter, from the RE & CBT point of view, both forms are closely scrutinized.

An example of a metaphor that was created in a session:

Therapist: Imagine a beautiful gold-colored horse, but she cannot run fast.
Client: Okay.
Therapist: Would you say that this horse was useless and worthless?
Client: Of course not. Horses are beautiful animals. She doesn't have to run fast.
Therapist: Let's apply this to your situation. You used to tell me you are not good enough at playing certain roles in plays you have acted in, because of your style.
Client: Yes.
Therapist: What would you think if I said that one of your 'bad' or 'inadequate' attempts does not 'delete' your 'good' skills? Can we use this metaphor? Do you think it would be appropriate for your situation?
Client: I guess so.
Therapist: Can you provide a metaphor using a dog?
Client: I have a dog that cannot bark. Is he still a good dog?
Therapist: Sometimes it is better than having a barking dog!
Client: (laughing) Yes.

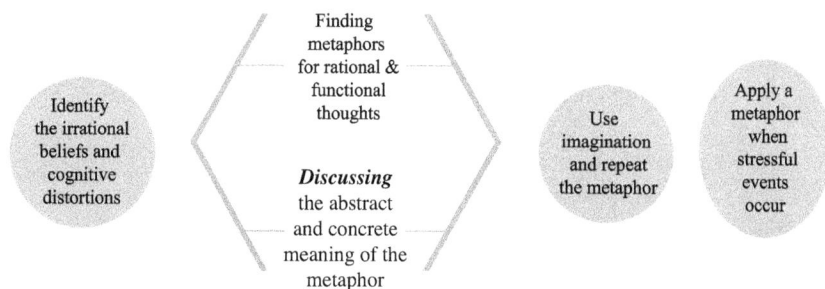

FIGURE 8.1 The *lct* technique.

Dr. Albert Ellis was also interested in clinical hypnotherapy, had a diploma in clinical hypnosis, and was a fellow of 12 divisions of the American Psychological Association. Self-hypnosis exercises (which can be done anywhere, easily!) are good tools to teach anxious clients to stop their anxiety or panic attacks. From the RE & CBT point of view, they are useful to treat *double* emotional disturbances, like 'fear of fear' or 'anger in panic.' Ellis wrote several chapters in his books and provided a clear hypnotic session structure.[16] When applying hypnosis, metaphors are used almost all the time. Other psychotherapy forms use metaphors in many ways, such as presenting alternative solutions to issues that are being struggled with, helping the client define her problem easily and appropriately, helping to develop self-awareness, expounding and expanding inspiration and motivation towards therapy or the goals of the treatment, and reframing and/or rethinking problems. For instance, the use of metaphors is an important technique in certain therapeutic approaches, such as Milton Erickson's. His approach during sessions is heavily dependent on hypnotherapy and using a great deal of metaphors is necessary.

Why Rational Beliefs?

In RE & CBT, using metaphors *only* for the rehearsal of rational beliefs and functional thoughts is a better idea than using them for pointing out dysfunctional thoughts, because metaphors are things to remember 'in the long run.' It is not necessary for a client to remember a metaphor for disputation. Disputation is a kind of attempt that forces the client to change her old, harmful beliefs and sometimes that is 'hard' to do. Using a metaphor helps a client better describe her old harmful beliefs, but nothing further. Furthermore, disputation methods may expire, when we achieve our goals as therapist and client. If the client does not have irrational beliefs then the therapist and client do not need to use disputations, but the client still needs to remember rational beliefs and functional thoughts. On the other hand, it is advisable that a client remembers his or her rational beliefs 'in the long run,' but neither for disputation nor for hypnosis, nor for bringing about a client's self-awareness of her irrational beliefs.

Here are some important principles, points, and guidelines before and during the use of metaphors in RE & CBT:

1. The brevity of the metaphor.
2. They do not have more than one message in them.
3. They are not made up of religious discourses.
4. They focus on what you mean, rather than emphasizing the importance of religion.
5. They should be summarized in such a way that they will not lose their originality.

> *Tbox: A meaningless or unused metaphor may lead a client to feel, 'Why bother?'*[1]

Finding appropriate metaphors for rational beliefs, or any other dysfunctional thoughts, requires a few important criteria:

1. What is the goal? What do we want to change in the client?
2. Before choosing or creating a metaphor, the therapist and client need to practice some metaphors in action.
3. Answering these questions may help to find a good metaphor:
    a. Does its expression parallel a new belief?
    b. Can it be used (in terms of brevity and ease of remembering) before, during, and after a stressful event?
    c. Does it contain words from daily language or sophisticated language?

This depends on the client; some clients do not find daily/street/slang language 'attractive.' They would rather use sophisticated words to keep the metaphor in mind. Some clients do not like, or prefer not to utilize, sophisticated words or meanings, such as proverbs, though there is nothing to stop either client or therapist from trying.

Humor and Stories

Dr. Ellis explained that it is crucial to 'attack' the client's *irrational beliefs* with humor, but not the client as a person. He clarified how humor and enjoyment are great instruments in treatment, and in particular, their use in REBT. He examined how we upset ourselves by taking A's (life, occurrences, events, situations, etc.) too seriously, or not taking many other things in our life seriously enough. As an alternative of wanting and desiring, individuals frequently command and demand (musts), which leads to defeat. It is the goal of therapy to combat over-seriousness, and utilizing humor is a convenient technique to do so. In addition, he talks about different ways to employ humor, including lessening ideas of foolishness, the use of puns, and the use of paradoxes.

Stories, when properly constructed and told, are usually more interesting than straightforward explanations of points one wishes to get across. Of course, it is possible to construct boring stories, or to tell great stories in a boring way, but well-thought-out, and well-narrated stories, told in the right setting, can inspire people to embrace errors and think about things they would not have considered before.[17] Stories have many layers of meaning when reading. Since they have hidden implications, upon presentation, they tend to be less threatening, but more memorable, than frequently pompous lecturing and articulate but mind-numbing expositions. This method of using humor in therapy will not harm the existing therapist-client compatibility—quite the opposite—and in fact, it may even bring about a greater camaraderie between the interlocutors. Metaphors in psychotherapy make the work rewarding in recommending solutions to real-life problems, helping individuals to recognize their 'self,' increasing inspiration, reframing and redefining problems[17] in a creative way, and reminding subjects of the benefits.

Dwairy recommends using metaphor therapy with Middle Eastern clients.[18] Many Middle Eastern people look positively at a *hodja* or other religious person's words when it comes to issues of 'trust.' In the Middle East, respected people in society are always listened to, just as Bill Gates or Warren Buffet are listened to by many people. Their word is important. For instance, if a respected person says something, people act on his or her word without questioning. There have been several important people in the Middle East who have a 'metaphoric effect' on clients. One of them is Nasreddin Hodja and another is Hajı Bektash Veli.

The following section provides examples of metaphors for irrational beliefs, as well as for cognitive distortions, such as over-generalizing, labeling, black and white thinking, and fortune-telling.

Humor and Nasreddin Hodja

In Turkish literature, the stories and tales of Nasreddin Hodja (AD 1208–1284) are very well known. Nasreddin Hodja was a philosopher and wise man with a witty sense of humor and a comical appearance ('hodja' means a kind of spiritual teacher, or wise man, in Farsi and Turkish). He was neither a spiritual teacher nor a clown but rather a 'funny' man. His stories have been told almost everywhere in the world, spread among the tribes of the Turkic World and into Persia, the Arabian Peninsula, northern Africa, along the Silk Road to China and into Indian culture, and later also to Europe. Shakespeare, Ibsen, and Chekhov are widely recognized in the Western world, but the year 1996 was proclaimed the year of 'Nasreddin Hodja' by UNESCO. Of course, all the stories currently attributed to the Hodja, over about 800 years, do not always originate from him. Most of them are the product of a collective humor, not only of Turks but also of other peoples of the world. A popular scholar, he was considered the foremost protagonist of comic tales, which included emotional content or propounded other messages.[19] The frequently satirical anecdotes about him focus particularly on love and praise, and gently mock both the main character and life.[19] He preferred to oppose the stricter elements of Islamic law with laughter, even self-mockery, and a desire to avoid using harsh words.[19] His words are a contradictory combination of the wise, ignorant, cunning, harmonious, insensitive, bashful, surprised, timorous, and dashing.

Another important element in Nasreddin Hodja's tales is a donkey, a reflection of the feelings of the people. It is impossible to imagine Nasreddin Hodja without his donkey, which is itself a vehicle of satire. The horse has pretty much no place in humorous tales invented by the people of Anatolia.[19] The donkey, with

FIGURE 8.2 Nasreddin Hodja (Bulent Kalaycioglu @123rf.com).

its suffering, pain, and the blows that are inflicted on it, is the most widespread symbol of the common man. No donkeys are to be found in humorous tales from the palaces,[19] since those that live there ride on horses.

From a RE & CBT point of view, it is easy to see in Nasreddin Hodja[20] and his stories that he created good metaphors for use in therapy. Nasreddin Hodja is a man who never catastrophizes or demands anything. In his stories, he always teaches people flexible thinking, in a humorous way. Nor does he awfulize anything in the world. With regard to frustration intolerance, he often shows how being impatient can harm people, or that 'deciding, without thinking' will probably cause a bad outcome. Giving clients homework to read Nasreddin Hodja stories may help them to get used to the rational beliefs of flexible thinking (preferences), anti-catastrophizing, high frustration tolerance, self, life, other acceptance, and overcoming black and white thinking and maximizing. His stories are also helpful in dealing with harmful core beliefs (lovability—'I am not lovable'; inadequacy—'I am not skillful,' and helplessness—'I am a failure').

Hajı Bektash Veli (AD 1209–1271)

Centuries ago, centers for religious thought in Middle Asia were created from institutions by wise men. Science, knowledge, and moral codes were spread from these centers. The administration encouraged holy men to settle in villages

FIGURE 8.3 Hajı Bektash Veli.

around Anatolia and through this newly created position of teacher, these men were afforded certain privileges. Consequently, even in desolate places in Anatolia, dervish lodges emerged. With the education they provided, a common cultural structure began to form.[21]

Hajı Bektash Veli came to Anatolia as a holy man. He was born in Afghanistan in AD 1248. He was educated in philosophy and social sciences as well as the sciences at the School of Hodja Ahmed Yesevi. He traveled to Iran, Iraq, and Arabia. Hajı Bektash settled in Sulucukarahöyük in central Anatolia around AD 1275 to 1280. He united the Christian residents of Anatolia and Turkoman migrants in various educational and developmental programs.[21] His role in forming a cultural unity cannot be understated. Over many years, the mystical Sufi order he inspired became influential throughout Anatolia and the Balkans. It was the official sect of the Janissaries, the elite Ottoman troops recruited among the Sultan's Christian subjects through the 'Devşirme' system of blood tribute. It has been suggested that the diverse belief system of the Bektashi, with its wide-ranging influences, may have appealed to men who had, in their early childhood, been Christian.

Many Alevi ('partisans' of the caliph Ali) people love to hear Hajı Bektash quotations relating to their problems. Ahead are some quotations from Bektash that we can use in therapy. Using quotations or other folk sayings may require imagination. Do not forget to include in any 'homework' that the power of the imagination must be utilized when suggesting quotations or other folk sayings.

- There exists in you a 'there is' to replace every 'there isn't' (anti-awfulizing).
- There is no rank or station higher than a friend's heart (unconditional acceptance).
- There is no repentance of repentance (unconditional acceptance).
- Let your heart, your hand, and your table be open to others (unconditional other acceptance).
- Whatever you seek, look within (unconditional self-acceptance).
- Do not forget your enemy is also a human being (unconditional other acceptance).
- If the path appears dark, know that the veil is in your own eyes (frustration tolerance).
- All blessings are granted to the one who overlooks another's shortcomings (unconditional other acceptance).
- Do not hurt others, even if you are hurt (unconditional other acceptance).

Atatürk

An important figure in history, for all Islamic countries, is Mustafa Kemal Atatürk. Atatürk's life can be used as a great example 'metaphorically' of 'high-tolerance skill,' anti-awfulizing, unconditional life acceptance, and flexible thinking for Middle Eastern nations. As mentioned in Chapter 6, he was not only the founder of the modern Turkish Republic but also an extraordinary reformer. He set up internal reforms to bolster the new direction of the country, and, with his colleagues, brought about an end to traditional costumes and the fez, changed the alphabet from an Arabic to a Latin-based one, introduced a new education system, changed a lot of the traditional rules, secularized the political and judicial systems, saw the end of the Ottoman Empire, repulsed an Allied invasion, and so forth. Two goals for the new republic were modernization and Westernization. Atatürk attempted to extricate himself from a pan-Turkic leadership and also from the rest of the Islamic world, despite a centuries-old relationship of Ottoman rule. Turkey's future role in the Middle East is likely to expand, but will it remain limited? Not for all, but for many, he is a respected leader for Islamic and other nations. What has this got to do with rational thinking? He was always an optimistic, brave, and hard-working man. He is therefore an excellent figure to use in a rational way of looking at life. Many of his works and quotations can be used to reinforce rational beliefs and functional thoughts in clients. He overcame many difficult situations with hard work.

Readers are encouraged to read his book *The Great Speech*, Lord Kinross's book, *Ataturk: A Biography of Mustafa Kemal, Father of Modern Turkey*, Andrew Mango and John Murray's book *Atatürk*, Andrew Mango's book *From the Sultan to Ataturk—Turkey*, and Edward J. Erickson's book *Mustafa Kemal Atatürk: Leadership-Strategy-Conflict*. Here are a few quotations[19] that can be used effectively when creating metaphors:

- 'Whoever tries hard is always stronger than someone who simply decides to do something but does not start doing it' (frustration tolerance).
- 'We are a people who prefer to do business instead of talking' (improving high-tolerance skills).
- 'Disasters should always lead people to make persistent and determined moves' (frustration tolerance).
- 'I never accept "being tired"' (frustration tolerance).
- 'I do not have an opinion about issues which I am not an expert in' (unconditional acceptance).
- 'It never hurts to criticize each other constructively.' (unconditional other acceptance).
- 'However, if you do the opposite (avoid or block any criticism), you will suffer a lot' (unconditional others/self-acceptance).
- 'You can't escape the facts. Put the facts in front of you. Look them in the eye!' (anti-catastrophising).

Applications

'Flexible Thinking'

Beliefs about the hereafter also have an important place in the tales, emphasized before, some of which are explicatory of feelings in the face of strict religious and traditional dogma.[20] Nasreddin Hodja's influence has spread to all sections of society. It has also led to the birth of other humorous tales reflecting the mind-sets of very different areas.[20]

1. *An irrational belief*: 'You must be quiet and respectful. Otherwise, I can't stand it.'

   A rational alternative: 'I would like you to be quiet and respectful; if you aren't, I can still deal with it.'

   A suggested metaphor: One day, some people said to the Hodja, 'Your wife walks around from house to house; tell her she mustn't walk around so much.' 'Alright,' said the Hodja, 'If she comes to our house, I'll tell her.'

2. *An irrational belief*: I must play appropriately.

   A rational alternative: I prefer to play appropriately; however, there is no rule saying 'I must.'

   A suggested metaphor.[22] At a gathering in the coffee house, they asked Nasreddin Hodja if he knew how to play the *saz* (a Turkish-Arabic instrument, similar to a guitar). Our Hodja, never one to disappoint his friends, said that he did. So, they gave him a *saz* and asked him to play. Nasreddin Hodja took the *saz*, placed it on his lap, then picked one string, and started to play that string. He did not move his fingers up and down, left or right; he simply plucked the same string on the same spot. 'Hodja Effendi, what kind of music is that?' protested the patrons of the coffee house. 'The real *saz* players move their fingers about, playing different strings. You hold on to one string and you do not let it go!' 'They move their fingers about because they are all looking for the right spot,' was the Hodja's explanation. 'I found it on my first attempt, why should I let it go?'

The story ahead can be used for the purpose of demonstrating demandingness.

   An irrational belief: 'People should act in accordance to strict principles.'

   A rational alternative: 'I wish people would follow rules and principles; however, there is no rule saying they "have to."'

   A suggested metaphor: Someone asked the Hodja, 'Nasreddin Hodja, why do people go in different directions when they leave their houses in the morning?' The Hodja answered without hesitation: 'If all of them went in the same direction, they would throw the world off balance!'

Unconditional Acceptance

In the story ahead, we find out how people react to appearances and the story should hopefully teach us the importance of our own self-worth and not our appearance.

1. *An irrational belief:* 'I must obtain approval from others.'

   A rational alternative: 'I would like to get the approval of others; however, I still accept myself, as I am, whatever others think of me.'

   A suggested metaphor:[23] One day the Hodja was invited to a wedding. Having arrived in his shabby clothing, nobody seemed to take any notice of him. Well, this wouldn't do. He bided his time and soon slipped out unnoticed. He returned wearing his best robe and a fine fur coat. From the entrance onwards, he was overwhelmed with compliments, given the best seat at the table, and urged to partake in the choicest morsels. Smiling, he began to dip the sleeve of his fur coat into the dishes, saying, 'Help yourself, my dear fur coat!' 'What are you doing, Hodja Effendi?' cried the host and guests, in alarm. 'Why, since it seems to command so much respect, I was merely inviting my fur coat to partake of these delicacies! A few minutes ago, without my fur coat, I wasn't even noticed. However, because of it, I am now overwhelmed with attention!'

2. The true story ahead shows that unconditional acceptance sometimes helps us to think about our weaknesses and failures, and to take action against them.

   A suggested metaphor: It was World War I and the Greeks and the Turks were fighting in Anatolia. The Greeks were making a final attack, in order to make sure of victory. They were marching towards the Turkish army, and the Turkish army, in its shattered state, could not hold them back. M. K. Atatürk ordered the army to retreat to the east of the Sakarya River. It seemed as if they were defeated. Some criticized such a move. He said, 'Let us unhesitatingly apply the lesson which military science dictates to us. We will take care of the other disadvantages later.' During the time that the wounded soldiers took to recover, new soldiers joined the forces. They were now preparing a final attack against the Greeks. The Turkish War of Independence under Atatürk's command then started. At the end of four weeks, victory was achieved.

3. Almost everyone in the US finds that the taste of tea makes no difference to their life. It is not a popular drink when compared to wine or coffee. For Eastern people the taste of tea is the same as for Westerners; however, the meaning is way different! '*A glass of tea*' is the best metaphor for unconditional others acceptance. Offering a cup of tea to a guest is a tradition in Middle East. Wherever you go, someone will ask you, 'Please take a seat, would you like to have a glass of tea?' You can hear this almost everywhere. And it has a message! 'We accept you unconditionally.' Drinking the proffered cup of tea means you accept the host unconditionally too. Likewise after a meal, especially dinner, you will, undoubtedly, be asked, if you would like to drink a glass of tea. If you say, 'Yes,' it means you liked the food, and especially the

service. If you say, 'No, thank you,' they question if anything was wrong with the food or the service and they become sorry.

4. A metaphor for UOA involving Aşık Veysel:

> Aşık Veysel was a blind man but one of the greatest poets in Turkish literature. His poems deal with the transitive nature of the world and thoughts and beliefs prevailing in traditional folk lore. He felt that his wife, Esma, had fallen in love with someone else and wanted to leave home. He became sad that his wife would leave him for another man. Since he could do nothing, as he was poor and blind and unable to provide a good life for his wife, he had no choice but to accept this situation. One day when he woke up in the morning, he called out to his wife, but there was no one at home. He understood that his wife had left the house. His wife and her lover went to another city and ran out of money. Esma said to her lover that there was some discomfort in her shoe and her foot was in pain. She took off her shoe and realized there was something inside it. When she lifted the lining of her shoe, she saw that there was some money in it. Aşık Veysel had put some money in his wife's shoe, in case she needed it, the night before she ran away from home.

Anti-awfulizing or Anti-overgeneralizing

If we do not catastrophize/awfulize, many things may turn out well, psychologically. Sometimes we create anxiety and catastrophe by ourselves without any real reason, as Albert Ellis pointed out. However, disputing irrational beliefs work may trigger catastrophe. For example, sometimes relaxation techniques trigger panic. This can give the impression like a malfunction of a function, and it is a frustration of intention. There will probably be trouble in a response to the sensation of losing control. Rather than using relaxation techniques or disputation interventions, using metaphors might be a more helpful method of overcoming 'awfulizing.'

1. *An irrational belief:* 'My thoughts say that life is chaotic.'

    A rational alternative: 'Sometime my thoughts say that life is bad and complex; however, it is not chaotic.'

    A suggested metaphor: An activity can be given to a client to imagine herself sitting on a bench at the edge of the Bosphorus (a strait in the center of Istanbul) and asked to watch the ships and boats pass by . . . some of them will be slow, others fast . . . all of them will move from right to left and from left to right . . . just follow them silently, with your eyes, she was told. Then she was instructed, Now . . . imagine all your catastrophic thoughts getting into those boats and watch them coming and going without bothering you.

The following metaphor shows us how anti-awfulizing works:

2. *An irrational belief:* 'If I am not getting what I want, it is awful.'

    A rational alternative: 'There is nothing awful in the world. I believe that I sometimes make things "awful."'

    A suggested metaphor.[22] At midnight the Hodja heard a noise. Two men were struggling outside. The Hodja got out of his bed, with a blanket to cover him, and went to the front of his house. He asked them why they were fighting. Without answering, one of the men took the blanket, and both of them fled. The poor Hodja returned to his bed again. 'What were they fighting about?' asked his wife. 'Our blanket,' said the Hodja. 'Now the blanket is gone and the struggle is over.'

3. *An irrational belief:* 'There is no solution for my problems and everything is a catastrophe.'

    A rational alternative: 'There is always a solution to all of my problems and, if there is no solution I can find, it may be a bad thing, but it is not a catastrophe.'

    A suggested metaphor.[21,22] *The missing leg.* The Hodja was a clever, though poor man, but never a miserly one. As a matter of fact, miserly people are never poor. One of the hodja's most important characteristics was his skill in 'anti-catastrophizing.' Anyhow, one day, the Hodja was going to visit the great emperor Tamerlane but he realized how unseemly it would look for him to go empty-handed. No, it wouldn't do . . .

    > He organized a beautifully roasted goose, placed it on a tray and started out on his way to the palace. After a while, the aroma of the roasted goose began to tell on him and, when he could bear it no longer, he broke off one of its legs and satisfied his desire. Tamerlane[24] when offered the gift, noticed at once that one of the legs was missing and, being lame in one leg himself, he thought this must have been done on purpose, to remind him of his disability. He was, of course, furious and the Hodja had never in his life been in greater danger.
    >
    > 'What is the meaning of this?' roared the tyrant. 'Where's the other leg of this goose?'
    >
    > 'Your Majesty, all the geese in Aksehir are one-legged,' replied the Hodja.
    >
    > 'That's preposterous! I've never heard such nonsense!'
    >
    > 'If your Majesty deigns to look out of the window, the geese near the water will vouch for me.'
    >
    > True enough, all of them were standing about in the sun, on one leg. He ordered an attendant to chase the birds away. They watched the attendant throw a large stick and then the geese ran away as fast as both their legs could carry them.
    >
    > 'You see, Nasreddin, you were lying. Those geese proved they have two legs apiece.'
    >
    > 'Those poor birds didn't prove a thing, your Majesty. If I were chased away with such a stick, I might grow two more legs myself.'

4. Some famous poets like Ahmed Arif (1927–1991) wrote "Don't self-destruct, you have to withstand with hope, with love, with dreams. . . ."[23] Nazım Hikmet (1902–1963) wrote poems that tell society that the future can be beautiful (*The Poet of Hope*). Hikmet had hope for humanity, for the future, for the youth and for love.[23] Such poems can be learned by the clients as metaphors. Though Albert Ellis advised his clients to write mockery poems as homework about their problems, these poems and poets, which are not funny but provide positive emotions, are available in the culture of the Middle East, and can be used in therapy.

Frustration Tolerance

People dealing with frustration may be disturbed by cognitive disputations because they may have a long history of seeing things as 'too difficult.' It is not only cognitive disputation but also more importantly disputing low tolerance, behaviorally, that is important. So, to increase tolerance, using behavioral homework is suggested. Low frustration tolerance is closely related to emotional intelligence. Most low frustrated people act based on their emotions rather than their thoughts. That is, it needs behavioral activity rather than a cognitive process to increase tolerance level. People say, 'I cannot stand it.' In order to be strong and increase your patience, you need to do something about what you are frustrated about.

For those who practice Islam in humility and peace, wherever they are in the world, the need for the most important activity to help rehearse rational beliefs of frustration tolerance (I can stand it) is 'fasting.' Fasting lasts for 30 days between sunrise and sundown. In poorer and hot countries, while working, this is very difficult. When being attacked it is more difficult. There are other fasting days, besides the main one, in the run-up to Ramadan or sweet festival. Many consider it an honor to fast. It is a holy duty, a time when Muslims learn how to contain their dysfunctional emotions, and thoughts, over a period of time. Neither eating nor drinking nor sex is allowed when you fast. A person who is fasting is not allowed to fight or even argue/swear with others. It is not scientifically proven, but fasting may regulate unhealthy emotions and irrational beliefs.

1. *An irrational belief:* 'I cannot stand failure.'
    A rational alternative: 'If I try hard enough I will learn how to overcome my problems. If I cannot overcome my struggles, at least I can learn how to stand failure.'
    A suggested metaphor: 'People trip each other up. When I fall, I have to get up again.'
2. In the Arabic world 'hadiths' are used as metaphors. According to the dictionary, hadiths are a collection of traditions containing the sayings of the prophet Mohammad that, with accounts of his daily practice (the Sunna), constitute the major source of guidance for Muslims, apart from the Quran. (This in itself is disputed—as mentioned elsewhere in this book.)
    An irrational belief: 'If I am not getting what I want it is awful.'
    A rational alternative: 'There is nothing awful in this world. I believe that sometimes I make them "awful."'

This is a *suggested hadith as a metaphor* (taken from https://hadithoftheday. com/patience/). Some people asked for some things from Mohammad (*SAW*) and so he gave them to them. They asked him again, and again he gave them to them. When they asked for them a third time he didn't have any more. Mohammad said,

> If I had more, I would not keep them back from you. Whoever abstains from asking others, Allah will make him contented, and whoever tries to make themselves self-sufficient, Allah will make them self-sufficient. Whomsoever remains patient, Allah will make him patient. Nobody can be given a blessing better and greater than patience.

3.   Dr. Ellis always pointed out the importance of poems in therapy, especially humorous ones. Poems can be great metaphors in therapy. A famous Turkish poet, Necip Fazıl Kısakürek, wrote,

> *The end of patience is peace,*
> *Oh, patience.*
> *You may say damn you!*
> *You salute the trouble!*[1]

Here Kısakürek shows us that our troubles (fears) make our life difficult, but we can 'salute!' our trouble and enjoy it.

Conclusion

The goal of this chapter was to show how metaphors can be used to demonstrate how to deal with work concerning rational beliefs. It is possible for the reader to reproduce samples according to the methods given in this section. Of course, the examples are just to get a flavor. A huge book could be written about it. It may be insufficient for some linguists, and even those who are interested in metaphors for use in therapy. It is self-evident that academic work in literature, linguistics, and semantics, as well as the work of colleagues and practitioners in other Middle Eastern countries, and elsewhere, is much deeper, but the reader should recognize this chapter as a window—a window to the Middle East.

Note

1. Kısakürek, N. F. (n.d.). *Sabır. Büyük Doğu Yayınları and Necip Fazıl Kısakürek Kültür ve Araştırma Vakfı.* İstanbul. (Reprinted with permission).

References

1. Dietrich, A., & Kanso, R. (2010). A review of EEG, ERP, and neuroimaging studies of creativity and insight. *Psychological Bulletin, 136*(5), 822.
2. Rogaeva, E., Meng, Y., Lee, J. H., Gu, Y., Kawarai, T., Zou, F., & Chen, F. (2007). The neuronal sortilin-related receptor SORL1 is genetically associated with Alzheimer disease. *Nature Genetics, 39*(2), 168.
3. Jung-Beeman, M. (2005). Bilateral brain processes for comprehending natural language. *Trends in Cognitive Sciences, 9*(11), 512–518.
4. Beeman, M. J., & Bowden, E. M. (2000). The right hemisphere maintains solution-related activation for yet-to-be-solved problems. *Memory & Cognition, 28*(7), 1231–1241.
5. Wehebrink, K. (2013). *Laterality in Metaphor Processing: A Unique Role of the Right Hemisphere?* Bachelor's thesis. Enschede, Netherlands. c
6. Vosniadou, S., & Ortony, A. (Eds.). (1989). *Similarity and Analogical Reasoning.* Cambridge: Cambridge University Press.
7. Gentner, D. (1983). Structure-mapping: A theoretical framework for analogy. *Cognitive Science, 7*(2), 155–170.
8. Moser, K. S. (2000, June). Metaphor analysis in psychology: Method, theory, and fields of application. *Forum Qualitative Sozialforschung/Forum: Qualitative Social Research, 1*(2).
9. Ottati, V., Rhoads, S., & Graesser, A. C. (1999). The effect of metaphor on processing style in a persuasion task: A motivational resonance model. *Journal of Personality and Social Psychology, 77*(4), 688.
10. Why Do Writers Use Metaphors? (2018). Retrieved from www.quora.com/Why-do-writers-use-metaphors
11. Lakoff, G., & Johnson, M. (2008). *Metaphors We Live by.* Chicago: University of Chicago Press.
12. Moser, K. S. (2000). Metaphor Analysis in Psychology-Method, Theory, and Fields of Application. Retrieved from www.qualitative-research.net/index.php/fqs/article/viewArticle/1090/2387
13. Bargh, J. A., Gollwitzer, P. M., & Barndollar, K. (1996). Social Ignition: The Automatic Activation of Motivational States. Unpublished manuscript, New York University.
14. Dweck, C. S. (1996). *Implicit Theories as Organizers of Goals and Behavior.* Guilford. New York
15. Barker, P. (1985). *Using Metaphors in Psychotherapy.* New York: Brunner and Mazel, p. 221.
16. Ellis, A., & Dryden, W. (1997). *The Practice of Rational: Emotive Therapy* (2nd ed.). New York: Springer.
17. Lapsekili, N., & Yelboğa, Z. (2014). Metaphor in psychotherapy. *Journal of Cognitive-Behavioral Psychotherapy and Research, 3*(2), 116–125.
18. Dwairy, M. (2009). Culture analysis and metaphor psychotherapy with Arab-Muslim clients. *Journal of Clinical Psychology, 65*(2), 199–209.
19. Baykal, A. N. (1990). *Yöneticiler için Yeni Bir Bakış Mustafa Kemal Atatürk'ün Liderlik Sırları* (200th ed.). Istanbul: Sistem Yayıncılık.
20. Nasrettin Hoca. (n.d.). Republic of Turkey Ministry of Culture and Tourism. Retrieved from www.kultur.gov.tr/EN-117878/life-of-nasreddin-hoca.html
21. Haci Bektaş Velî Külliyesi. (2009). Republic of Turkey Ministry of Culture and Tourism. Retrieved from http://aregem.kulturturizm.gov.tr/TR-12047/haci-bektas-veli-kulliyesi.html

22. Nasreddin Hoca Stories. (n.d.). Retrieved from http://salpagarov.narod.ru/kultura/hoca/Jokes-Anecdotes.htm
23. Some Famous Stories of Nasreddin Hodja. (n.d.). Retrieved from www.sivrihisar.net/stories.htm
24. Timur. (2018). Retrieved from www.britannica.com/biography/Timur

9

MIDDLE EASTERN IDIOMS, PROVERBS, AND FOLK SAYINGS

Out of suffering have emerged the strongest souls; the most massive characters are seared with scars.
—Khalil Gibran

Although proverbs are a written-symbolic and metaphorical language, they can serve as visual 'packages' for mental healing. They usually take fundamental effect immediately, in psychotherapy, if used properly. They may also shorten the hours needed for therapy. However, whether you are a clinician or a client, and like to use idioms, proverbs, or folk sayings as a therapeutic tool, you should be careful to acknowledge that a huge number of proverbs may contain irrational beliefs, over-generalizations, depreciation and self-downing, others-downing, or shame-inducing characteristics that cannot be used for healing. There are, of course, a multitude of 'positive' and 'motivational' proverbs, and they may support the client to adapt to new healthy thoughts and beliefs, for a beneficial effect. Providing reason and empathy, proverbs, idioms, and folk sayings help to identify rational and useful thoughts and beliefs within a number of cultures. There has been research on the usage of proverbs in therapy but not in the Middle East. *(Please note that from now on, in this chapter, idioms, proverbs, and folk sayings are referred to as 'wise old sayings.')*

This section will include examples of Turkish and Arabic 'wise old sayings' for rational beliefs. Some suggestions will be given for using 'wise old sayings' for understanding some components of REBT. An explanation of how to use them to support clients will also be discussed.

One of the differences between RE & CBT is the distinction between hot and cold cognitions. Cold cognitions are located on the surface of a person's cognitive level, such as automatic thoughts, while hot cognitions are part of the lower layers of cognitive structure that are not often pronounced, such as irrational beliefs. So, hot cognitions are thoughts and beliefs that we do not usually say aloud in everyday language. During disputation interventions (restructuring clients' thought systems/schemas) in REBT, the therapist focuses on hot cognitions instead of cold ones. A way of understanding hot cognitions and assimilating rational hot cognitions is to use 'wise old sayings' in the 'B' of the ABC model. Most clinicians assume that understanding abstract meanings of 'wise old sayings' requires a different sort of higher-order cognitive ability.[1] Understanding and interpreting the proverbs are assumed to reflect executive functions.[2] A variety of empirical evidence suggests that the ability to understand many 'wise old sayings' reveals the presence of metaphorical schemes that are ubiquitous in everyday thought.[1]

Choosing Proverbs

It is important to be judicious when choosing proverbs because not every proverb contains rational expressions. On the contrary, there are many proverbs with irrational expressions and cognitive distortions. Ahead are examples of negative, unmotivating, and unusable proverbs. They have been translated to get as close to the original in spirit as well as meaning:

- *He who laughs much weeps much.*
- *Revenge is sweeter than honey.*
- *Like the donkey's tail, he neither grows longer nor shorter.*
- *He who knows much errs much.*

Proverbs, as well as extracts from the Quran, have prospered as a means of shortcut communication, throughout history, in the Middle East. As such, they have developed into adages or regularly utilized words, phrases, sound bites, sentences, and expressions in everyday dialogue. They are inserted into a way of life, which metamorphoses into a way of thinking, or even an attitude, for want of a lack of a system of critical thinking and scientific discovery—although Middle Easterners will cite Nobel prize winners to disprove a rule!

Middle Eastern proverbs have come about as the result of a culture with a history going back several thousand years. They mirror the cultural ride and 'esteem framework' held by the general population. For instance, Turkish proverbs were used to conceptualize notions like controlling, competency, mastery, and being prosperous.[3] The metaphorical propositions elicited from cultural schemas embedded in Middle Eastern proverbs reveal that in the society, for instance, a *horse* is associated with words like 'precious,' 'master,' 'valuable,' 'friend,' 'hard-working,' and 'unpredictable danger.'[3] Middle Eastern axioms or regular adages are those that mirror the psyche of the people—communicating the generally shared belief system and theory that have more than once been utilized, screened, and held up as an indisputable truth by numerous people over many centuries.

The style and usage of 'wise old sayings,' in a session, are also important. They express thoughts utilizing a chronicled story, in representative statements, with philosophical ramifications. At the point where proverbs may be used to recognize issues that a patient is enduring, the treatment is, or ought to be, imparted by implication, without directly remarking on the patient's personal situation, so that she will feel less humiliated or hurt. The patient becomes more amenable when the 'pressure' appears to be off, once 'wise old sayings' are used, and she may feel less restricted and freer to discuss problems more openly.

Tbox: After homework is completed, getting feedback from the client about whether she wants to continue to work with 'wise old sayings' is important. If she does not find it useful, after a few attempts, the application should be stopped.

Tips for Application

First, discuss with a client why 'wise old sayings' in a session are helpful and why they are needed. In the cognitive behavior therapy model, the ABC model, 'wise old sayings' are used for 'B' only, not for 'C' (emotions).

Second, remember that when you use any 'wise old saying,' say it directly at the beginning, but do not explain the meaning. Give clients a chance to think about its meaning, and then discuss it.

Third, the therapist needs to be ready to provide some 'wise old sayings' to clients. Also, if it is possible, an explanation of the origin of the proverbs (from Turkish, Arabic, Persian, etc.) may need to be provided by the therapist.

Fourth, for clients, the procedure using 'wise old sayings' in model B will help in replacing irrational beliefs by embracing rational beliefs. The purpose of using 'wise old sayings' is to ensure rational beliefs are memorable so that a deeper meaning can also be ascertained. As mentioned in previous chapters, remember that irrational beliefs comprise a demandingness IrBel, and three evaluative IrBels (awfulizing, frustration intolerance, and self/other depreciation). The alternative to these irrational beliefs is rational beliefs: (1) preferences (nondemanding wants and wishes), (2) anti-awfulizing (realistic negative evaluations), (3) frustration tolerance (high-tolerance beliefs), and (4) acceptance beliefs (of self, others, and life) (or, as proposed in this book: love of self, others, and life beliefs).

1. Activating event: Take the most stressful event as a starting point. Do not forget to underline the 'critical A,' which is the most disturbing point inside the 'A.'
2. Identify the IrBels: Choose demandingness and one of the three evaluative IrBels.

3. Find out what the RaBels could be. Once you agree with the IrBels and RaBels go ahead to the next stage.
4. Use some disputation techniques (e.g., functional or semantic) to challenge IrBels.
5. Come up with a proverb related to RaBels.
6. Remember the 'A' and think about how it is related to RaBels.
7. Do homework to produce other possible 'wise old sayings' relating to RaBels.
8. Return to IrBels to check whether the IrBels have still influenced your behaviors and emotions.

Until the client's IrBels are changed, she must continue to repeat the same circle with additional 'wise old sayings' until her emotions become healthy.

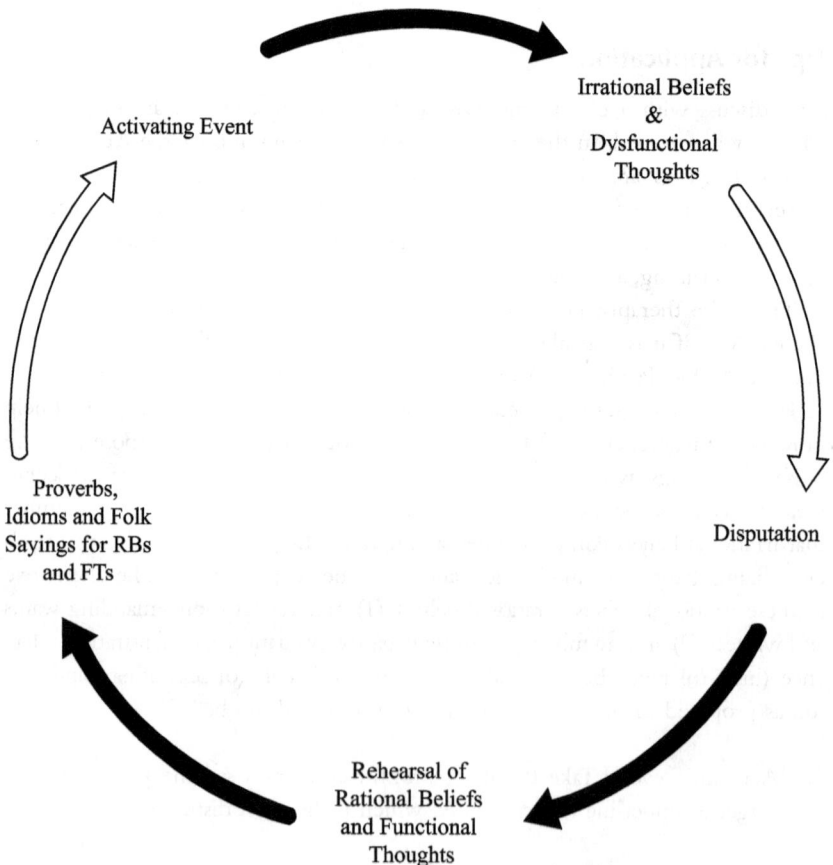

FIGURE 9.1 The A-B-A circle for usage of 'wise old sayings.'

Therapeutic Relationship

'Wise old sayings' help to maintain a therapeutic relationship with the client, because the words of powerful men and women are viewed as very valuable in Middle Eastern and Asian cultures. The basic components of a fruitful psychotherapy session are a stronger collaboration between all parties concerned, mindfulness, understanding, giving valuable comments, and making remarks on observed and observable changes, efficacious proposals and propositions to clients, reflection, and treating the patient for development. A socially pertinent connection with clients is imperative. With regard to Turkish clients (and maybe those from Middle Eastern, African, and Asiatic cultures), 'wise old sayings,' as metaphors, are a useful guide that can be used in therapy. The clients may also take advantage of bibliotherapy interventions.

'Rational and Inspiring'

Some Middle Eastern idioms, proverbs, epithets, aphorisms, and sayings may be used to demonstrate how rational demandingness (logical, realistic, healthy, flexible wishes and wants) can be addressed. It is important to understand and reflect on the pervasiveness and breadth of Middle East culture over many centuries (before and after Islamization), because Islamic teaching has helped humanity to be calm and flexible. Islam gives people a different perspective that emphasizes the importance of peace and acceptance. On the other hand, strangely, Middle Eastern people always say this but they are sometimes very aggressive. However, generally speaking religious messages may help society to become calm and flexible in a stressful situation.

Rational Demands, Preferences, Wants

As mentioned in Chapter 3, demandingness can be conceptualized as rules of life that include inferences, evaluations, and/or philosophical biases using modal verbs 'should be,' 'ought to be,' 'must be,' and 'need to be.'

The demands of life in non-first-world countries are considerably more taxing than in first-world ones, though this is neither a criticism nor an excuse. It is self-evident that there are geopolitical reasons for this. These demands necessitate a far greater resilience to the day-to-day strains of what life has to offer, what dreams can be made, and what needs to be done in order to meet them. For instance, demandingness may reflect the belief 'I want to be successful and therefore I must be.' Here are some translations and transliterations of the first of our Turkish 'wise old sayings' in this chapter. Some may be hard to grasp as translation is not an exact science and meaning can be obscure and obfuscated. From an REBT point of view the following Middle Eastern 'wise old sayings' examples can be used to replace irrational demandingness beliefs or, from a CBT point of view, 'absolute thinking' cognitive distortions.

1. 'Eyes know no bounds' *(Desire has no rest).*

This is for clients who are not aware of their irrational demandingness. It can be used as a reminder (or warning sign) of having irrational demandingness in different situations. Assume that a client wants to be perfect at all times. She thinks that whatever she does needs to be done perfectly and you can remind her, 'Eyes know no bounds!'

IrBel: Her irrational belief was 'I must be perfect at all times; otherwise I cannot stand it!'

RaBel: Rational beliefs can be 'I prefer to be perfect at all times, but if I am not, then I believe it is not a "must." I can still stand it!'

2. 'The chicken that goes far away from its coop gets dirt in its feet.'

This proverb means that even if you have sufficient food and material wealth, you still look for more in other places. For instance, a client comes to therapy with problems of enviousness or jealousy. The meaning of the proverb in the session can be discussed. Some may agree, but this doesn't deal with greed, nor does it deal with aspiration.

3. 'The best of everything is in the middle.'

Imagine a person who has just started her career after graduation from university and who comes to therapy. After assessments, a therapist finds she has 'irrational demandingness beliefs' for certain things in her life. She says that she must be successful at all costs in her new job. She is anxious about whether she will be able to perform at her desired standard, well or at all.

4. 'They do not give cloth (suitable) for everybody' loosely meaning 'One cloth fits all,' or rather doesn't, may be the nearest to it in the Western world. This idiom refers to and is a deep-rooted saying linked to the famous Silk Route of yore, where merchants and traders from the Far East made their way across Asia, without modern conveniences, which most people now take for granted—a place where basic human needs must be met in order not to die. We can see everyday examples of these harsh lands on the news every day. Things in life rarely go to plan, but rules cannot be broken according to the needs and requirements of each individual. Such an idea is narcissistic. It is incorrect to expect a situation to occur according to how one would necessarily like it to, even with careful planning. It must be recognized that although the desired extent of a situation may not be attained, any benefit or usefulness of the necessary dosage can be reached, even though this may require some flexible thinking.

5. 'A hungry man puts his hand in the flame' is a close relative of 'Necessity compels' or 'Needs must.' In current usage, this phrase is usually used to express something that is done unwillingly, but with an acceptance that it can't be avoided; for example, *I really don't want to cook tonight, but needs must.* Shakespeare used the phrase several times—for example, in *All's Well That Ends Well:*

Countess: Tell me thy reason why thou wilt marry?

Clown: My poor body, madam, requires it: I am driven on by the flesh; and he must needs go that the devil drives.

The phrase became pared down to 'needs must' during the twentieth century and even in that short form is rather archaic-sounding and fading from popular use, despite a high-profile appearance on TV in *Blackadder II* (1985): '*Needs must when the devil vomits into your kettle.*'

6. There is a Turkish proverb that represents demandingness from life: 'A person who is hungry thinks "I will never be satisfied," a person whose stomach is full thinks, "I will be never be hungry again."' This is the same as the irrational belief that 'Life should be easy and it should provide me with whatever I want with no exceptions.' However, there is an additional part to this saying: 'Less is more' or 'Too much of a good thing is bad.' This implies the notion that simplicity and clarity lead to good design, which is, sadly, frequently lacking in modern Turkish culture, together with the rarely used word 'class.' In the field of music, however, we can see this is not the case, even though that Turkishness may be exemplified by an Armenian named Ziljian!

7. Some idioms (not proverbs) frequently used in daily conversations can be included in therapy by a therapist.

> '*Speak logically*' *(mantıklı konuşmak) means when you say something, please give some evidence of what you are saying.*
>
> '*Weigh up what you are saying*' *(tartarak konuşmak) means that before you say something 'think twice!'*

Taken from a part of a session:

C: They made me angry and I cursed them. They called security! I tried to explain what happened but the security guys didn't listen to me.

T: If you spoke logically in the first place or, if you could weigh up what you were saying, what would happen instead of facing unfairness?

C: Yes, it was my mistake; I should have spoken to them calmly. I always make similar mistakes, acting impulsively without thinking.

Frustration Tolerance

In therapy, increasing the strength of the client to cope with stressful situations and helping her to increase her high tolerance beliefs and skills can be one of the most troublesome issues, because events have already made things very difficult for her. The client would not have come to receive support if she had been able to tolerate the situations anyway. A therapist's task is to support the client to have frustration tolerance (high tolerance) beliefs. It can be achieved with behavioral, cognitive, and emotional methods. However, it is obvious that simply repeating rational beliefs, such as 'I can bear it' or 'I can stand it!,' may not always be adequate to help clients. Proverbs can be used when undertaking cognitive homework. In many cases, proverbs will help clients when completing behavioral homework. For a homework assignment in treatment, a client can remind herself of proverbs to increase her tolerance before, during, and after unbearable situations. Some proverbs that will help raise the tolerance level are as follows:

1. 'He who has never tasted what is bitter cannot truly appreciate what is sweet.'

'The greater the storm, the brighter the rainbow.'
'Every big thing consists of small things.' *(Small steps make a long journey.)*
'Time is the medicine; have patience with it.'

Case example: A 26-year-old client, who had never worked, could not manage to find a job, after graduation from his university. He was afraid of what he would have done if he had got hired. The foregoing three proverbs, to dispute his irrational beliefs, were discussed and a replacement with rational beliefs was considered.

2. A client found these proverbs beneficial in healing frustration intolerance beliefs. She had a problem with procrastinating, and saw every task as a big obstacle. She repeated a proverb every day. She wrote an essay for each one and explained how they were related to her problems.

'One who has not burnt in the sun does not appreciate the shade.'

'Do not leave the business of this evening to the morning'—that is, don't put off till tomorrow what you can do today.

'Nothing is difficult for a willing mind.' ('No pain, no gain').

'Someone who wants to eat honey must bear the sting of the bees.'

3. Some of the proverbs can be useful, as a reminder, when tasks are 'difficult' for clients. One of the ways to maintain high frustration tolerance is to act patiently and stubbornly. Some clients only get 'benefit' from doing things that they find 'difficult,' rather than changing their thoughts about certain situations. For instance, the only way to get a student to perform a difficult homework was to get her to do it, rather than procrastinate. Students, therefore, can learn high frustration tolerance by 'doing' it rather than cognitively changing their minds.

Turkish proverbs with animal metaphors can be used:

'Today's hen is better than tomorrow's goose'—Patience is a virtue. Trying to obtain more may cause us to lose everything.

'One goose is better than 40 sparrows'—Dealing with one big task is better than dealing with many small tasks. Small steps are better than big steps, so we need to be careful not to 'rush' and look for quick results.

Anti-Catastrophizing/Awfulizing

Not many proverbs can be used for therapeutic purposes. There are many wise old sayings that represent catastrophic beliefs or maximization and over-generalization as cognitive distortions, such as 'Once you are under the waves, does it matter if you are ten inches under or ten feet?' or 'An ember burns where it falls' (*Nobody will understand what I am going through*). The client will need to pay attention to the proverbs that will help her own catastrophizing/awfulizing beliefs and cognitive distortions, and ignore the proverbs that have disguised discourses in them. The proverbs ahead will not provoke irrational beliefs and cognitive distortion; on the contrary, they will help clients deal with dysfunctional thoughts.

1. 'Every bad thing has a worse alternative.'

In REBT, as a technique in therapy, therapists use a catastrophe scale. There are two stages to this scale. A couple of folk sayings can be used to support the main idea (Figure 9.2).

First, the client is asked to rate the 'bad' things or 'possible, bad' things in her life. Second, 'whatever her particular problem' is, she is asked to place it on the scale. The purpose of this workout is to show the client that there is nothing in this world that is '101%' bad, as Albert Ellis pointed out many times in his lectures and books. An example of a suggested activity: Imagine a problem you think is a catastrophe. Place it on the scale ahead, from not too bad to completely catastrophic.

2. 'A single stone suffices to scare away a thousand crows.'

'A carefree head is to be found only on a scarecrow.'

'If you do not know a tunnel, go over the bridge.'

'One who comes on like a torrent, goes away as a stream.'

'A landslide takes from a hill and fills the creek at its bottom' *(There is no great loss without some gain)* can be used with functional disputation.

'One crow does not make a winter' can be used with evidence-based disputation. Crows roosts are primarily a fall and winter thing. Numbers peak in winter. It appears that all crows will join winter roosts. Most breeding crows sleep in their territories during the breeding season, but join the roosts afterward.

3. 'Do not burn the blanket to get rid of a flea.'

This proverb may be suitable to use in catastrophic beliefs or over-generalization as a cognitive distortion that causes feelings of 'hurt.' For instance, after 'being hurt' in a broken relationship, a person may tend to disbelieve in 'love.' A client may have the cognitive distortion of 'a drop of ink that discolors a beaker of water.'

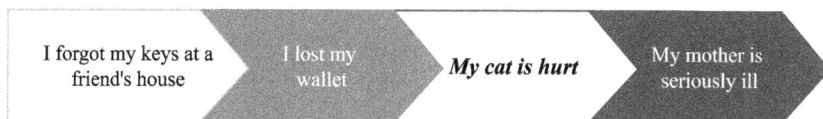

FIGURE 9.2 A catastrophe scale used in REBT.

Unconditional Self-acceptance

A self-depreciation belief could be: 'When I fail, it means that I am a complete failure,' whereas other forms of depreciation could reflect a belief: 'When others treat me poorly, it proves they are bad people.' From a CBT point of view, cognitive distortions that reflect the concept of unconditional acceptance may be self-blaming ('It is all my fault') and labeling ('I am stupid'). These proverbs can be used against such cognitive distortions. Repetition will allow clients to better understand and adopt new, rational acceptance beliefs. An example exists at the end of this chapter of how clients and their therapist may apply such intervention.

Here are some great wise old sayings that represent and reinforce USA:

'No son of Adam is without fault.'
'No one can do a man as much harm as he does to himself.'
'Every man is the blacksmith of his own fortune.'
'Everyone has his own way of eating yoghurt.'
'The crown of maturity is humility.'

Unconditional Other Acceptance

Another depreciation belief is towards other people. It is usually seen in anger problems and narcissistic personality disorders. Such people criticize, dislike, or downgrade others around them. The following examples can be given to them to change their beliefs and thoughts towards others.

'One will have no friends if looking for a perfect person.'
'He who is looking for a friend with no failures will remain without a friend.'
'Five fingers are not alike.' *(This implies that there is no equality in our skills.)*

Unconditional Life Acceptance

A client may believe that life is not worth living. She usually has the cognitive distortion of disregarding the positive and focusing on the negative in others or all-or-nothing thinking. In depressed clients, the most widely held belief is life depreciation (downing) IrBels.

'The rose springs from the thorn, the thorn from the rose.'
'If you do not know a tunnel, go over the bridge.'
'A bird in the hand is better than ten on the tree.'
'Let it wound your heart rather than go out and cause a scandal.'

Homework

Example Homework Assignment 1

TABLE 9.1 Example homework assignment

A: Activating event or situation	Irrational beliefs, negative automatic thoughts, cognitive distortions	Suggested proverbs
1. My friend didn't invite me to the birthday party.	IB: I am a worthless person. NAT: I hate myself. CD: Nobody loves me.	'Do not burn the blanket to get rid of a flea.' 'If you do not know a tunnel, go over the bridge.'

TABLE 9.2 Client form

IrBels—Please write your irrational beliefs and negative automatic thoughts	**RaBels**—Please write your rational beliefs and alternative non-harmful automatic thoughts	Write your favorite proverbs

Homework Assignment 2

Meditate for one or two minutes, keeping the 'rational and inspiring' wise old sayings in mind. During this time, instead of thinking about the meaning of the proverb, or something having to be inferred, it is enough to repeat the proverb and try to remain calm and quiet.

References

1. Gibbs, R. W., & Beitel, D. (1995). What proverb understanding reveals about how people think. *Psychological Bulletin, 118*(1), 133.
2. Leyhe, T., Saur, R., Eschweiler, G. W., & Milian, M. (2011). Impairment in proverb interpretation as an executive function deficit in patients with amnestic mild cognitive impairment and early Alzheimer's disease. *Dementia and Geriatric Cognitive Disorders Extra, 1*(1), 51–61.
3. Pourhossein, S. (2016). *Animal Metaphors in Persian and Turkish Proverbs: A Cognitive Linguistic Study* (Yayınlanmamış Doktora Tezi). Ankara, Turkey: Hacettepe Üniversitesi.

10

SESSION STRUCTURES AND EXAMPLES

Emotions are the fuel of your behavior. No behavior can be emotionless. Watch out for the fuel you fill your heart with.

The purpose of this chapter is to provide some guidance to clients, therapists, and other readers with real in-session demonstrations. In this chapter, readers will find (1) an experimental study with cultural contents and methods, (2), two culturally redefined RE & CBT session protocols (with step-by-step guidance), (3) some dialogues from sessions with Turkish and other Middle Eastern clients, and (4) examples of culturally redefined self-help forms.

Empirical research in REBT practice has been evaluated in a great deal of research under the auspices of CBT. Studies were applied to RE & CBT interventions together.[1,2] Many experimental studies show that RE & CBT were used together successfully to treat clients in Western society.[3,4,5]

RE & CBT is an effective treatment in the West. Experimental studies, such as the work of Shelley, Battaglia, Lucey, Ellis, Opler, and Center on schizophrenia,[6] Sava, Yates, Lupu, Szentagotai, and David on major depressive disorders,[7] David, Szentagotai, Lupu, and Cosman on non-psychotic major depressive disorder,[8] and other many REBT researchers show evidence that REBT is a (moderately to highly) effective therapy. Furthermore, REBT treatment successfully reduces the anxiety of the students.[9] Aler, Leiva, Bonet, Ortega, Puertolas, and Izquierdo found that REBT is effective for the treatment of dysthymia compared with standard care.[10] A meta-analysis of psychotherapy outcome studies indicated that REBT has the second highest effectiveness and usefulness in terms of effect size after systematic desensitization and before behavioral modification, Adlerian therapy, client-centered, psychodynamic, transactional analysis, and eclectic therapies.[11] A meta-analysis of 70 rational emotive therapy (RET) outcome stud-ies, a total of 236 comparisons of RET to cognitive behavior modification, behavior therapy, and other psychotherapies were examined by Lyons and Woods.[12] The results showed that participants receiving REBT benefited from the treatment over baseline measures and control groups. Other recent meta-analysis has been done mostly on CBT treatment. According to many experimental research results, the effect of CBT treatment is very strong.[13] Cognitive behavior therapy (CBT) in the treatment of major depression disorder (MDD), generalized anxiety disorder (GAD), panic disorder (PAD), and social anxiety disorder (SAD) was examined in 144 different trials around the world (184 comparisons). The results indicated that CBT is an effective treatment.

REBT is the oldest CBT therapy and is criticized by some practitioners of cognitive behavior therapy. According to many CBT therapists although all cognitive therapists are in debt to Ellis, his work did not have as great an effect as Beck's approach (CT), in research and practice, due to his rejection of seem-ingly academic and *theoretical* REBT work on limited cognitive distortions (e.g., catastrophizing, absolute thinking), although Ellis's students have filled the gap of scientific and practical applications with many control trials in the last 15 years. Unlike REBT, which mostly focuses on the four irrational beliefs and their rational alternatives, CBT works on various cognitive distortions to treat a large amount of disorders.[14] Ellis's approach differs from CBT, in terms of focusing mostly on demandingness and the three evaluation beliefs (awfulizing/ catastrophizing, frustration intolerance, and self-others-life downing/condemna-tion), discussing philosophical change, and replacing certain dysfunctional emo-tions (unhealthy negative emotions) with functional emotions (healthy negative emotions).

REBT determines a distinction between evaluative cognitions and perceptions/ inferences. Unlike CBT, REBT strongly emphasizes the philosophical basis of emotional regulations. REBT therapists are suggested to be more active and directive than CBT therapists. However, both REBT and CBT therapists appear to be co-discoverers or collaborators with clients on a path of treatment. REBT prescribes certain emotions to work on (e.g., anger, guilt, anxiety, jealousy), while CBT does not specify any emotions, but rather allows the client to name an emotion as being functional or dysfunctional. Lastly, the conceptualization of unconditional acceptance and frustration intolerance is another distinct feature of REBT.

A Study in Istanbul

A total of 21 outpatients (8 females, 13 males) at the Affiliated Center of the Albert Ellis Institute in Istanbul were included in the study. The participants were divided randomly into an experimental and a control group. They were all patients with mild depression and some had symptoms of general anxiety disorders. Three clients in the REBT group and four clients in the control group had received treatment in the past. None of them were on medication at the time.

For the experimental group each treatment took eight weeks—meeting once a week. Each therapy session lasted 50 minutes. The author had created a *culturally adaptable RE- & CBT-based manual.*

1. The ABC model was introduced to the clients.
2. The clients were informed about irrational and rational beliefs. The meaning of the B-C connection and dysfunctions/unhealthy emotions, and their effect on our behaviors, was taught using a blackboard.
3. Sufism (e.g., a brief history, the most used definitions, such as *nafs*, love, and surrendering, philosophy, Mevlânâ's statements) was included in the presentation when introducing USA, UOA, and ULA.
4. Logical, functional, semantic, philosophical, and other disputation techniques in classical RE & CBT were used. However, the therapist disputed mostly didactically, teaching rational beliefs (preferences, anti-catastrophizing, frustration tolerance, and an explanation of USA/UOA and ULA) with 'wise old sayings'—for instance:

    4a. I'd better be successful in what I do; however, there is no 'must' saying that I have to be successful (preferences).

    'Eyes know no bounds' (*Desire has no rest*).—A proverb

    4b. I want to be successful and, if I am not, it will be a bad thing. However, I cannot say that it will be 'awful.'

    'If you do not know a tunnel, go over the bridge.'—A proverb

    4c. I can still stand it if I am not successful.

    'Whoever tries hard is always stronger than someone who simply decides to do something, but does not start doing it' (*frustration tolerance*).—M. K. Atatürk

    4d. *If I am not successful, life is still valuable.* Others who cause my failure are still valuable people.

5. A metaphor was used: Aşık Veysel (for the short story see Chapter 9).
6. In order to reinforce rational beliefs, short stories were used from Nasreddin Hodja and the words of Haji Bektash Veli as metaphors.
7. The goals of culturally redefined RE & CBT therapy: Rather than seeking only functionality in a client, clients were encouraged to seek meaningfulness in their life, learning love of self/others/life, maintaining peace and what motivates them—based on self-determination theory (the need for autonomy, competence, and relatedness).

8. The practitioner suggested that clients work with metaphors, proverbs, idioms, and other folk sayings.
9. Two summarized books on Sufism, by the author, were given to the clients as a reading assignment.

Starting the Treatment

Clients spoke about their problems in the first session. The therapist introduced the ABC model and the importance of the B-C link, and also explained the differences between irrational and rational beliefs. The therapist and the clients worked on identifying unhealthy emotions and irrational beliefs. To collect data about the clients' irrational beliefs, homework was given in the shape of a self-help report form.

In the second session the goals of meaningfulness in their lives, the motivational aspects (three psychological needs) of human behaviors, maintaining peace, and love of life were discussed with the client.

During the third session, the therapist explained the difference between hot and cold cognitions and the importance of using proverbs, idioms, folk sayings, and Sufism. Sufism was explained briefly, and, as homework, ten pages of Sufist readings were assigned to the clients in the experimental group.

In the fourth session, clients were asked to observe their thinking patterns regarding the difference between the A-C and B-C link. Clients were provided

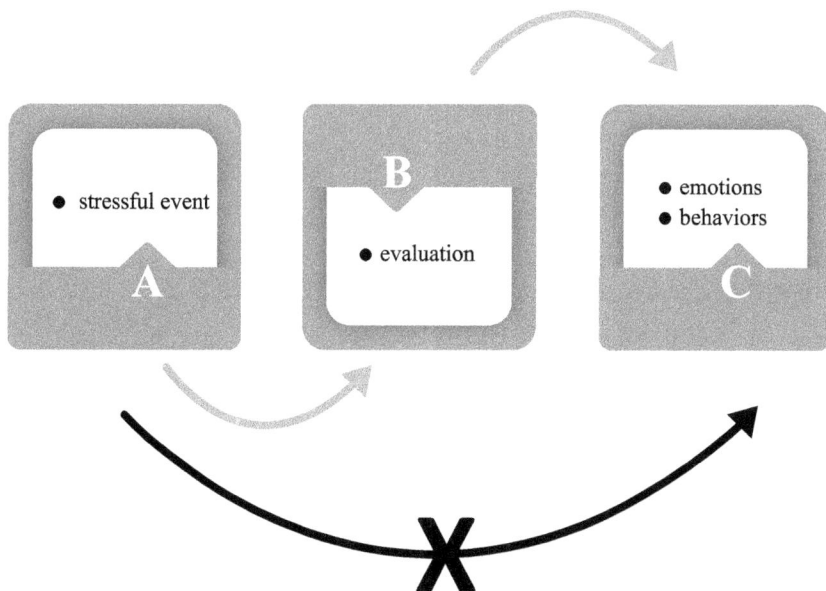

FIGURE 10.1 Importance of B-C link.

with a list of proverbs, idioms, and some quotations by Rumi. As in session activities, the ABC model was applied using metaphors, proverbs, and Rumi's teachings. Clients were provided with a 15-slide PowerPoint presentation to take with them to read at home.

In the fifth and sixth sessions, when necessary, logical, functional, semantic, and philosophical disputations were used. All disputations were matched with rational beliefs, Sufism, and 'wise old sayings.'

During the seventh session, using a didactic approach and role plays (and reverse role plays), a rehearsal of rational beliefs was applied. Unconditional acceptance (and love) beliefs and Sufism were deeply discussed with clients and some readings were given as homework.

During the eighth session, the therapist checked the homework assignments and then summarized the sessions. He then opened a discussion on how REBT affects their lives and their problems. The therapist then terminated the treatment by informing them that the research was completed and if any further psychological service was required then they could continue with therapy elsewhere, which is standard practice.

Control Group

While the experimental group was exposed to an example of culturally redefined RE & CBT therapy, the control group received conventional therapy. Two therapists, who had previously been trained in basic counseling skills and mid-level client-centered therapy, were assigned to provide psychological counseling for the control group sessions. They were not allowed to apply any specific therapeutic approaches, including CBT interventions. Clients were encouraged to talk openly about their problems and asked to give feedback. Each treatment took eight weeks—once a week for 50 minutes. Data was collected before and after the treatment with no follow-up in either the control or the experimental group. It was suggested that they continue therapy after the end of the sessions by providing at least two psychologists' names and contact numbers.

Results

According to the outcome of this experimental research, the participants in the experimental group improved *significantly* compared to the control group, which made little improvement. Please note that the study and its quantitative outcomes will be published in a scientific journal in 2020. The outcome suggested that culturally redefined RE & CBT works! Some clients gave feedback since, as mentioned elsewhere in this book, they liked to hear some of the cultural aspects of the therapy. Others said that they were 'positively' surprised about the cultural content (e.g., proverbs, metaphors) in treatment. Some said they were not expecting that this type of homework (culturally redefined goals and activities) would help them to improve. One of the clients with no religious background (he was an atheist) told the practitioner that he would prefer to use only the ABC model and contemplate rational beliefs, rather than work on Sufism and metaphors. However, he reported that he found proverbs and folk sayings were somewhat beneficial. One of the clients said she found it hard to understand the goal of being autonomous. Yet another one liked the idea of Sufism being integrated with unconditional acceptance and self-love, but once, in the session, she thought that she needed to become a nun to heal. Later she understood it was nothing to do with being religious.

An Example of a Session's Structure—I

An example is given ahead as to what is involved in the structure of a session for culturally redefined RE & CBT. A session may cover the following stages, respectively, but not necessarily in the same sequence. There is no necessity to finish all the stages in a single session: it can take 8–16 sessions to complete all the stages.

1. Listening to the client's problems and bringing up the event or situation that most disturbs the client within this problem.
2. Determining what 'most' bothers the client in a certain case/situation. Finding the 'critical A' involves a discussion between client and therapist.
3. Introducing the client to the ABC model. A self-help form is given to the client.
4. Introducing irrational and rational beliefs and other cognitive distortions. The therapist opens a discussion on the B–C link (how our thoughts determine our emotions and behaviors).
5. Working on identifying the client's irrational beliefs and other cognitive distortions. The following table should be used in session and outside a session.

   A RE & CBT form for thought record:

Activating event	Automatic thoughts & inferences	Irrational beliefs	Cognitive distortions	Feelings & behaviors

6. Teaching the client unhealthy negative emotions and how they are dysfunctional in our lives. An introduction to healthy negative emotions is given.
7. Finding the goals of the therapy. Besides philosophical change and being functional, a client is encouraged to add the following three goals to her

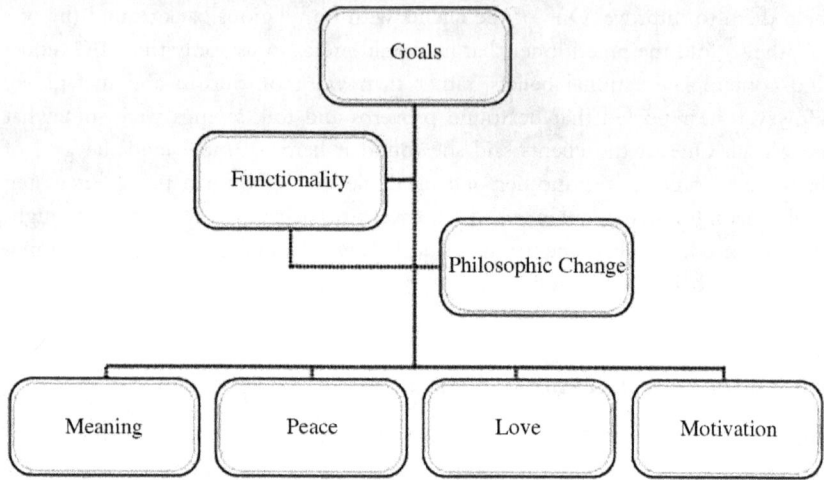

FIGURE 10.2 Culturally redefined goals for Middle Eastern clients.

agenda: (1) meaningfulness in her life, (2) maintaining peace, and (3) what motivates her, based on self-determination theory (needs of autonomy, competence, and relatedness).

Questions for clients to think about:

- How do my irrational beliefs and cognitive distortions disturb my functionality?
- What are my irrational beliefs about myself, others, life, things in life, and the future? How do they affect me in the long term?
- What kinds of irrational beliefs and cognitive distortions do I have that become blocks to finding the meaning in my life?
- What are the thoughts and beliefs I hold that create chaos in my life and become a barrier to maintaining peace in my life?
- How can I satisfy my basic psychological needs? What kinds of irrational beliefs do I hold that block me from satisfying my need for autonomy, competence, and relatedness?

8. Helping the clients find rational beliefs to their problems.
9. Introducing the core of the treatment to the clients: Metaphors, Sufism, proverbs, idioms and folk sayings, along with rational beliefs.

   a. Preferences/flexible thinking ability
   b. Anti-catastrophizing/realistic evaluation of 'badness' (anti-exaggerating or anti-dramatization)
   c. High frustration tolerance (practicing being patient)
   d. Unconditional self/others/life acceptance (love of self/others/life; practicing Sufism)

Clients can use this table:

	Automatic thoughts & inferences	*Rational beliefs*	*Cognitive distortions*
Client's report			
Suggested proverbs			
Suggested other 'wise old sayings'			

10. Emphasizing the importance of the B–C link and connecting rational beliefs to healthy emotions and behaviors. Discussing how Sufism, metaphors, proverbs, idioms, and folk sayings can be used for this purpose. Explaining to the client how to adopt healthy negative (functional) emotions, such as annoyance, sadness, disappointment, sorrow, and concern about a relationship, but leading them away from unhealthy negative (dysfunctional) emotions, such as anger, anxiety/panic, depression, shame, hurt, and jealousy.

    At this stage, talk about how these rational beliefs will provide healthy emotions, while assessing the same events.

11. Giving a client homework: Metaphors, idioms, folk sayings, and proverbs can be introduced here. Sampling the homework in the session may be attempted. Finding out which proverbs and folk sayings match with positive or healthy thoughts and beliefs. Making a list of possible 'wise old sayings':

    a.
    b.
    c.

12. Discussing with the client how, when, and how often she will complete homework.

13. Controlling new rational beliefs with Sufism, idioms, proverbs, or metaphors and *providing a suggestion that the client could provide examples of new, healthy emotions.*

14. Summarizing the session and giving the client time to ask questions.

15. Termination of the session and summarizing the therapeutic journey with the client.

An Example of a Session's Structure—II

'Using Sufism in RE & CBT therapy'

Each session should be 50 minutes in length. A nine-session protocol is suggested. (Please read Chapter 7 before reading this section.)

Session 1: Using this book to learn about what RE & CBT are. How the ABC model functions, what the meaning of the B–C link is, what irrational beliefs and rational alternatives are, and what unhealthy and healthy emotions are.

Session 2: Practice monitoring your activities and moods during the upcoming week using an activity monitor (see the end of the chapter). In this way you can determine what irrational beliefs and emotions are and which ones you have.

Session 3: Introduction to Sufism-Related RE & CBT

Some brief information about Sufism is presented. Sufic writing memorization is introduced. Some readings about Sufism and RE & CBT need to be read (using this book). The author recommends additional reading about Mevlânâ and other Sufists, their lives, and their sayings.

Session 4: Applications

Clients are taught that a key way to begin to change their irrational beliefs and negative automatic thoughts and perspectives is by replacing the idea of *unconditional acceptance (love)* with what is written in Sufic teachings, and clients are provided with various books on them.

Session 5: Emotions

This involves taking notes about when we perceive Sufism as 'B' and how our life will be changed by means of experiencing emotions. Discussing *unconditional acceptance (love)* and a healthy emotions link is also touched on. A basic understanding of the treatment rationale and further refinement of a client's ability to self-monitor her beliefs, moods, and behaviors are discussed.

Session 6: Disputations

This involves using disputation techniques, changing unhelpful thoughts and irrational beliefs. When disputing, Sufism can help the client to rationalize new helpful thoughts. Semantic and functional disputing is especially useful at this stage. Clients are asked to memorize key passages of scripture, in Sufism, that can be used to challenge negative thoughts.

Session 7: Challenging Unhelpful Thoughts

7a. Acting as if you are a Sufist (!)
   There are similar techniques used in CBT, such as '*act as if . . .*' A person plays a desired role. For instance, a role might be being rational all day without allowing oneself to be irrational. In this way, you are not just challenging unhelpful thoughts and replacing them with more positive thoughts by acting as if you are a Sufist but also adding or replacing your negative thoughts with the true words of Sufists.

7b. Surrendering

Surrendering the need to have things 'be' a certain way helps us begin the process of letting go. It is important to remember that active surrender is different from giving up. Active surrender involves a conscious decision to release, or let go of those things that one does not have the power to change. Noticeably, surrender is paradoxical—the Buddha said that much *dukkha* or stress has to do with our need for things to happen in a certain way. In Buddhist terms, 'surrender' is not surrendering the 'will' to God (or Mother Nature) but rather surrendering, or letting go of, one's identity, with the core of the ego, or the identification of the self, with a source of pain, or a source of desire.

Session 8

8a. The ABCDE method is used to help the client see the situation from the offender's perspective, aiding in the development of empathy, and the alignment of feelings with the decision to forgive.

8b. The client is introduced to the notion of expressing generosity and engaging in altruistic acts. A religious motivation is provided for helping others (e.g., the great commandment of doing unto others as you would have them do unto you).

Session 9: Video

Clients make a video, or voice recording, of what they have learned about during the sessions. The client explains the concepts of Sufism in the video as if she or he is teaching someone else; then whoever is closest to her or him, she or he will show them the video and discuss it with them.

An Example of a 'Self-Therapy' *for Clients*—III

In this particular session protocol, a short-term Sufism + RE & CBT intervention is introduced to clients who are interested in self-therapy.

Step 1: Read About RE & CBT

To learn about RE & CBT:

1. Use this book, and read Chapters 1–5 to get a flavor of RE & CBT.
2. Seek more info about REB and CB therapies—Google them! Or watch a couple of videos on YouTube.
3. Recommended books about RE & CBT include: *A Practitioner's Guide to Rational Emotive Behavior Therapy* (Third Edition). Authors: Raymond A. DiGiuseppe, Kristene A. Doyle, Windy Dryden, and Wouter Backx.

Step 2: Assessment and Introduction

Self-monitor yourself for your negative emotions and irrational beliefs or negative automatic thoughts. You can use the forms at the end of this chapter.

Step 3: Learning the Model

Stick with the ABC model (see Chapters 1 and 2): the B–C connection (see Chapter 3), B's cognitive distortions (Chapter 3), the role of negative automatic thoughts, irrational and core beliefs, and dysfunctional emotions (unhealthy negative emotions). This will help to put your thought processes in order, so that you can think of any event according to the ABC model in your daily life.

Step 4: Identify Your Goal

Categorize your goals into three parts:

1. Practical life goals (e.g., coping with relationship problems, work/life problems).
2. Emotional goals (e.g., getting rid of unhealthy negative emotions and having healthy negative emotions and maybe, if possible, positive emotions).
3. Culturally adaptable goals: Find the meaning and peace in your life and a way of getting motivated.

Step 5: Positive Thinking and Bibliotherapy

Remember or search for your cultural values and significant people (e.g., thinkers, scientists, authors, artists) in your history. Take notes from your readings. Encourage yourself; you have a powerful history that can help you think rationally, functionally, and even positively about your psychological problems.

Step 6: Dealing With the Stress

Practice USA, UOA, and ULA or unconditional love of self/others/life. Surrender the need to have certain things be a certain way, which helps us begin the process of letting go. In Sufic terms, 'surrender' is not only surrendering the 'will' to God but also surrendering, or letting go of, identity, with the core of the ego, or the identification of the self, with a source of pain or a source of desire.

Step 7: Improve Your Coping Skills

Improve your coping skills with 'wise old sayings,' metaphors, and the teaching of Sufism (you may want to read Chapter 7).

Make a list of Sufic statements. Using flashcards will be helpful.

Front of Flashcards:

1. I must be successful in this exam.
2. Otherwise it will be catastrophic.
3. I cannot stand being unsuccessful.
4. I will be a failure if I do not pass this exam.

Back of flashcards:

1. It seems I need to be successful, but there is no reason I *must* be.

    Sufis say, *Raise your words, not your voice. It is rain that helps flowers grow, not thunder.*

2. It's very unfortunate to fail at this exam; however, it is not catastrophic if I fail.

    Sufis say, *The cure for pain is in the pain.*

3. I can still stand being unsuccessful.

    Sufis say, *The pains you feel are messengers. Listen to them.*

4. I still believe that I am worthy as a human.

    Sufis say, *If you are irritated by every rub, how will your mirror be polished?*

Session 8: Writing a Letter

Write a letter and show gratitude, praise, or thankfulness for any effort so far. Joy can be found in deeds that benefit others but for which there is no reward. In the REBT letter homework (Letter to Mr. Rational), the writer strives to write only rational expressions, forcing herself to face the most stressful situations and emotions that bother her most. Note: the letter should contain *no* irrational beliefs at all. Not only rational beliefs should be written in the letter but also reasons and evidence need to be found for such rational beliefs. Practice USA, UOA, and ULA and unconditional love of self/others/life. Remember any attempts to change any irrational beliefs and unhealthy negative emotions to rational beliefs and healthy negative emotions.

Example statements for the letter. Fill in the blanks where necessary:

*   Actually the _____was bad, but it was not *awful.*
*   I could stand it when _____occurred.
*   Actually, I would like to do _____but there is no reason I 'must.'
*   I hope I will succeed in _____but it doesn't mean I have to succeed.
*   I made a mistake in doing/acting _____but I am still worthy/I still love myself.

- It is a very difficult situation but I can bear _____ because I think I have some personal skills.
- The situation looks bad; however, I think there are many other reasons to make this 'un-awful' because _____.
- I can provide _____ as proof of why saying 'have to' or 'must' is not functional.

Case Examples

Session Example 1: Using Proverbs

The client is a 28-year-old female. She has problems with her boyfriend. She can't stand some of his behavior, such as 'He doesn't call,' and 'He's careless of my romantic needs.'

Therapist:	How often do you feel frustrated?
Client:	Every day.
T:	As you recall, we talked about your frustration intolerance beliefs in previous sessions.
C:	Yes.
T:	Would you like to practice some Turkish proverbs regarding them?
C:	Sure.
T:	What do you think about the proverb: *Patience is bitter, but its fruit is sweet?*
C:	I guess everything needs time.
T:	Does this tell you anything about your frustration intolerance beliefs?
C:	Yes, the proverb tells me that if I am patient with my dysfunctional emotions, I will be better able to deal with them.
T:	Do you think it is easy to remember the proverb and repeat rational beliefs of frustration tolerance, such as 'I can stand it' or 'I can deal with the uncomfortable feelings'?
C:	Actually, I like the phrase 'Patience is bitter, but its fruit is sweet.' Yes, I like it. And yes, it is easy for me to remember.
T:	I would like to point out that our aim with proverb workouts is not only that it is easy to remember them, but also that they will aid you in increasing the intensity of rational belief statements.
C:	Okay, I understand.

Session Example 2: A Metaphor

The client is a 17-year-old student who is preparing for the national entrance exam to university (a kind of SAT, GRE, A-level exam).

Client: *It was born inside me* (I can feel it in my bones) that I will be successful in this exam.

(The client means she hopes she will be successful in the exam.)

T: It is good to be motivated. However, let us check and see if you really are ready to pass the exam! 'It was born inside me' is a kind of cognitive distortion—the distortion of *emotional reasoning*. Thinking something must be true because you 'feel' it strongly, ignoring or discounting evidence to the contrary, is irrational.

C: You mean that I need to think logically rather than reasoning with my emotions.

T: A metaphor about emotional reasoning or logical thinking can be found in a Nasrettin Hodja story:

Some people ask the Hodja, 'Hodja, is the moon or the sun more useful?' 'Of course the Moon,' replies Hodja. 'While the sun lightens the earth during the daytime, the moon illuminates it during the night.'

Yes, emotions, or our sixth sense, illuminate our nights and they seem more useful. However, rational beliefs and logical thinking actually brighten our daytime. Can you think about 'nights' as unclear situations, or times when there is darkness? You may need the sun in the daytime to see things more clearly.

C: It is very interesting to hear that. Thank you. Emotions help us to see during the nights; however, a more logical and realistic thinking helps us to see things as they are in the daytime.

T: Exactly! Could you remember this metaphor during the week, to deal with your emotional reasoning distortions?

C: Yes, I definitely won't forget.

Session Example 3: The Goal of the Therapy

A 28-year-old client is having a hard time finding a direction in her life. She mostly stays at home and has symptoms of depression, such as fatigue, spends too much time sleeping, and feels hopeless.

C: I'm always empty. I don't know what to do about my life.

T: You say you're having a hard time making sense of life.

C: Yes, I haven't found my purpose in life for the past ten years. Since I was a teenager.

T: Let us assume that irrational beliefs prevent you from finding the meaning of life. What kind of irrational beliefs may you have?

C: Maybe thinking that if I decide something, I'm going to lose the other choice, and I might be worried about it.

T: So, is it a kind of 'catastrophe' irrational beliefs?

C: Could be.

T: Well, suppose that you make a decision, what could be the worst that could happen?

C: I would have wasted my time.

T: By making no decision, are you saving time?

C: Hmm. I am already losing time. Making no decision is also bad?

T: Which is worse? Making no decision or making a wrong decision?

C: I guess making no decision.

T: Without knowing right or wrong.

C: Yes.

T: Let's assume that you make a decision and see that it is wrong for you. What could happen?

C: I guess I would need to decide something else.

T: So the purpose of life can be found only by trying. Do you agree?

C: I agree.

T: If I give you a proverb by Atatürk, can you apply it to your situation?

C: Sure.

T: 'You can't escape the facts. Put the facts in front of you. Look them in the eye!' It means that you must try to have a purpose in life. You may fail, but you also need to look it in the eye. You don't know, yet, if it is a 'wrong decision'!

Session Example 4: Sufism

Before the session ahead, the therapist gave the client a Sufism reading as a homework activity. The client has some irrational demandingness beliefs about his career. He is anxious because he is not working at the desired level he wants in his company.

T: In the last session we talked about how Sufism may help you. For instance, rational beliefs of unconditional self, others, and life acceptance/love can be found in the core of Sufic teaching. In the previous session you talked about some of your rigid 'demands,' such as your boss should understand you, your job position should change, and your salary should be increased. Sufism can teach you flexible thinking and unconditional love. After you did your homework, what did you think about Sufism, flexible thinking, and unconditional love and acceptance?'

C: I found it very useful. I still think I deserve better in my job. However, after reading some Sufic texts, I know demandingness is a kind of poison that makes my life miserable. However, I don't think unconditional acceptance is possible at this moment in my life. However, I like the idea of unconditional love of self.

T: Yes, it is difficult to understand *unconditional acceptance.* However, I have hope that you will learn it too.

TABLE 10.1 Example Workout With Self-Help Form 1.

Culturally Redefined RE & CBT Assessment Self-Help Form: Please fill in the first form and step up to the second form. Some examples are given.

Activating event (stressful situations)	What are my thoughts? Negative automatic thoughts, perceptions, assumptions.	What are my beliefs? (How do I evaluate the A?) Choose some of the four irrational beliefs.	What are my unhealthy (dysfunctional) emotions? Primary and secondary emotions.	What are my unhelpful behaviors? And any physical symptoms.	My goals: 1. Practical solutions 2. Functional emotions 3. Helpful behavior	Culturally redefined goals: Meaning, peace, love, motivation
Having bad moments at work. Missing an important appointment. Not passing the exam. Having a financial crisis.	Life is difficult. People are unbearable. I cannot find my 'true' self. My future is in darkness.	Life should be easy. I cannot stand people around me. I am a worthless person. I don't even know who I really am. It is awful that my future is not secure.	Depression; anxiety; guilt; shame; anger; jealousy	Avoidance; withdrawing from social life; smoking; eating junk food; having back pain; frequent headaches	1. Find a new occupation to fit my personality and change my job 2. Concern, regret, annoyance 3. Doing some exercise, eating healthily	**Meaning:** Building a family and rearing a child **Peace:** Finding my true career path **Love:** I want to enjoy life **Motivation:** Being independent, being a skillful person, having sincere and good friends

TABLE 10.2 Example Workout With Self-Help Form 2.

Culturally Redefined Goals Definition Self-Help Form:

Please write what the meaning of your life is, how you can gain peace, what role 'love' plays in your life, and whether you satisfy your three psychological needs: autonomy, competence, and relatedness in your life. Some examples are given.

Problems with **meaning in** my life?	What is missing for your inner **peace**?	How can I find **'love'** in my life?	Are you **autonomous/ free/independent in your life**?	Are you satisfied with your **competency**?	Do you have close and sincere **relationships**?
I am concerned about my future; I don't know what I want to do with my life;	I am always stressful in my workplace;	I have always doubted myself and feel insecurity with others. I can't fall in love;	I am not fully free and independent due to people around me (e.g., my boss, my partner).	I am not satisfied with my position in my job; I have doubts if I am a good parent;	I don't have a real friend in this life; I am alone; I suffer lack of good and quality
I cannot find the values that I seek in my partner. Why are we alive and what is the purpose of life?	I want some changes in my life but I don't know exactly what makes me satisfied; I don't have economic freedom. Therefore, I am uneasy.	I only love animals but the rest of the world seems to be an enemy to me. It would be enjoyable and lovely to travel	I would like to travel the world—it is my dream. However, my family don't allow me to do so.	I have a lot of anxiety about this exam. I'm not intelligent enough to pass the exam!	relationships in my life; I have no one with whom I can have sincere and intimate or close conversations
I want to know why these things are happening to me.	My ex-husband/ wife makes my life miserable.	and see new cities and people.			with.

TABLE 10.3 Example Workout With Self-Help Form 3.

Culturally Redefined Rational Beliefs Form: Some examples are given here.

Activating event (stressful situations)	Functional, beneficial, and realistic thoughts, rather than negative automatic thoughts, assumptions.	Choose the rational beliefs that are alternatives to your irrational beliefs.	What should my healthy (functional) emotions be?	Make a list for your practical needs.	Your meaning, peace, love, autonomous, competency; relationships.
Having bad moments at work.	I need to stop complaining and have some plans for my future.	I wish life was easy, but I don't say it absolutely *must* be easy.	Concern but not anxiety.	Having a stable job.	Doing something that I have always wanted to do for my entire life.
Missing an important appointment.	Yes, sometimes people make mistakes.	In some way I can still manage my relationships with people around me.	Annoyance but not anger.	Having a fit body. Going on vacation.	Finding the right partner and living a peaceful life.
Not passing the exam.	Life is hard but not so difficult.	Regardless of everything, I am a worthwhile person.	Sadness but not depression.	Passing the exam. Solving my relationship problems with my partner.	Learning to love life and have a good time.
Broken relationship.	I need to find my 'true' partner.	However bad things are in life, nothing is awful.	Regret but not guilt.		Being economically free, having good times with friends, learning new skills.

TABLE 10.4 Example Workout With Self-Help Form 4.

Culturally Redefined RE & CBT Practical Application Form. Some examples are given here.

My negative automatic thoughts, assumptions, irrational beliefs.	Try to do self-disputing—challenge your irrational/dysfunctional thoughts and beliefs—logically, semantically, functionally, using evidence-based techniques, and maybe using humor.	Find possible 'wise old sayings' (idioms, proverbs, and other folk sayings).	What can be learned from unconditional life/others and self-love? If possible, read about Sufism or related teachings (e.g., Buddhism).	Use metaphors, including humorous ones (e.g., short stories and tales) or read about the lives of significant people. Try to relate them to your problems and solutions.
Life is difficult. People are unbearable. I cannot find my 'true' self. My future is in darkness.	I agree that I prefer life to be easy; however, who says that life should be completely easy (logical disputation)? What do I mean by 'difficult'?	If the path appears dark, know that the veil is in your own eyes (anti-awfulizing).	Please go back and read Chapter 7 and additional sources on Sufism. Do activities at the end of Chapter 7.	Please go back and read the metaphors in Chapter 8. Find more metaphors about anti-awfulizing, frustration tolerance, unconditional acceptance.
	My current situation makes my life unclear; however, even if it is a bad thing, not to know what my future will be is not 'awful!'	I never accept 'being tired' (frustration tolerance).		
	Does continuing to say, 'Life is difficult' lead to my goal in life?	Make a list of inspiring and rational 'wise old sayings' against your irrational beliefs.		

References

1. Meaden, A., Keen, N., Aston, R., Barton, K., & Bucci, S. (2013). *Cognitive Therapy for Command Hallucinations: An Advanced Practical Companion.* Abingdon, UK: Routledge.
2. Gaviṭa, O. A., David, D., Bujoreanu, S., Tiba, A., & Ionu iu, D. R. (2012). The efficacy of a short cognitive-behavioral parent program in the treatment of externalizing behavior disorders in Romanian foster care children: Building parental emotion-regulation through unconditional self-and child-acceptance strategies. *Children and Youth Services Review, 34*(7), 1290–1297.
3. Montgomery, G. H., Kangas, M., David, D., Hallquist, M. N., Green, S., Bovbjerg, D. H., & Schnur, J. B. (2009). Fatigue during breast cancer radiotherapy: An initial randomized study of cognitive-behavioral therapy plus hypnosis. *Health Psychology, 28*(3), 317.
4. Mersch, P. P. A., Emmelkamp, P. M., Bögels, S. M., & Van der Sleen, J. (1989). Social phobia: Individual response patterns and the effects of behavioral and cognitive interventions. *Behaviour Research and Therapy, 27*(4), 421–434.
5. Gould, R. A., Buckminster, S., Pollack, M. H., Otto, M. W., & Massachusetts, L. Y. (1997). Cognitive-behavioral and pharmacological treatment for social phobia: A meta-analysis. *Clinical Psychology: Science and Practice, 4*(4), 291–306.
6. Shelley, A. M., Battaglia, J., Lucey, J., Ellis, A., Opler, L. A., & Center, B. P. (2001). Symptom-specific group therapy for inpatients with schizophrenia. *Einstein Quarterly Journal of Biology and Medicine, 18*(1), 21–28.
7. Sava, F. A., Yates, B. T., Lupu, V., Szentagotai, A., & David, D. (2009). Cost-effectiveness and cost-utility of cognitive therapy, rational emotive behavioral therapy, and fluoxetine (Prozac) in treating depression: A randomized clinical trial. *Journal of Clinical Psychology, 65*(1), 36–52.
8. David, D., Szentagotai, A., Lupu, V., & Cosman, D. (2008). Rational emotive behavior therapy, cognitive therapy, and medication in the treatment of major depressive disorder: A randomized clinical trial, posttreatment outcomes, and six month follow up. *Journal of Clinical Psychology, 64*(6), 728–746.
9. Eifediyi, G., Ojugo, A. I., & Aluede, O. (2018). Effectiveness of rational emotive behaviour therapy in the reduction of examination Anxiety among secondary school students in Edo State, Nigeria. *Asia Pacific Journal of Counselling and Psychotherapy, 9*(1), 61–76.
10. Aler, C. R., Leiva, M. F., Bonet, X. F., Ortega, J. A., Puertolas, O. C., & Izquierdo, S. E. (2016). Effectiveness of rational emotive behaviour therapy in clinical social work: Impact on frequency of visits and use of psychopharmacological treatment. *International Journal of Integrated Care, 16*(6).
11. Smith, M. L., & Glass, G. V. (1977). Meta-analysis of psychotherapy outcome studies. *American Psychologist, 32*(9), 752.
12. Lyons, L. C., & Woods, P. J. (1991). The efficacy of rational-emotive therapy: A quantitative review of the outcome research. *Clinical Psychology Review, 11*(4), 357–369.
13. Hofmann, S. G., Asnaani, A., Vonk, I. J., Sawyer, A. T., & Fang, A. (2012). The efficacy of cognitive behavioral therapy: A review of meta-analyses. *Cognitive Therapy and Research, 36*(5), 427–440.
14. Leahy, D. J., Aukhil, I., & Erickson, H. P. (1996). 2.0 Å crystal structure of a four-domain segment of human fibronectin encompassing the RGD loop and synergy region. *Cell, 84*(1), 155–164.

INDEX

Note: Page numbers in *italics* refers to figures and **bold** refers to tables.

For Product Safety Concerns and Information please contact our EU
representative GPSR@taylorandfrancis.com
Taylor & Francis Verlag GmbH, Kaufingerstraße 24, 80331 München, Germany